What is *Radical Politics Today?*

'This is a bold, brave and timely book. As we emerge, blinking into the light after three decades of neo-liberal darkness, Jonathan Pugh has put together a collection of essays that will provoke and provide clues to the question of what comes next; what indeed *is* radical politics today?'

Neal Lawson (Chair, Compass)

'Jonathan Pugh gathers some of the most innovative and insightful voices from Britain and beyond to stage a series of debates on the central issues facing radical politics today. This collection is a model for the kinds of discussion we need to move forward.'

Michael Hardt, co-author of *Empire, Multitude* and *Commonwealth*

'At a time when all ideologies are either exhausted or have become irrelevant, the need for a truly radical politics can hardly be exaggerated. Radical politics is about rethinking the common sense, the taken for granted assumptions, of the age. This timely and well-planned collection of essays by distinguished and concerned scholars throws much new light on where we should be looking for new ideas. It represents a major contribution to the ongoing debate on the problems of our times.'

Lord Bhikhu Parekh

'In the present moment of rapid and fundamental political and economic change we need sustained critical discussion of the kinds of alternative politics available to us. In *What* is *Radical Politics Today?* leading political theorists initiate this timely discussion by addressing both possibilities and obstacles from a wide range of perspectives.'

James Tully (University of Victoria)

'As the most immediate effects of a global economic and financial crisis seem to be ebbing from our consciousness, the authors in this collection identify the urgent need for a different kind of politics. One after the other they draw a picture of a world ill at ease with itself: addicted to consumption yet unjust in its rewards; obsessed with the idea of the global at the expense of an engagement with the real; aware yet narcissistic. Helpless with fear, paternalism and debt. But the book is, above all, in the words of one contributor "a challenge to fatalism". The chapters sketch out a radical politics for the 21st century based on the rediscovery of our human powers to invent and adapt – a rebuilding of the state's management and redistributive capacities, a revaluing of autonomous behaviour and critical judgement, the prioritising of a "social planet" over a "social state" and even, a repudiation of near-sacrosanct institutions. No doubt some injunctions will rile, but though this book may fail to comfort, it will not fail to challenge or provoke.'

Catherine Fieschi (Director, Counterpoint,
The Think Tank of the British Council)

'With impeccable timing, this volume provides a stimulating range of perspectives on what radical politics can offer during this period of crisis and change. It deserves to be widely read and debated.'

Ruth Lister (Loughborough University)

'There's a world to win, but only if the Left is possessed of bright ideas, inspiring aspirations and brilliant strategies. This book – rich in insight – assembles some of our leading thinkers to consider what sort of Left can unlock the progressive potential contained in this moment of early 21st-century crisis. Has the mainstream Left conceded far too much to the liberals and conservatives this last 30 years? If so, what sort of Left can win hearts and minds in this moment of crisis? The answers to these important questions are the stuff of this excellent book.'

Noel Castree (Manchester University)

'The current era presents a mixed picture for the possibility of radical politics. Old radical solutions are failing, the Left is on the retreat in many countries and regions, and urgent global problems, from financial market regulation to climate change threaten to disrupt and disorganise progressive coalitions. On the other side, the Western economic and political consensus of the last 30 years is in disarray. In this context, the task of renewing the nature and form of radical politics is both pressing and demanding. This new book is a welcome step in the right direction.'

David Held (London School of Economics)

'This is a wonderfully salutary and visionary collection of widely different opinions on how we can think about our world in these "interesting" times.'

Emily Young (Sculptor, and of Penguin Café Orchestra)

'Like an exploding star, the radical Left in the UK has disintegrated and its fragments have flown off in all directions. People who once thought they were engaged in a common project can no longer agree about where they are going, let alone how they should get there. If you feel radical but confused read these essays. They may make you even more confused, but they may also help you decide where to go next.'

Bob Rowthorn (Cambridge University)

'With the aim of understanding the forces and boundaries of a genuinely radical politics, this volume begins to interrogate the models, figures and reach of the structureless moment that currently commands political tropology and life.'

Avital Ronell (New York University)

'If you are looking for a rich diversity of views and fierce arguments about radical politics today, then this is the book for you!'

Achin Vanaik (Delhi University)

'Timely, engaging and bold. This book provides intellectual, moral and political challenge for any reader on a question which urgently needs lucid answers: what *is* it to be radical today?'

Tom Bentley (Policy Director for Australia's Deputy Prime Minister)

What *is* Radical Politics Today?

Edited by

Jonathan Pugh

Senior Academic Fellow in Territorial Governance
Newcastle University, UK

palgrave
macmillan

First published 2009 by
PALGRAVE MACMILLAN

Palgrave Macmillan in the UK is an imprint of Macmillan Publishers Limited,
registered in England, company number 785998, of Houndmills, Basingstoke,
Hampshire RG21 6XS.

Palgrave Macmillan in the US is a division of St Martin's Press LLC,
175 Fifth Avenue, New York, NY 10010.

Palgrave Macmillan is the global academic imprint of the above companies
and has companies and representatives throughout the world.

Palgrave® and Macmillan® are registered trademarks in the United States,
the United Kingdom, Europe and other countries.

ISBN 978–0–230–23625–7   hardback
ISBN 978–0–230–23626–4   paperback

This book is printed on paper suitable for recycling and made from fully
managed and sustained forest sources. Logging, pulping and manufacturing
processes are expected to conform to the environmental regulations of the
country of origin.

A catalogue record for this book is available from the British Library.

A catalog record for this book is available from the Library of Congress.

10 9 8 7 6 5 4 3 2 1
18 17 16 15 14 13 12 11 10 09

Printed and bound in Great Britain by
CPI Antony Rowe, Chippenham and Eastbourne

Contents

v

List of Figures

Acknowledgements

We are at a watershed moment in the history of radical politics. Given that radicals have not produced a clear alternative to the present crisis in neo-liberalism, the question arises: what *is* radical politics today? What is the nature of contemporary radical politics? Is it effective; if so, how?

The idea for a survey into the character and spirit of radical politics in our times first came to me while in a debate with Tony Benn, Hilary Wainwright, David Chandler and Bernard Crick, in London, August 2007. We were discussing the many different ways in which Left-wing radical politics takes place in the twenty-first century. As the global economic crisis was to unfold only a few months later, and a clear alternative to the status quo was not forthcoming from the radical Left and progressives, the need for this survey became even more apparent.

Many people have made this book possible. My sincere gratitude firstly goes to the contributors. All leaders in their fields, they represent a formidable range of often conflicting perspectives on the spirit of contemporary radical politics. Thanks to all of you for putting up with my regular emails, as I tried to coordinate the project. I hope you like the final product.[1]

Thanks to Alison Howson, commissioning editor from Palgrave Macmillan, for her vision and continuous attention to detail; for reading each chapter, often a number of times. Gemma d'Arcy Hughes from Palgrave Macmillan is also to be thanked for taking the project to completion, making the whole process run smoothly, and I am also grateful to Jo North for her outstanding editorial work on the book as a whole. Alex Suermondt, from 'questioncreative.co.uk', has produced a great cover, illustrating how this book is aimed at both public and student audiences.

Thanks to Alastair Bonnett, Andy Gillespie, Steve Juggins and Helen Jarvis for inviting me into the creative atmosphere of the School of Geography, Politics and Sociology, Newcastle University. To Chantal Mouffe, Doreen Massey, Grant and Erin Henderson, David Chandler, Ben Allen, Nick Megoran, Deborah Thien, Steve Aggett, Yvonne Pugh, Alex Hall, Simon and Georgie McCann for their friendship and support throughout the two years it took to produce this book.

Thanks also to the Economic and Social Research Council, the British Academy, the Barry Amiel and Melburn Trust, Newcastle University and

The Great Debate for their financial support of some of the many public debates which also helped shape this book. Finally to Zoe, Mum and Dad, for their help in this and every project I undertake.

Since the completion of this book, I have launched an ongoing survey of radical politics today. This is via a free, online, multi-media magazine, entitled *Radical Politics Today*. It can be found on 'The *Spaces of* Democracy and the *Democracy of* Space' international network website (see http://www.spaceofdemocracy.org). If you are interested, please feel free to email me (Jonathan.Pugh@ncl.ac.uk).

Note

1. In the interest of stimulating debate about the radical Left, I have sought to open up the question What *is* radical politics today? The views expressed in this volume of contrasting opinions are therefore not necessarily my own.

Notes on Contributors

Dora Apel is Associate Professor and W. Hawkins Ferry Chair of Modern and Contemporary Art History at Wayne State University. She is the author of *Memory Effects: the Holocaust and the Art of Secondary Witnessing*; *Imagery of Lynching: Black Men, White Women, and the Mob*; and *Lynching Photographs* (with Shawn Michelle Smith).

David Bates is a PhD student at the University of Sunderland, writing a thesis on *Multiculturalism and Asylum Policy*.

Zygmunt Bauman is Emeritus Professor of Sociology, University of Leeds. His forthcoming publication is *Living on Borrowed Time: Conversations with Citlali Rovirosa Madrazo* (Polity Press).

Alastair Bonnett is Professor of Social Geography at Newcastle University. He is the author of a number of books on anti-racism, whiteness and ideas of the West. His next book, *Left in the Past: Radicalism and Nostalgia*, will be published by Continuum.

David Boyle is a Fellow of the New Economics Foundation and the author of a number of books about history and the future, including *The Tyranny of Numbers* and *Authenticity*. He is the founder of London Time Bank and has stood for Parliament as a Liberal Democrat.

Terrell Carver is Professor of Political Theory at the University of Bristol, UK. He has published extensively on Marx, Engels and Marxism, and sex, gender and sexuality, and his latest books include *The Postmodern Marx* (1998) and *Men in Political Theory* (2004). He is also co-general editor of Rowman & Littlefield's book series *Globalisation*.

David Chandler is Professor of International Relations at the University of Westminster and founding editor of the *Journal of Intervention and Statebuilding*. His recent books include: *Hollow Hegemony: Rethinking Global Politics, Power and Resistance* (Pluto, 2009); *Empire in Denial: the Politics of State-building* (Pluto, 2006) and *Constructing Global Civil Society: Morality and Power in International Relations* (Palgrave, 2004). http://www.davidchandler.org.

Nick Cohen is a British journalist, author, and political commentator. He presently writes mainly for *The Observer, London Evening Standard* and *Daily Mail*; and previously for the *New Statesman*. Since May 2008 he has been the television critic for *Standpoint* magazine. Cohen has written four books, including *What's Left?* (HarperPerennial, 2007), and has been shortlisted for the Orwell Prize.

Alejandro Colás teaches international relations at the School of Politics and Sociology, Birkbeck College, University of London. He is author of *Empire* (Polity, 2007) and *International Civil Society: Social Movements and World Politics* (Polity, 2002), and is on the editorial board of the journal *Historical Materialism*.

Jason Edwards is Lecturer in Politics in the School of Politics and Sociology, Birkbeck College, London. His research focuses on both the history of political thought and issues in contemporary political and social theory, including problems with current ideas about radical democracy. He is author of *The Radical Attitude and Modern Political Theory* (Palgrave Macmillan, 2007).

David Featherstone is Lecturer in Human Geography at the University of Glasgow. His research interests include transnational political activism, geographies of resistance, subaltern political ecologies and the relations between space and politics. He is the author of *Resistance, Space and Political Identities: the Making of Counter-Global Networks* (Wiley-Blackwell, 2008).

Frank Furedi is Professor of Sociology at the University of Kent in Canterbury. In recent years his work was devoted to an exploration of the workings of the culture of fear. He is now engaged in a study of the relations between changing ideas of authority and the meaning of subjectivity.

Jeremy Gilbert is Senior Lecturer in Cultural Studies at the University of East London. He has written widely on music, politics and cultural theory, and is author of *Anticapitalism and Culture* (Berg, 2008). He is one of the editors of *New Formations*.

James Heartfield has written widely on environmental movements and architecture in *The Times Higher Education Supplement*, *Spiked Online*, *Blueprint*, the *Telegraph*, *The Times*, the *Architects' Journal*, *Art Review*, *Review of Radical Political Economy* and *Cultural Trends*. In May 2006, with Julia Svetlichnaja he interviewed the Russian dissident, Alexander Litvinenko. The interviews were only published after Litvinenko's death.

Will Hutton is former editor-in-chief of *The Observer* and currently Chief Executive of The Work Foundation (formerly the Industrial Society). In 1992, he won the What The Papers Say award for Political Journalist of the Year. He has authored many books including *The Writing on the Wall: Why We Must Embrace China as a Partner or Face It as an Enemy* (2006) and *The State We're In: Why Britain is in Crisis and How to Overcome It* (1995).

Sheila Jasanoff is Pforzheimer Professor of Science and Technology Studies at Harvard University's John F. Kennedy School of Government. She previously founded and chaired the Department of Science and Technology Studies at Cornell University and has held visiting positions at MIT, Yale, Cambridge, Oxford and Kyoto universities and the Berlin Institute for Advanced Study. She has written widely on the role of science and technology in modern democratic societies.

Paul Kingsnorth is the author of *One No, Many Yeses*, and *Real England*. He was deputy editor of *The Ecologist* from 1999 to 2001 and writes widely on environmental politics and related issues. His website is http://www.paulkingsnorth.net.

Jo Littler is Senior Lecturer in Media and Cultural Studies at Middlesex University. She is author of *Radical Consumption: Shopping for Change in Contemporary Culture* (Open University Press, 2009) and co-editor, with Roshi Naidoo, of *The Politics of Heritage: the Legacies of 'Race'* (Routledge, 2005). She is currently writing a book about celebrity.

James Martin teaches political theory at Goldsmiths, University of London and is co-director of the Center for the Study of Global Media and Democracy. He has published research on Italian political thought and contemporary radical political theory. He is currently writing a book on politics and rhetoric.

Doreen Massey is Professor of Geography at the Open University and joint founder of *Soundings*: a journal of politics and culture. Her most recent books are *For Space* (Polity, 2005) and *World City* (Polity, 2007).

Gregor McLennan is Professor of Sociology at the University of Bristol. He has written widely on Marxism, pluralism, ideology, sociology and politics. He is currently engaged on a book-length treatment of 'post-secularism' in social and political theory.

Tariq Modood is Professor of Sociology, Politics and Public Policy and the founding Director of the Centre for the Study of Ethnicity and Citizenship at the University of Bristol. He is a regular contributor to the media and to policy debates in Britain. His most recent books are *Multiculturalism: a Civic Idea* (Polity, 2007) and, as co-editor, *Secularism, Religion and Multicultural Citizenship* (Cambridge University Press, 2009).

Chantal Mouffe is Professor of Political Theory at the Centre for the Study of Democracy, University of Westminster. She co-authored *Hegemony and Socialist Strategy: Towards a Democratic Politics* (Verso, 1985) with Ernesto Laclau, and sole authored other books, including *The Democratic Paradox* (Verso, 2000) and *On the Political* (Routledge, 2005). She has taught at Harvard, Princeton and the Collège International de Philosophie (Paris).

Saul Newman is a Reader in Political Theory at Goldsmiths University of London. He is the author of a number of books on radical political theory, including: *From Bakunin to Lacan* (Rowman & Littlefield, 2001), *Power and Politics in Poststructuralist Thought* (Routledge, 2005), *Unstable Universalities* (Manchester University Press, 2007), *Politics Most Unusual* (Palgrave, 2008) and *The Politics of Postanarchism* (forthcoming Edinburgh University Press, 2009).

Jonathan Pugh is Senior Academic Fellow, Newcastle University. He is founding director of 'The *Spaces of* Democracy and the *Democracy of* Space' network. He has written some forty articles on radical politics, and in 2009 founded *Radical Politics Today* magazine (http://www.spaceofdemocracy.org).

Amir Saeed is a Senior Lecturer in Media and Cultural Studies at the University of Sunderland. His interests are in 'race' and racism.

Saskia Sassen, Columbia University, is the author of *The Global City* (2nd edn, Princeton, 2001), *Territory, Authority, Rights: From Medieval to Global Assemblages* (Princeton, 2008) and *A Sociology of Globalisation* (Norton, 2007), among others. Her website is http://www.columbia.edu/~sjs2/.

Clare Short (Member of Parliament) is a member of the British Labour Party. She is currently the Independent Member of Parliament for Birmingham Ladywood, having been elected as a Labour Party MP in 1983, and was Secretary of State for International Development in the UK Labour government from 3 May 1997 until her resignation on 12 May 2003.

Edward W. Soja is Distinguished Professor of Urban Planning at the University of California, Los Angeles (UCLA). He has written a series of books promoting an assertive spatial perspective, including *Postmodern Geographies* (1989), *Thirdspace* (1996) and *Postmetropolis* (2000). He is currently completing a book to be published by the University of Minnesota Press on *Seeking Spatial Justice*.

Jason Toynbee is Senior Lecturer in Media Studies at the Open University. His most recent books include *Bob Marley: Herald of a Postcolonial World?* and *The Media and Social Theory* (with David Hesmondhalgh). A member of the Socialist Party, Jason has campaigned, among other things, against privatisation of public services and the invasion of Gaza.

Nigel Thrift is Vice Chancellor, Warwick University. Co-author, author or co-editor of over 35 books, he is credited with coining the phrase 'soft modernity' and coming up with 'non-representational theory'. Nigel has been awarded numerous prizes, including the Royal Geographical Society Victoria Medal, and is a Fellow of the British Academy.

Hilary Wainwright is co-editor of *Red Pepper*, Research Director of the New Politics Programme of the Transnational Institute, and Senior Research Associate at the International Centre for Participation Studies. Her most recent books are *Public Service Reform But Not As We Know It!* (UNISON and Compass, 2009) and the paperback update of *Reclaim the State: Experiments in Popular Democracy* (Seagull, 2009). Her books also include *Arguments For a New Left: Answering the Free Market Right* (Blackwell, 1994).

Michael J. Watts is Class of 63 Professor of Geography, and Chair of Development Studies at the University of California, Berkeley, where he served as the Director of the Institute of International Studies from 1994–2004. The author of eight books and over 100 articles, he was awarded the Victoria Medal by the Royal Geographical Society in 2004.

Ken Worpole is the author of a number of books on architecture, landscape and public policy. He is Senior Professor at The Cities Institute, London Metropolitan University. Ken has lived in Hackney, east London, for the past forty years and is married to the photographer, Larraine Worpole (http://www.worpole.net).

What *is* Radical Politics Today?

Jonathan Pugh

A crisis makes you rethink your life. The recent economic crisis is no exception. All of us are now thinking how our lives could be run differently. This recession seems to be giving more cause for reflection than most – not only about how the economy is managed, but also about the environment and society more generally. Neo-liberalism has governed our lives for nearly thirty years. Many feel that its Right-wing ethos of deregulation, privatisation and liberation of corporate power has not only failed the world's financial systems, but more fundamentally degraded the environment and the social fabric of life. Despite all the expert predictions, history did not in fact end in 1989 with the triumph of neo-liberalism.

While there is much to despair at in our current situation, there is also an underlying sense of anticipation – change is coming. Specific events are certainly contributing to this mood: not only the collapse of the global financial systems, but the mobilisation of people in protests on ever larger scales, the symbolic and historic election of Barack Obama, the end of the George W. Bush presidency, changing international relations with the Middle East and Asia, the rising power of China and some countries in Latin America, to name just a few.

Before we get too excited though, the 'revolution' is not coming anytime soon. No grand alternative ideology or movement of the masses is waiting in the wings, ready to seize the opportunity. This leads to the obvious question of this book: What *is* radical politics today? What is the spirit and nature of radical politics in our times? For this particular book, what *is* Left-wing and progressive radical politics? Where they once offered the grand ideology of socialism, what do they offer now? This book is a broad survey, a step into the character of radical politics today.

1

Let's start this survey with a general definition: What constitutes a 'radical politics'? The term was originally coined to describe a politics which gets to the roots of a problem. The Latin noun 'radix' means 'root'. But radical politics not only gets to the roots of a problem. If it is effective, it also turns over, or 'roots out', and redefines how society functions. This of course does not have to mean revolution, in the sense of a communist or Islamic state revolution for example. It does not mean that radical politics is confined to particular causes or issues. To take just a few examples, in our definition of 'radical politics' we could include the radical impact of feminism, modernism, Islam, mass education and health care, Christianity, neo-conservatism, the Chinese model, feudalism, Right- or Left-wing radicals. All have caused radical changes in society.

We look to radical politics to provide an alternative view of the world, when that world is in trouble. Indeed, if we remember, neo-liberal capitalism was once a radical alternative to the problems of nearly forty years ago. The 1970s were defined by inflation, increased accumulation of capital, unemployment and a variety of fiscal crises. Neo-liberalism beat the other main radical contender at the time, socialism, in apparently getting to the root of the problem, overturning it, and redefining how society functions. Neo-liberal capitalism was developed by leaders like Ronald Reagan, Margaret Thatcher and a network of powerful international institutions, such as the World Bank and International Monetary Fund. Often called the 'American Model', low wages and high inequality are not central concerns for this system, whose primary function is the liberation of corporate power. Neo-liberalism and free market forces became the organising framework for society; from the deregulation of finance, to privatisation of health care and educational systems. By the mid-1980s it was no longer radical, but the accepted norm.

I believe that the end of this decade will be singled out by historians as a defining moment in radical politics. We will talk of 'post-2009' in times to come, but not because there has been a 'grand radical moment'. This moment is significant precisely because people will look back and ask: what *was* radical politics then? Given the lack of a clear alternative to neo-liberalism when the financial crisis and recession hit, historians will pay great attention to the spirit, disposition and temperament of radical politics in our times. They will consider such prominent examples as today's anti-globalisation movements, anti-capitalists and environmentalists. Historians will explore the character of radical neo-conservatism, the Chinese model and radical Islam. They will examine the spirit of the anti-war protests, peace and justice organisations. They will interrogate the radical impact of multiculturalism, identity politics and non-governmental development agencies, as the fortunes of these ways of doing politics rise and fall.

But we should not wait for historians. We should begin this survey now. In the crucial years of a crisis which has affected the lives of so many people, it is important to understand the nature of radical politics, today.

The first major challenge we encounter in our survey has already been implied. There are apparently many ways of being radical today. Some argue that this is the weakness of contemporary radical politics. It has split into too many different factions, or is dominated by people who are disconnected from the rest of society. Here the examples of creative artists, suicide bombers, anti-capitalists, tree-huggers and anarchists, incapable of mobilising under a single banner, are often used as illustrations. But so are the small group of out-of-touch elites who ran Bush's radical neo-conservative agenda, or the dictators of the Chinese or Islamic state projects. In short, many think radical politics today does not have support from broad sections of society.

Others say that this fragmentation is the strength of radical politics. It provides an opportunity for different groups to challenge the status quo – those environmentalists, feminists, peace movements, for example, which are slowly chipping away at specific injustices. Moreover, many also argue that grand visions of society – like socialism, neo-liberalism or the Islamic state – oppress those who don't believe in them, as much as they support those who do. A grand alternative is therefore not the answer at this time of crisis. In today's diverse cultures, many believe it is better to deal with injustices as they arise in particular situations, rather than produce a single radical solution for all. These people believe radical politics should be creative, taking many different forms, as 'women', 'Muslims', 'Christians', 'the poor', respond to the different circumstances which they face. They argue that it is neither possible nor desirable to produce a one-size-fits-all vision for society.

However, others think that today's radicals do not work hard enough at reaching out to different parts of society, at bridging the gaps; that they are not seriously committed to their radical causes. The modern protest – such as Live8 and Make Poverty History – is often seen as illustrating this. At these protests people meet up with their friends for the day, listen to Bob Geldof or Bono talk about poverty, and express their personal outrage at the world. But when it comes to actually working collectively for instrumental change and rolling up their sleeves, these protesters are much less interested. They are more worried about being seen at the right protest, wearing the right coloured bracelet.

The supporters of these media events instead say that while this may be true to a certain extent, something needs to be done. They draw our attention to the effectiveness of modern protests in other areas; for example, their creativity in drawing our leaders' attention to important issues, like mass starvation in a globalised world. In a 24/7 media-driven society, it is necessary to put on ever more elaborate events, in order to grab our attention, money and time for radical causes.

From just these brief examples, it should be clear that there are many ways of thinking about radical politics today. Its spirit is broad and diverse. Written for students and the general public, this book is not concerned with complex theoretical debate. Rather, it presents conflicting and contradictory, often provocative characterisations of radical politics today. It includes original works from leading commentators (mainly from the Left and progressive politics residing in the USA and England). These gradually build up a broad picture of radical politics today.

The book is structured by the following four themes:

1. The place of grand visions in contemporary radical politics;
2. New forms of radical politics;
3. Radicals' response to diversity and difference in society; and
4. What today's radicals think about the state.

The importance of an overarching 'big idea' or 'grand vision' of how society should function varies between individuals and to a large extent depends on their political allegiances. Unlike neo-conservatism and Right-wing Islam for example, Left-wing and progressive radical politics today do not, in general, offer *grand visions* for change. Instead, their *new forms of radical politics* tend to focus upon particular issues, contexts and events – including wars in Iraq and Afghanistan, the environment, or the injustices of sweat shops and animal experimentation. There is also an emphasis upon specific identities, such as expressing the concerns of interest groups like 'Muslims', 'women' or 'the disabled'. There is no obvious alternative overarching plan for society, coming from the Left and progressives.

This also illustrates how contemporary radical politics is dominated by the themes of *diversity and difference*, in what is perceived to be an increasingly complex world. Societies are often fragmented; communities and individuals disconnected from each other. Many radicals therefore see it as their role to articulate the claims of people that are not being heard. In turn, *the role of the state* is increasingly to mediate between these different, often competing interest groups. Against this backdrop, to some radicals the state is the problem, to others the solution; to some it is irrelevant, and to others it is indispensable in creating the radical changes that society needs today.

1. Grand visions

In his contribution **Zygmunt Bauman** argues that radical politics today is often not that radical. He ascribes this to our addiction to debt and industrial growth. Most solutions to the present crisis, which have come from both government and society, will push us further into debt, since they generally rely on returning us to the status quo and guaranteeing the availability of limitless credit. Yet radicals on the Left have not developed a grand counter-vision to this. For Bauman, we specifically need to develop radical international organisations which impose limits on consumption, raising the revenue needed to deal with the environmental crisis and social exclusion at a global level. A truly radical politics – which curtails exploitative attitudes – is lacking. In direct contrast, **Frank Furedi** argues that the rise of environmentalism and the precautionary principle are obvious examples of where radical politics has gone wrong. For Furedi, such risk-averse ideals form the basis of a reactionary approach, pervasively holding back radical politics today. Instead we should confront the limitations on development, tackling those who put the economic and environmental crisis down to human selfishness and greed. For Furedi the issue is not whether radical politics comes from the Right or Left; both have become risk averse, neither is therefore radical.

Paul Kingsnorth agrees that politics today lacks a radical edge precisely because it is locked into Left/Right history, but for very different reasons to Furedi. For Kingsnorth, both Left and Right are against 'Deep Green' ideology – whose grand vision puts nature resolutely above human progress, uplifting it to a spiritual level. This form of radical politics, dominant in radical debate in the 1960s, has more recently been sidelined. While in agreement with Kingsnorth, **James Heartfield** reaches the opposite conclusion. He says that in putting nature first, although limited in number, deep green campaigners manage to oppress the working masses. They directly attack workers whose jobs rely upon environmental destruction (coal miners, for example). For Heartfield, this shows how radical politics today is dominated by environmental elites who show disdain for ordinary people. Heartfield, like a number of contributors, argues that radical politics today betrays 'the workers', because it is disconnected from the public.

It is therefore interesting to note that while Right-wing neo-conservatism was the most powerful form of radical politics in recent memory, **Terrell Carver** comments that it never had broad-based support from the public. Rather, with a lack of a credible alternative from the Left, elite neo-cons in Washington manipulated systems of government with devastating consequences. So in her contribution **Clare Short** does not celebrate the transformative powers of non-governmental organisations, such as the green parties, development, environmental, anti-war and peace activists. For nowhere have they managed to break through, achieving significant change or political progress. This means that the Right, in the form of neo-conservatism and increasingly Right-wing versions of Islam, has simply stepped into the vacuum. Indeed, Short believes that the radical Right will strengthen in coming years, reinventing itself, as people look for a compass to orientate them out of this crisis.

Edward Soja, however, says that in the wake of the economic crisis of 2008, radical politics does not 'revolve around absolute or categorical choice, such as that between capitalism and socialism. More than ever before, this is not a simple either/or choice.' He argues that 'Whatever happens in the aftermath of these epochal events, radical politics today is shifting its focus, moving away from an all-embracing anti-neoliberalism towards a renewed hope that radical change is possible.' In his contribution, which goes against the grain of authors like Furedi and Heartfield, Soja does not look to grand visions, but instead to the emergence of diverse ways of resisting spatial inequalities across the world, as radical politics today takes on many new forms.

2. New forms of radical politics

David Chandler, in contrast, argues that many new forms of radical politics are dominated by personal and isolated protests. While this makes protesters feel better about themselves, it does not meet the demands of real political change. He says the 2003 anti-war march, anti-capitalism and anti-globalisation protests, the Make Poverty History campaign at the end of 2005, the World Social Forums or the radical jihad of Al-Qaeda, are all illustrative of highly individualised protests. There is no attempt to build a social or collective movement. And so, theatrical suicide, demonstrating, badge and bracelet wearing become ethical acts in themselves: personal statements of awareness, rather than attempts to engage politically with society.

Contradictory judgements are a theme of this book. In her contribution **Hilary Wainwright** is more supportive of new forms of radical politics today. She says that they reflect a move away from a hierarchical view, with knowledge being the exclusive privilege of a few (the leaders of a party, for example), to an understanding of diverse and plural sources of knowledge and resistance. From the 1968 student movements and the 1970s women's movement, to the World Social Forum and anti-war campaigns, the emphasis is upon developing inter-communication, through complex networks of resistance. In examining performative artworks, **Dora Apel** discusses the type of protests which contributors like Chandler would surely criticise. But Apel says that while 'protest actions, performative artworks and images by themselves arguably have limited ability to effect direct political change, their power should not be underestimated'. For example, such acts held the American government to account for their actions in Abu Ghraib.

Michael Watts is therefore drawn to the following question. Can radical politics, often geographically dispersed and fragmented as it is today, amount to a significant challenge to the status quo? While the answer is not clear, Watts argues that resistance to neo-liberalism – if we are to chart the larger landscape – is heterogeneous and worldwide. The recent revolts in France, the factory occupations in Argentina, the oil nationalisation in Bolivia, and the insurgencies in Iraq are all symptomatic, even if the national and local dynamics differ greatly. For Watts, we should not be gloomy; he sees regular opportunities as neo-liberalism constantly fails.

Jason Toynbee, however, is more sanguine about new forms of radical politics. Reflecting upon crisis and political transformation at this watershed moment, Toynbee says that: 'There's no guarantee, or even likelihood, that recession and the more intense poverty it brings will lead to a resurgence of working-class consciousness and resistance. As the 1980s showed all too well, recessions can weaken resistance by making solidarity more difficult to build.' Toynbee's chapter shows how, as Part II unfolds, this interrogation of the spirit of social engagement and commitment in radical politics is intensifying today.

The following three chapters highlight a range of concerns in this regard. **James Martin** acknowledges that the test of today's radical commitment is not that of the last century: namely, demonstrating allegiance to a party or social group. Yet without a programme and organisation to bring the different groups together, many radicals are failing. The proliferation and pluralisation of new forms of radical politics – from internet blogging to diverse ways of protesting – has meant that commitment 'flattens out'. The challenge for radicals is to find new but serious radical commitment, leading to meaningful political change.

In their contribution **Jeremy Gilbert** and **Jo Littler** take the example of the Green New Deal, produced by the New Economics Foundation. This shows how some radicals are practically trying to address the real worry over fragmentation and gesture politics. The Green New Deal aims to move against the anarchic withdrawal that characterises and alienates so much of radical politics today. It instead seeks to engage with a wide range of people, from civil society, through to the state, via a broad range of strategies, in order to address the environmental and economic crisis simultaneously.

The general thrust of **Doreen Massey's** chapter, which closes Part II, is that the crisis presents an opportunity for disparate forms of radical politics to come together. She points out that neo-liberalism only became the norm because so many people worked hard collectively, through a broad range of strategies, to make it so. It will therefore take collective effort to turn over and uproot. Massey, like Gilbert and Littler, talks about the Green New Deal. In doing so she highlights how concern with more than 'one off' stunts is becoming increasingly important for those interrogating the spirit of radical politics in our times; particularly post-crisis. The nature of collective action is being seriously examined.

The first and second parts of the book highlight that today's radicals are sometimes criticised for not being committed enough; for being reactionary, or disengaged from the general public. While several commentators lament the death of grand visions, others count this as a blessing. Some believe that radical politics is most effective when experimental and creative, and is better able to deal with the particularity of injustice. Others say that the possibilities for universal transformation are reduced post-crisis, as radical politics focuses too much upon the micro level.

Others still are beginning to discuss how the present crisis may be a turning point: an opportunity for collective action to be reinvigorated through invention and hard work, and renewed social engagement around newly constituted publics. From this departure, the third section explores how contemporary radical politics deals with diversity and difference within society.

3. Diversity and difference

This is a prevailing theme for many authors, as in radical politics today widespread attention is given to multiculturalism, identity politics and more recently violence and Islam. As in the previous parts of this book, many contributors are poles apart in their perspectives.

Most agree that as the second millennium ended identity politics gained influence in radical politics, replacing other grand visions. **Gregor McLennan** is concerned that this has brought radical politics to a crucial juncture. Too much, and for too long, has the 'politics of difference' dominated. For it is not possible to run organisations – like schools or hospitals – through pressure-group politics alone. So McLennan reflects a mood of restlessness around endless pluralism; calling for a turn towards a majoritarian, broadly secularist radical politics, uplifting people's capacities.

However, **Tariq Modood** goes against this emerging grain within radical politics, arguing for multiculturalism *as a* radical politics. Multiculturalism, despite what others say, has a radical content. Modood asks us to think about the many Muslims adopting multicultural, rather than the violent, less democratic, approaches in recent years. For Modood, a successful multicultural ethos shows how Muslims can be radical, engaging peacefully in passionate debates, while living in diverse societies. However, **Nick Cohen** argues that there is a different side to multiculturalism. He says: 'postmodern multiculturalists have taken the liberal idea of tolerance and pushed it into an extreme relativism which holds that it is wrong for liberals to attack previously disadvantaged groups – "the other" – even when "the other" espoused ideas which were anti-liberal. In short, it has become racist to oppose sexists, homophobes and fascists from other cultures.' Cohen argues that many Left-wing, liberal-minded people don't oppose certain abhorrent aspects of radical Islam. Radical politics today is worse off as a result.

Coming from a different perspective, **Amir Saeed** and **David Bates** point out the similarities between Muslim beliefs and the traditional Left. They have more in common than what divides them. In turning to multiculturalism, they say, 'Right-wing commentators fear the concept of multiculturalism because it implies an erosion of core, national values in favour of diverse cultures. Whilst more liberal commentators appear to suggest that the concept actually creates divisions in society by emphasising difference rather than stress the common ground.' The challenge is to bring together like-minded Muslims and non-Muslims, offering an alternative to free market capitalism.

Alastair Bonnett takes yet another tack on this issue of multiculturalism. He writes that multiculturalists draw upon the myth of a departed universal fellowship, in order to critique the lack of coherence in society. Indeed, Bonnett points out that all radical politics is generally nostalgic for lost utopias and universal aspirations that provide it with direction.

This opens up a new concern for our survey and interrogation of radical politics today – what is radical politics becoming nostalgic for post-crisis? In his contribution **Ken Worpole** gives one answer. Like many others in this book he says radical politics needs to return to a belief in universal needs and conditions. This is illustrated by the example of modern childhood and education. Reminding us that poverty and lack of opportunity still blight the lives of millions, Worpole demonstrates how difficult it has become to create collective, progressive visions for change through educational systems. Yet he also points to how few radicals in recent years have been concerned with such universal aspirations.

Illustrating this point **Sheila Jasanoff** questions those who claim that education, science and technological innovation are universally to the benefit of all. Drawing upon examples such as Harvard University, she argues that the new knowledge economies and technological innovations are locked into dominant imaginations, which drive us in particular directions, heedless of history, culture or social context. Jasanoff writes that there are two ways to respond – one modest, the other radical. The modest approach maintains the dominant narrative of progress; that of the North of the globe. The radical approach politicises innovation, where political alliances are built by disparately concerned people, challenging those who claim that technological innovations are 'universally' good for all.

Nigel Thrift also explores the tensions between universality, the university and radical politics. Weighing up the pros and cons of universities, he argues that they need to be defended because of their radical potential to drive society collectively forward for the better, particularly at a time of stagnation and despair. However, Thrift wonders whether many so-called combative radicals from the Left fully realise this point. For to say that universities are vital civilisational forces, without which we would all be worse off, can sound fey and oppressive to the full-blooded Left-wing radical. Thrift, however, believes that this reveals a lot about the nature of such radicals today. It demonstrates a narrow focus upon critique, and a suspicion of authority and expertise.

As **Will Hutton** points out, radical politics on the Left needs a strong, unifying utopian vision. It also needs to be more supportive of the state and institutional structures. When the economic crisis hit, most people turned to the state, not the market, to step in. It is also important for radical politics on the Left to develop strong, overarching narratives, as a response to the rise in ugly Right-wing nationalisms, and the failures of the centre ground in mainstream Western politics. Hutton argues that such countervisions are necessary to mobilise people's imaginations and desires; to seize the present opportunity for progressive change. But they can only be achieved through the development of strong institutional structures.

4. The role of the state

Further conflicting perspectives are brought out in the last part of the book. Turning to the theme of anarchism, **Saul Newman** acknowledges that radicals have tended to look upon it less favourably in the last few years. Nonetheless, he encourages the reader to take a closer look at its successes. Newman says withdrawal from collective representation, the state and institutions is strictly the only proper radical act. He calls for celebration of such experiments today, saying: 'this is not an escape from politics – precisely the opposite: it is an *active withdrawal* that fundamentally calls into question the symbolic authority of the state'. **Chantal Mouffe** disagrees in her contribution. Mouffe distinguishes between two approaches dominating contemporary radical politics: the first as 'critique as withdrawal' from the state; the second as 'critique as engagement' with it. She is unequivocal: withdrawal leaves a vacuum, which is frequently filled by the Right. Despite this, a significant number of contemporary radical theorists still believe withdrawal is more valuable. Turning against this tide, she supports those who extend a 'war of position' deep into unjust state practices, building coalitions across a range of geographical sites, not an exodus. Mouffe thereby illustrates how some leading postmodern and radical thinkers today are looking more favourably upon the state as an agent of positive change.

David Featherstone specifically targets Chantal Mouffe for criticism however, saying she sees: 'the national as the key site where political antagonisms are to be constructed and negotiated primarily through parliamentary politics'. Featherstone believes this makes it tricky to recognise and engage with key contemporary movements bringing neo-liberalism into contestation; namely, the transnational counterglobalisation movements. In contrast to Featherstone, **Alejandro Colás** and **Jason Edwards** explicitly agree with Mouffe's sentiments about the nation state. These contributors write that 'without the powerful resources of the modern state – its capacity to collect and reinvest revenue; to regulate the economy and redistribute wealth; to provide for or coordinate the delivery of the necessary infrastructure in securing basic human needs – struggles for radical democracy can get stuck in the debilitating treadmill of constant protest, perpetual mobilisation and ubiquitous antagonism.' Mouffe, Colás and Edwards alike criticise those who seek to operate too much outside the state.

However, **David Boyle** points out that many people are concerned with the way in which the state has over-centralised many services, prescribing ever more regulations and statistics to discipline ordinary life. Boyle's chapter reveals a wider desire for authentic social interaction, connection and engagement within radical politics today. This seeks to act against what many radicals see as the overbearing control and power of the state.

In contrast, in the last chapter of the book **Saskia Sassen** explores how state power can be used for progressive means, particularly in the sphere of international human rights. She says the recent crisis demonstrates that the state is increasingly the main agent for global change (notably in the USA). With the growing power of state intervention, radicals have once again been re-thinking their stance towards government. Sassen asks of the USA: 'could the emergent internationalism of the executive branch, now used to further the global corporate economy, be used for addressing some of our pressing global challenges?' Such provocative statements, contentious within this book of conflicting opinions, demonstrate the diverse but open possibilities within radical politics today.

5. Initial reflections

We are at a watershed moment for radical politics. Despite a global crisis, there is no obvious alternative to neo-liberalism for people to mobilise around. Given that the dominant institutions of politics have visibly failed us all, radical politics is being forced into the spotlight. For after the spectacular collapse of neo-liberalism, everyone is reflecting upon the radical alternatives. The question – what *is* radical politics today? – is no longer of peripheral concern to the population at large. This is a sobering time.

As an important aside for students, we should remember that in the 1980s and 1990s large amounts of money were injected into Right-wing think tanks and educational institutions (particularly in the USA). Whereas the Left was uncertain about its educational agenda, the Right certainly was not. This meant that educational institutions focused upon the (now discredited) theories underlying neo-liberalism. Neo-liberal ideology filtered through the educational system, which became a point of indoctrination. Given that neo-liberalism is now discredited, millions of people educated in the 1980s and 1990s, in turn, naturally have a sense of alienation from both education and politics. Because when the economic crisis came, these were not places where seriously discussed alternatives to neo-liberalism could be found.

This book therefore seeks to reinvigorate the importance of a critical survey into the spirit of radical politics in our times. As will now be seen, there is a wide range of perspectives to reflect upon.

Jon Pugh, Director, 'What *is* radical politics today?' project[1]
Newcastle University
England

Note

1. If you are interested in this ongoing project, please email: Jonathan.Pugh@ncl. ac.uk. Or respond through the magazine, found at: http://www.spaceofdemo cracy.org

Part I
Grand Visions

1
Getting to the Roots of Radical Politics Today

Zygmunt Bauman

Lives on credit

This chapter answers the question 'what *is* radical politics today?' by drawing attention to how so-called radical alternatives to the present global crisis are not radical. They do not get to the root of the problem: namely our addiction to a particular lifestyle.[1]

The current credit panic offers a striking illustration of what 'reaching the roots' in politics ought to mean but all too often, contrary to its self-presentation and perhaps also its self-illusion, does not. The present-day credit crunch is not an outcome of the banks' *failure*. On the contrary, it is a fully expectable, even if by and large unforeseen, fruit of their outstanding *success*: success in transforming a huge majority of men and women, old and young, into a race of debtors: debtors forever, once the condition of 'being in debt' has been made self-perpetuating, and as long as more debts keep being offered as the sole realistic salvation from the debts already incurred. In the last three decades, entering that condition has become easy as never before in human history; whereas escaping that condition has never been so difficult. Whoever could be made into a debtor, and millions of others, for instance the 'sub-prime mortgage' recipients, who could not and should not be lured into playing the lending/borrowing game, have been enticed and seduced into going into debt. And just as shoeing of all or almost all barefoot people spells trouble for the shoe industry, so the indebting of all or almost all debt-free people spells disaster for the loan industry. Rosa Luxemburg's famous prediction has come true once more: habitually behaving like a snake devouring its own tail, capitalism is now again dangerously close to an unwitting suicide by managing to exhaust the supply of new virgin lands for exploitation.

In the USA, the average household debt has risen in the last eight years – the years of apparently unprecedented prosperity – by 22 per cent. The total sum of unpaid credit card loans has increased by 15 per cent. And perhaps most menacingly, the overall debt of college students, the future political, economic and spiritual elite of the nation, has doubled. Training in the art of 'living in debt', and living in debt permanently, 'till death do us part', has been incorporated in the curriculum of national education. A very similar situation has been reached in Great Britain. The rest of Europe follows suit, not far behind. The banking planet is running short of virgin lands, having already recklessly adopted for exploitation vast expanses of the endemically barren.

The reaction so far, impressive and even revolutionary as it might appear once recycled into the media headlines and politicians' soundbites, has been 'more of the same': an effort to *re-capitalise the money lenders and to make their debtors credit-worthy once more*, so that the business of lending and borrowing, as well as of falling in debt and staying there, could return to normal. The welfare state for the rich (which, in a stark distinction from its namesake for the poor, has never been in danger of being put out of operation) has been brought back to the showrooms from the service quarters to which its offices were temporarily relegated to avoid invidious comparisons. To be sure, restoring it to public approval and acclaim was not extended to the welfare state for the non-rich: to that welfare state, the emphatic statement made by John McCain, the US Republican presidential candidate, before the credit crunch hit the headlines – that 'it is not the duty of government to bail out and reward those who act irresponsibly' – surely stands (*New York Times*, 28 March 2008).

The state's muscles, long unused for that purpose, have again been publicly flexed; this time for the sake of continuing the game that makes flexing them resented – yet also, abominably, unavoidable; a game that, curiously, cannot bear the state flexing its muscles yet cannot survive without it. Note that the American government took action only once the suicidal tendency of rampant globalisation and of the wholesale deregulation of global financial markets was experienced first-hand, and so noticed, by the *first-league* players of the free-market and free-capital-flows game. All the measures which have been suddenly, and in sharp contradiction to all their previous professions of faith, undertaken by the federal authorities, are aimed at salvaging the high and mighty from the catastrophe they visited upon the lowly and weak, and at allowing them to recover from present and future 'hiccups' and play the globalisation game with yet greater stamina, determination, self-abandonment – and profit.

The measures have been introduced to save the sharks, not the minnows on which they feed, and once reassured and reinforced, sharks are the last creatures likely to demand constraints on hunting in global waters. In the flowery phrase of the *Financial Times* of 20 September 2008, 'global markets roared in approval' at the American line of action, which in the sober estimate of the same paper was meant to 'allow banks to stem their losses, re-capitalise and return to business' (Guha et al., 2008). Note: not to change their, the banks', routine methods – but to make the banks able, once more, to follow them, reassured and hoping that they will be bailed out from the consequences of their greed with which they were previously supposed (and conceitedly demanded) to deal by their own means (insufficient, as it now transpires) and according to their own judgement (wrong, as it now appears). As Alistair Darling, responsible for British financial policy, told *Sky News* on 8 October 2008, the successive (one is tempted to say 'serial') 'Black Wednesday', morning: 'we want to make sure that we can get the system going again'.

What is joyously (and foolishly) forgotten is that the nature of human suffering is determined by the way humans live. The roots of the currently lamented pain, like the roots of all social evil, are sunk deep in our mode of life by our carefully cultivated and by now ingrained habit of running for consumer credit whenever there is a problem to face or a difficulty to bypass. In August 2007, mortgages, loans and credit card debts in Britain overtook the entire gross domestic product: the British, one may say, live on credit – spending money they have not earned and less and less able to repay from their earnings. Like many drugs, life on credit is addictive, and decades of lavish supply of a drug cannot but lead to shock and trauma when the supply grinds to a halt. We are now proposed the apparently easy way out of shock that afflicts both drug addicts and drug pushers: through resuming the (hopefully regular) supply of drugs and preventing the addiction from being cured.

Tackling the roots of the problem which, unintended by the principal political actors, has been now pulled out of the 'top secret' compartment into the focus of public attention, is the only solution likely to be adequate to the enormity of the task, in order to survive the intense, yet comparatively brief agonies of withdrawal. Yet, like all radical solutions, it is not an *instant* solution. It will need more thought, more action and more time than a feverish attempt to 'recapitalise' the money-lending and debt-promoting banks and make their debtors 'credit-worthy' once more (but for how long?), in still-born hope of refreshing, instead of cutting, the roots from which if 'things are going well' germinate and sprout up, simultaneously, the fabulous (even if short-lived) profits of the banks and the misery of their borrowers.

None of the radical political undertakings required are instant solutions; measures hoped to be instantly effective as a rule aim at mitigating (again as a rule temporarily) a crisis – at trimming the 'abnormalities' and restoring the *status quo ante* dubbed 'normality'. Instant solutions, however extraordinary and bold, are essentially *conservative*, intended to restore the conditions responsible for the crisis. For that reason, they cannot come anywhere near the 'roots' of the trouble and therefore fail to prevent the crisis from returning with a vengeance. Indeed, they store up trouble for the (not very distant) future. That applies to the ingrained habit and institutionalised necessity of living on credit – but also, and in equal measure, to the roots of other social evils which present-day radical politics must tackle. A few of them will be briefly discussed below.

Lives to waste

With its compulsive and obsessive urge to modernise, our world creates two mass industries of 'human waste'. One industry is order-building (that cannot but massively produce human *rejects*, the 'unfit' who are excluded from proper and orderly, 'normal' society). Another, called 'economic progress', turns out huge quantities of human *leftovers*: humans for whom there is no place in the 'economy', no useful role to play and no opportunity to earn a living, at least in the ways defined as legal (recommended or just tolerable). The social (welfare) state was an ambitious attempt to phase out those two industries. It was a project of inclusion for all, and of bringing to an end the practices of social exclusion. In many respects successful, though not without its shortcomings, the social state itself is now being phased out – while the two industries of human waste are back in operation in full swing, the first producing the 'aliens' (*sans papiers*, illegal immigrants, false asylum seekers, and all sorts of other 'undesirables'), the other producing flawed consumers, and both together producing the underclass: not the lower class at the bottom of the class ladder, but people for whom there is no place in *any* social class, people cast *outside* the class system of 'normal society'.

The state is today unable, and/or unwilling, to promise its subjects existential security ('freedom from fear', as Franklin Delano Roosevelt famously phrased it). Gaining existential security – obtaining and retaining a legitimate and dignified place in human society and avoiding the menace of exclusion – is now left to the skills and resources of each individual on his or her own; and that means taking enormous risks, and suffering harrowing uncertainty which such tasks inevitably induce. The fear which the social state promised to uproot has returned – with a vengeance. Most of us, from the bottom to the top, now fear being excluded, shown to be inadequate to the challenge, denied dignity and humiliated.

On the diffuse and misty fears that saturate present-day society, politicians as much as the consumer markets are eager to capitalise. The sellers of consumer goods and services advertise their commodities as foolproof remedies against an abominable sense of uncertainty and ill-defined threats. Populist movements and populist politicians pick up the task abandoned by the weakening and disappearing social state, and also by much of whatever remains of the by and large bygone socialist Left. But in stark opposition to the social state, they are interested in *expanding*, not *reducing* the volume of fears; and particularly in expanding fears of the kind of dangers they can be seen on TV to be gallantly resisting and fighting back and all in all protecting the nation from. These seldom, if ever, happen to be the real dangers that lie at the roots of popular anxiety and fear. However successful the state might be in resisting the advertised menaces, the genuine sources of anxiety, uncertainty and social insecurity – those prime causes of fear endemic to the modern capitalist way of life – will remain intact and if anything be reinforced.

In times of globalisation, directing resentment towards migrants particularly captures the public imagination and is therefore politically profitable. In some perverted way migrants are seen to represent everything that breeds anxiety and horrifies in the new variety of uncertainty and insecurity that has been and continues to be prompted by mysterious, impenetrable and unpredictable global forces. Migrants embody, bring 'into one's backyard', render palpable and all-too-visible the horrors of destroyed livelihood, enforced exile, social degradation, ultimate exclusion and relegation to a 'non-place' outside the universe of law and rights – and so they incarnate all those half-conscious or subconscious existential fears that torment men and women of a liquid modern society. Chasing the migrants away, one rebels (by proxy) against all those mysterious global forces that threaten to visit on everybody else the fate already suffered by the migrants. There is a lot of capital in that illusion that can be (and is) adroitly exploited by the politicians and the markets alike.

As far as the bulk of the electorate is concerned, political leaders, present and aspiring, are judged by the severity they manifest in the course of the 'security race'. Politicians try to outdo each other in their promises to be tough on the culprits of insecurity – whether genuine or putative, but always those that are near, within reach, can be fought and defeated or at least deemed to be conquerable and presented as such.

Forza Italia or the Lega may win elections promising to defend the hard-working Lombardians against being robbed by lazy Calabrians, to defend both against the newcomers that remind them of the shakiness of their own position, and to defend every voter against obtrusive beggars, stalkers, prowlers and muggers. The genuine threats to human decent life and dignity will emerge from all that unscathed.

Freedom fatigue

Democracies are at risk, but only partly due to the *state governments* desperately seeking to legitimise their right to rule and to demand discipline – through flexing their muscles and showing their determination to stand firm in the face of endless, genuine or putative threats to human bodies – instead of (as they did before) protecting their citizens' social usefulness, their respected place in society, and promoting insurance against exclusion, denial of dignity and humiliation. I say 'partly', because a second threat to democracy is what can only be called 'freedom fatigue', manifested in the placidity with which most of us accept the process of the step-by-step limitation of our hard-won liberties, our rights to privacy, to defence in court, and to being treated as innocent until proven guilty. Laurent Bonnelli (2008) recently coined the term 'liberticide' to denote that combination of states' new far-reaching ambitions and citizens' timidity and indifference. He asks what are the true, even if undeclared, targets of the new 'securitarian' policies: 'L'antiterrorisme contre les libertés civiles?'

A while ago I watched on television many thousands of passengers stranded at British airports after another 'terrorist panic' – when flights were cancelled after an announcement that the 'unspeakable dangers' of a 'liquid bomb', and a worldwide plot to explode aircraft in flight, had been discovered. Those thousands lost their holidays, and missed important business meetings and family reunions. But they did not complain! Not in the least. Neither did they complain of having been sniffed all over by dogs, kept in endless queues for security checks, or submitted to body searches that they might well consider offensive to their dignity. On the contrary – they were jubilant: 'We have never felt so safe as now', they kept repeating. 'We are so grateful to our authorities for their vigilance and for taking such good care of our safety!'

Keeping prisoners in camps without charge for years on end has prompted an occasional murmur of protest, but not a public outcry. We console ourselves that all those violations of human rights are aimed at 'them', not 'us' – at different kinds of humans (are they indeed human?!);

those outrages will not affect us. We have conveniently forgotten the sad warning of Martin Niemöller, the Lutheran pastor and a victim of Nazi persecution, in his 1976 poem:

> When the Nazis came for the communists,
> I remained silent;
> I was not a communist.
>
> Then they locked up the social democrats,
> I remained silent;
> I was not a social democrat.
>
> Then they came for the trade unionists,
> I did not speak out;
> I was not a trade unionist.
>
> Then they came for the Jews,
> I did not speak out;
> I was not a Jew.
>
> When they came for me,
> there was no one left to speak out for me.

Global problems, local solutions

In an insecure world, security is the name of the game. Security is the main purpose of the game and its paramount stake . . . It is a value that in practice, if not in theory, dwarfs and elbows out all other values – including the values dearest to 'us' while hated most by 'them', and for that reason declared the prime cause of 'their' wish to harm 'us'. In a world as insecure as ours, personal freedom of word and action, right to privacy, access to truth – all those things we used to associate with democracy and in whose name we still go to war – need to be trimmed or suspended. Or at least this is what the official story, confirmed by official practice, maintains.

The truth, however, is that we cannot effectively defend our freedoms here at home while fencing ourselves off from the rest of the world and attending solely to our own affairs. There are valid reasons to suppose that in a globalised world, in which the plight of everyone everywhere determines the plight of all the others while being determined by them in turn, one can no longer assure freedom and democracy 'separately' – in isolation, in one country, or in a few selected countries only. The fate of freedom and democracy in each land is decided and settled on the global stage; and only on that stage can it be defended with a realistic chance of lasting success. It is no longer in the power of any state acting singly, however resourceful, heavily armed, resolute and uncompromising, to defend chosen values at home while turning its back on the dreams and aspirations of those outside its borders. But turning our backs is precisely what we, the Europeans, seem to be doing, when keeping our riches and multiplying them at the expense of the poor outside.

At an earlier stage, modernity raised human integration to the level of *nations*. However, before it finishes its job, modernity needs to perform one more task, yet more formidable: to raise human integration to the level of *humanity*, inclusive of the whole population of the planet. However hard and thorny that task may yet prove to be, it is imperative and urgent, because for a planet of universal interdependency it is, literally, a matter of (shared) life or (joint) death. One of the crucial conditions for this task being undertaken and performed is the creation of a *global* equivalent of the 'social state' that completed and crowned the previous phase of modern history – that of the integration of localities and tribes into nation states. At some point, therefore, the resurgence of the essential core of the socialist 'active utopia' – the principle of collective responsibility and collective insurance against misery and bad fortune – would be indispensable, though this time on the global scale, with *humanity as a whole* as its object.

At the stage that the globalisation of capital and commodity trade has already reached, no governments, singly or even severally, are able to balance the books – and without the books having been balanced the continuation of 'social state' practices effectively cutting at the roots of poverty and preventing inequality trends from running wild are inconceivable. It is also difficult to imagine governments able, singly or even severally, to impose limits on consumption and to raise local taxation to the levels required by the continuation, let alone further expansion, of social services. Intervention in the markets is indeed badly needed. But will *state* intervention bring tangible effects? Rather, it will be the work of *non*-governmental, state-independent and perhaps even state-dissident initiatives. Poverty and inequality, and more generally the disastrous side-effects and 'collateral damage' of global *laissez faire*, cannot be dealt with effectively separately from the rest of the planet in one corner of the globe (unless at a human cost that the North Koreans or the Burmese have been forced to pay). There is no decent way in which a single or several territorial states can 'opt out' from the global interdependency of humanity. The 'social state' is no longer viable; only a 'social planet' may take over the functions it not so long ago tried, with mixed success, to perform.

I suspect that the vehicles likely to take us to that 'social planet' are not the territorially sovereign states – but rather, and from the start, extra-territorial and cosmopolitan non-governmental organisations and associations; those that reach directly to people in need, above the heads of and with no interference from the local 'sovereign' governments.

This is, not necessarily by our choice, the substance of 'radical politics'. As Karl Marx memorably observed, humans make their history, but not in conditions of their choice.

Note

1. Acts, undertakings, means and measures may be called 'radical' when they reach down to the *roots*: of a problem, a challenge, a task. Note, however, that the Latin noun 'radix', to which the metaphorical uses of 'radical' trace their pedigree, refers not only to *roots*, but also to *foundations* and to *origins*. What do these three notions – root, foundation and origin – have in common? Two features:

   One: under normal circumstances, the material referents of all three are hidden from view and impossible to examine, let alone to touch directly. Whatever has grown out of them (their 'outgrowth' – like trunks or stems in case of roots, edifices in case of the foundations, or consequences in case of the origins), has been superimposed on top, or emerged after covering them and hiding them from view – and so it has first to be pierced, cast out of the way or taken apart, if one wishes the objects targeted when thinking or acting 'radically' to be reached.

   Two: in the course of blazing trails to those targets, their outgrowth needs to be notionally deconstructed, or materially 'pushed out of the way' or dismantled. Probability is high that from the work of deconstruction/dismantling the targets will emerge once and for all disabled, and for all practical purposes incapacitated: they might be no longer able to give birth to, offer a site for, or start off, another growth – particularly an outgrowth replicating the one that has been decomposed or stifled. Taking a 'radical' stance signals an intention to *destroy* – or, at any rate, the readiness to *take the risk* of destruction; more often than not, a radical stance aims at a '*creative* destruction' – destruction in the sense of 'site-clearing', or turning over and loosening the soil, in order to prepare for another round of sowing or planting and make the ground ready to accommodate another type of root. Politics is 'radical' if it accepts all those conditions, and if it guides itself by all such intentions and objectives.

   Having said this, however, leaves the criteria of recognising the claim to radicalism sorely under-defined. The radicalism of a specific policy is as a rule an 'essentially contested' issue – and no wonder, considering that the reputation of radicalism in politics is a widely coveted badge of honour and so tends to be an object of intense competition. In political rivalry, to possess an opinion of 'radicalism' is an asset; to be charged with 'superficiality' or 'irrelevance' (the opposites of 'radicalism') is a liability. What, however, is believed/presented by some as 'reaching to the roots of the matter', may well be decried and deprecated by some others as a mere 'surfing', 'quibbling' or 'leading astray', or otherwise misconceived and irrelevant.

Each policy rests its claim to radicalism on an overtly spelled out or tacitly assumed theoretical model – of the society to which it is addressed and of the cause-and-effect chains underlying its operation. More often than not, theoretical models are themselves 'essentially contested' propositions and the contentiousness of claims to 'radicalism' is a derivative of that fact. Whatever the models' truth value, their selection, and consequently the definitions of 'roots' and their outgrowth, are in the last account matters of political choices: the choices most radical of all political decisions.

References

Bonnelli, L. (2008) 'Antiterrorisme en France, un système liberticide?' *Le Monde*, 11 September 2008.
Darling, A. (2008) *Sky News* 8 October.
Guha, K. (in Washington), F. Guerrera and M. Mackenzie (in New York) and G. Tett (in London) (2008) 'Global markets roar in approval', *Financial Times*, 20 September http://www.ft.com/cms/s/0/fcfd84aa-86ac-11dd-959e-0000779fd18c.html?nclick_check=1
New York Times (2008) 'Equity Loans as Next Round in Credit Crisis', 28 March.
Niemöller, M. (1976) *First They Came*, http://en.wikipedia.org/wiki/First_they_came...

2
What Happened to Radical Humanism?

Frank Furedi

This chapter explores the nature and character of radical politics today, by drawing out one central and overriding trend: the lack of a radical humanism. In one important sense the current economic crisis is different to any other that has erupted since the beginning of capitalism. In contrast to the past there is little in the way of any fundamental critiques or alternatives to the system. The predominant response has been to perceive the current crisis as if it was brought on by an act of nature. Most of the criticism takes the form of superficial denunciation of individual greed, financial manipulation and of obsessive consumption. Instead of a socio-economic interrogation of the system critics have attacked the psychology of selfishness. Anyone perusing the radical press would assume that if it was not for greedy bankers, excessive executive bonuses and the reckless manipulation of financial instruments then everything would be all right. Worse still some so-called anti-capitalist commentators have actually welcomed the recession on the grounds that it will force people to cut down on their consumption and presumably live a more wholesome life. Some environmentalists have expressed the hope that today's turbulent global economy will be hospitable to a green agenda and that capitalism could be open to becoming recognised on a more 'sustainable' basis. Of course since nothing is more sustainable than stasis an indefinite depression can be presented as a positive outcome.

One reason why the response to the present crisis is so incoherent is because anti-capitalist ideas and politics have lost their critical and progressive edge. The term 'anti-capitalism' today is rarely associated with the claim that this system of production lacks a dynamic towards development. On the contrary, the focus of criticism of radical and Left-wing activists is that capitalism develops far too much and far too fast and that this has destructive consequences for both the environment and for people. The fear today is that there is far too much development and that capitalism produces too many things. 'Today, with its dysfunctional side effects, we are more aware of the dangers; we now experience the inexorable development of productive forces and the global expansion of western civilization more as threats' argues Jürgen Habermas (1997: 37), a leading German Leftist social theorist. If anything, for Habermas capitalism has become much too efficient. 'One can no longer coax an unredeemed promise from the production-centred capitalist project' he complains.

In direct contrast to the traditions of the nineteenth- and twentieth-century radical movement, those who define themselves as Left wing today are weary of economic and technological development. One recent attempt to give some content to the meaning of 'Left wing' argued that the orientation towards production was a characteristic feature of the politics of the Right. It argued that 'needless to say, the neo-liberal Right supports the present dominance of the productivist logic, whereas the Left struggles for a shift from the present gross imbalance to a balanced co-existence of the above values/rationalities' (Mouzelis, 2001: 447).

Apprehension about fast rates of economic growth and the development of new technology is linked to a sense of insecurity regarding change. In what constitutes a dramatic reversal of roles the Left appears to be more uncomfortable in dealing with change than the Right. Organisations like the World Social Forum appear more hostile to change than the targets of its criticism. For example, Samir Amin disputes what he calls the 'dominant right wing discourse', which argues that change is always for the better and happens spontaneously. As a result, Amin (2004: 7–8) contends that 'we now have to look at what is new in a different way'. He asks 'how can popular forces reorganise to reduce the damage associated with global capitalist expansion?'

Apprehension concerning development has been reinterpreted by today's cultural and political elites as a risk. Human progress, once embraced as a wholly desirable enterprise, is today represented as a risk to be avoided. Paradoxically, it is those who call themselves Left wing who have become most risk averse and most vociferous in denouncing the idea of progress. In the nineteenth century, the association of anti-capitalism with hostility to progress was confined to the Luddites and the conservative reaction to modernity. Radicals, liberals and socialists were for progress. Today, the most bitter opponents of progress are the radical anti-capitalist critics of production and development.

In previous times, radical opponents of capitalism denounced the system for failing to provide people with the material possessions they required for a decent life. Today's anti-capitalists believe that we (at least in the West) have too many possessions and reject the 'mindless consumerism' perpetuated by the market. Not surprisingly, in an era of 'conspicuous consumption' the problem of poverty has become a less fashionable issue. The term 'child poverty' can still exercise a bit of concern but poverty as such is off the political radar.

An anti-modernist critique of mass society often lurks behind the label of anti-capitalism. In the first half of the twentieth century anti-modernist sentiments tended to be linked to the conservative reaction to change. In Europe, conservative thinkers felt uncomfortable with new forms of popular culture and regarded Hollywood, jazz and the crass materialism of the USA with dread. Today this response of interwar Little England conservatism is frequently proclaimed by the lifestyle politics of radical activists. Hating MTV, Nike, Coca Cola, McDonald's or Starbucks has become a defining feature of the message. As one advocate of this approach argues 'attaching political messages to corporate brands becomes a useful way to carry often radical ideas into diverse personal life spaces, as well as across national borders and cultural divides' (Bennett, 2004: 2).

The conservatism of fear disposes both radical critics of the status quo and the upholders of the establishment to become preoccupied with what they see as the mounting dangers facing human existence. Again, in a reversal of roles, Leftist commentators are often more promiscuous in their doom-mongering than are conservative commentators. They revel in stories about *X-Files* style cover-ups over poisoned food, lethal pollutants, new diseases and other threats to human health. Throughout most of the past 300 years, conspiracy theories were frequently used by the Right to explain unexpected and unpleasant developments. Blaming outside agitators, Jewish and Masonic conspiracies for violent upheavals and disorder was part of the repertoire of the Right-wing political imagination. Today, conspiracy theory has become appropriated by Left-wing commentators. Major events such as the war in Iraq or against terrorism as well as the 2004 election of George Bush are portrayed as the outcome of a plot hatched by a small cabal of neo-conservatives.

It seems that, regardless of their point of departure, commentators of different shades of opinion are now likely to arrive at a strikingly similar conclusion: that the world is an increasingly dangerous, out-of-control place. All sides promote the politics of fear. The target of their concern may differ – some are anxious about the rise of street crime, while others are obsessed by the variety of abuses that children face. The Right is apprehensive about the threat of terrorism; the Left is anxious about some impending environmental catastrophe. What seems to divide political figures is what and how they should fear.

For a radical humanism

We need to retrace our steps to the time before there was a Left and Right – to recover the progressive legacy of the past. We do this not because we want to escape from politics but because we live in pre-political times that require the recovery of ideas through which a challenge to fatalism can be mounted. They demand that we let go of the categories that helped illuminate political life in the last century. The line of division that matters today is between those who subscribe to the conformist embrace of the present and those who want to mobilise the past experience of humanity to influence the future. In particular we need to challenge the prevailing interpretation of change that assigns human beings a passive role in the making of history. Human beings are viewed as extraneous to the process of change and therefore are seen to exercise little influence over their destiny. Back in the eighteenth century, the German philosopher Immanuel Kant recognised that it was the emergence of the condition where individuals could pursue their destiny unimpeded that constituted the point of departure of the Enlightenment. Experimentation and the pursuit of knowledge are not simply good in and of themselves, they give freedom and democracy real content.

Kant (1784) claimed that the 'enlightenment is man's emergence from his self-imposed immaturity'. By immaturity he meant 'the inability to use one's understanding without guidance from another'. According to Kant this immaturity was self-imposed and its 'cause lies not in lack of understanding, but in lack of resolve and courage to use it without guidance from another'. And confronting his reader with what he characterised as the motto of the Enlightenment – *Sapere Aude* or Dare to Know – he challenged them to use their understanding. Today, when the Precautionary Principle constantly communicates the prejudice that science threatens to run ahead of society and that those mounting experiments are 'playing God', daring to know is often represented as an act of irresponsibility. Kant would have been perplexed by contemporary society's uneasy relation with science and knowledge.

Of course our ambiguous relationship with knowledge and reason is not due to the failure of individual character but the outcome of a more deep-seated process of cultural disorientation. Unfortunately

Kant's diagnosis of self-imposed immaturity is more pertinent to contemporary times than to the circumstances he faced. At a time when the claims of knowledge and science are regarded with mistrust and cynicism the motto *Sapere Aude* goes against the grain of contemporary cultural sensibility.

Contemporary cultural norms even in their radical form are highly sceptical of the ideal of individual autonomy. To be sure, even at the best of times, individual autonomy is an ideal that can at best be realised inconsistently. People live in a world not of their own making and in circumstances that often elude their aspiration to determine their affairs. The exercise of autonomy has always come up against external constraints – natural obstacles, economic exigencies, wars and conflict and social dislocation. Today it also faces a cultural climate that is deeply suspicious of the aspiration for autonomous behaviour. It also has few friends among those who call themselves radical.

Human action often results in unexpected outcomes, some of which are uncomfortable to live with. Nevertheless the pursuit of the ideal of autonomy offers people the promise of choices and frequently results in progress. It is precisely because some individuals have taken this ideal seriously that they successfully challenged repressive institutions and the use of arbitrary powers that sought to thwart their ambition. An enlightened society needs to harness the ideal of individual autonomy to create the optimum conditions for human development. Societies that fail to valorise this ideal end up dominated by a culture of fatalism and risk collapsing into a state of stasis.

The Enlightenment ideal of individual autonomy insists that society and the state must recognise the independence of each individual. As Bronner (2004: 136) argues, 'autonomy originally implied the right for each to have his or her faith'. Such a perspective puts into question the right of the state to promote a particular faith – be it in the form of a traditional religion or the lifestyle crusades associated with the current policy of behaviour modification. Recognition of the ideal of individual autonomy – an important component of the legacy of the Enlightenment – represents the foundation for choice-making, moral and political decision-making and political action.

Popular suspicion towards the exercise of human agency means that the ideal of individual autonomy is frequently dismissed as an illusion fostered by apologists for the free market. It is argued that in a society which is dominated by the media, big corporations and forces unleashed by globalisation, individuals lack the capacity for autonomous action. Moreover, as diminished or vulnerable subjects, people do not so much choose their faith as have it foisted on them. That is why the Enlightenment model of the autonomous and responsible citizen is displaced by a more passive disoriented individual who requires the 'support' of public institutions. What we are left with is a regression to the condition of the immature self of the pre-Enlightenment era.

The mood of cultural pessimism does not leave society untouched. It has a profound impact on how people see themselves. It is difficult to Dare to Know when our culture continually transmits the signal that risk-taking is irresponsible and that caution and safety are the principal virtues of our time. Such signals serve as an invitation to people to constrain their aspirations and limit their actions. If people are repeatedly told that not much is expected of them and that indeed they are vulnerable individuals in need of support – they will frequently begin to play the part that is assigned to them. Today the promise of individual autonomy is contradicted by the reality of a culture that is uncomfortable with its exercise. As a result, individual existence is experienced not so much through the prism of autonomy but through that of isolation.

The lack of validation accorded to the ideal of autonomy goes hand in hand with a lack of respect for democracy. Powerful anti-democratic sentiments have been institutionalised by public bodies that are devoted to treating adults like children. Public policy is frequently inspired by the belief that the electorate cannot be relied on to figure out what is in its best interest. The politics of fear provides one instrument for 'raising the awareness' of people about what's good for them. In the twenty-first century it is not politically correct to refer to people as 'mentally children or barbarians'. Nevertheless the representation of grown-up citizens as 'vulnerable' people fuels the profound anti-democratic ethos that we discussed previously. Their orientation interacts and reinforces the feeble sense of personhood that prevails today. It is this pre-Enlightenment story of personhood that constitutes the first and arguably principal obstacle to the restoration of political life.

Humanising personhood

The version of personhood that is most consistent with the ideals of autonomy, the exercise of choice and history-making, is that given by the legacy of the Enlightenment. Risk-taking, experimentation, the exercise of critical judgement and reason are some of the important attributes of historical thinking and agency. The exercise of these attributes is the precondition for the reconstitution of public life. Through such human activities people develop an understanding of how purposeful public activity may lead to positive results in the future. Without a sense of agency personhood lacks the imagination one associates with political engagement. Humanising personhood requires challenging the prevailing paradigm of vulnerability and gaining acceptance for the humanist concept of personhood.

The humanist and vulnerability paradigms of personhood (Figure 2.1) never exist in a pure form. Since the rise of the modern era every culture has internalised elements of both. But nevertheless cultures discriminate when they communicate stories about which forms of behaviour they value and which ones they don't. For example, throughout most of the nineteenth and twentieth centuries the ideals of self-help and self-sufficiency enjoyed cultural affirmation. Today, it is help-seeking that benefits from cultural validation. In contrast to the celebration of the risk-taking in former times, society today has turned safety into a veritable religion. The ideal of experimentation has been displaced by the conformist embrace of caution, which has been institutionalised through the precautionary principle. The values associated with the humanist paradigm of personhood are not entirely absent, but they have become subordinate to ones that promote the sensibility of vulnerability.

Humanist paradigm	Vulnerability paradigm
Valorises autonomy	Valorises help-seeking
Orientation towards reasoning	Scepticism towards the efficacy of knowledge
Search for universal values	Affirmation of identity
Positive attitude towards risk taking	Strongly risk-averse
Valuation of experimentation	Celebration of caution and safety
Belief in capacity to change and alter circumstances	Change is perceived as precursor of negative outcome
Oriented towards the future and upholds achievements of the past	Frozen in the present and estranged from the past
Expectation that community possesses coping skills	Anticipation that individuals/ communities are unlikely to cope
Believes that humanity possesses capacity to overcome adversity	Believes that people are defined by their state of vulnerability

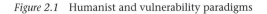

Figure 2.1   Humanist and vulnerability paradigms

Fortunately, human society can never entirely accept the fatalistic dogma of 'There is No Alternative'. Nor can it frame its ideal of personhood entirely based on the paradigm of vulnerability. That is why sections of society continue to look for a more positive version of personhood. Conflicting ideas about the paradigm of personhood are today the equivalent of past clashes of ideologies and political alternatives.[1] They touch upon such fundamental questions as what it means to be human, the meaning of human nature and the relationship between the individual and public institutions. Ideas about the paradigm of personhood constitute the point of departure for the formulation of policy and the creation of norms – informal and formal – that regulate people's relationship and individual behaviour. The meaning of personhood has important implications for how we view the relationship of people to history and the potential for changing and altering circumstances. Our attitude towards personhood informs how we make sense of the exercise of choice and of individual responsibility, our capacity to know, to reason and gain insights into the truth. Ultimately different ideas about personhood lead to conflicting ideas about public life. Whether people are perceived as the problem, or as the solvers of problems, depends on which paradigm one subscribes to.

In our era of political exhaustion the challenges that face us are characteristically pre-political ones. It makes little sense to develop an ambitious political philosophy when the sense of human subjectivity exists in a diminished form. Politics represents the negation of fate and its existence depends on the prevalence of the belief that what people do can make a difference. That is why today the challenge facing those interested in the reconstitution of public life is not the discovery of a Big Idea or the invention of a new political doctrine or philosophy. In the absence of a more robust sense of human agency that can act on such ideas, such doctrine would have a formal and platitudinous character. Does that not mean abandoning any hope of re-engaging with political life? Not at all. For the most immediate task facing those interested in the recovery of the Enlightenment sensibility towards the future is to contribute to the promotion of the humanist version of personhood. Before politics can be reconstituted we need to foster an intellectual climate that is hospitable to sentiments that directly challenge the prevailing paradigm of vulnerability. Humanising personhood is the most pressing issue and practical question facing those concerned with challenging the prevailing culture of fatalism.

Aside from the exhaustion of the traditions associated with Left and Right there is another reason why we need to stake out a new terrain for the development of public life. With the prevalence of the paradigm of human vulnerability, politics (Left or Right) has little practical consequences. What matters is whether people are prepared to accept the conformist ethos that freezes society in the present and deprives us of both our past and future. No doubt in the future there may be plenty of doctrinal issues to fight about. But perversely for now the genuine conservative and liberal and socialist have more in common than they suspect. The task of restoring a more human-centred public culture should engage the energies of all those who are inspired by the traditions associated with the historical movement from the Renaissance through to the Enlightenment and twentieth-century modernism. Despite profound political differences, we all have a common interest in rescuing the humanist tradition, and reconstructing it in a form appropriate to provide a progressive critique of the contemporary global crisis.

Note

1. These conflicts underpin some of the clashes of the so-called Culture Wars. See Furedi (2006) for a discussion of these trends.

References

Amin, S. (2004) 'For Struggles, Global and National: Samir Amin Interviewed by V. Sridhar', in J. A. Sen, A. Anand, A. Escobar and P. Waterman (eds), *The World Social Forum: Challenging Empires* (New Delhi: Viveka), http://www.choike.org/documentos/wsf_s102_amin.pdf

Bennett, W. (2004) 'Branded Political Communication', in M. Micheleti, A. Follesdal and D. Stolee (eds), *The Politics Behind Products* (New Brunswick: Transaction Books).

Bronner, S. (2004) *Reclaiming the Enlightenment: Towards a Politics of Radical Enlightenment* (New York: Columbia University Press).

Furedi, F. (2006) *Politics of Fear: Beyond Left and Right* (London: Continuum Press).

Habermas, J. (1997) 'Popular Sovereignty as Procedure', in J. Bohman and W. Rehg (eds), *Deliberative Democracy: Essays on Reason and Politics* (Cambridge, MA: MIT Press).

Kant, I. (1784) 'An Answer to the Question: "What is Enlightenment?"', http://eserver.org/philosophy/kant/what-is-enlightenment.txt

Mouzelis, N. (2001) 'Reflexive Modernization and the Third Way: the Impasse of Giddens' Social Democratic Politics', *The Sociological Review*, 49(3): 436–56.

3
Victim of Success: Green Politics Today

Paul Kingsnorth

My answer to the question – what *is* radical politics today? – is relatively straightforward and uncompromising. Green politics today, whilst often thought to be radical, is usually not so in practice. It has been watered down to such an extent, that it is undeserving of the description 'radical politics'. I start to explain this point, by way of a simple illustration.

A few years ago, I taught a class in environmental politics at a London college. I started the class by drawing a large circle on the blackboard. This, I told the students, represented industrial society. Within this circle I drew two smaller ones. One of them represented the political Left, one the political Right.

I then drew another circle, just outside the first one but meeting it at the edges. This, I said, was where green politics sat. It was not part of the conventional argument about how to divide up the spoils of industrial progress. Its purpose was to argue that the definition of progress itself was the problem to be solved: that industrial society, as currently constituted, was a threat not only to the individual freedom cherished by parts of the Right and the social justice cherished by parts of the Left, but also to the global ecosystem – what both sides referred to as the 'natural world', as if somehow humans were 'unnatural' and apart from it – which both were frantically destroying in the name of that progress. In this sense, I said, green politics was more radical than the teachings of either Marx or Hayek.

In explaining this, I was outlining one of the founding concepts of the green movement, as it had begun to take political form in the 1970s: that from an 'ecocentric' perspective – one which puts the wider world, rather than human interests, at its centre – the similarities between Left and Right are greater than their differences. This idea was, for example, outlined a quarter of a century ago by Jonathon Porritt (1984: 44) in his book *Seeing Green*, which introduced the then fairly novel concept of environmentalism to a wide audience:

> Both [capitalism and communism] are dedicated to industrial growth, to the expansion of the means of production, to a materialist ethic as the best means of meeting peoples' needs, and to unimpeded technological development. Both rely on increasing centralisation and large-scale bureaucratic control and co-ordination. From a viewpoint of narrow scientific rationalism, both insist that the planet is there to be conquered, that big is self-evidently beautiful, and that what cannot be measured is of no importance.

This argument is – or should be – at the core of green politics. It is a political and ethical philosophy which sees humanity as part of the web of life, not as a separate entity which can control and direct something called 'nature' with no consequences for itself. It stresses the ecological limits within which humans operate, and the need for an ecocentric – Earth-centred – rather than an anthropocentric – human-centred – standpoint. Finally, it stresses that human politics as currently constituted is fundamentally ill-equipped for this task – and that what is often regarded as political radicalism is in fact a reordering of the same anthropocentric development paradigm, in which the fruits of the destruction of global ecosystems are simply distributed to more humans than before.

Whatever happened to ecocentrism?

Today, forty years after green politics began to coalesce into a serious political force, its case has been spectacularly proven. The fallout from industrial progress is all around us, and it is tragic: a quarter of the world's mammals are currently threatened with imminent extinction; an acre and a half of rainforest falls every second; humanity consumes 25 per cent more of the ecosystem's products than the Earth can replace – a figure which is predicted to rise to 80 per cent by mid-century; 75 per cent of the world's fisheries are on the verge of collapse. And above it all looms runaway climate change, which threatens to render all human political projects irrelevant.

While socialism languishes sullenly in the shadows, communism remains in fatal shock after a century of brutal failure and capitalism undergoes its biggest structural crisis for at least half a century, it is easier than ever to argue that environmentalism is the most urgent and relevant political movement of the age. Yet in its current success may lie the seeds of its potential destruction.

In less than a decade, environmentalism in the West has moved from being a fringe concern to a fashion statement. Its influence can be seen everywhere: from burgeoning farmers' markets to organic food on supermarket shelves; from daily newspaper headlines about climate change to 'celebrities' hymning their new Toyota Prius. Recently, the *Independent on Sunday* treated its readers to a list of 'Britain's top 100 environmentalists'. Highlights included media mogul James Murdoch, model Lily Cole, a former head of the CBI, Page 3 girl Keeley Hazell and the Queen (*Independent on Sunday*, 2008). The greens, it seems, are being tamed. Capitalism, always so effective at absorbing and defanging dissenters, is transforming an existential challenge into yet another opportunity for shopping.

This is not to say that 'radical' has to mean marginal, nor that environmentalism should be the preserve of hatchet-faced puritans exhorting the proles not to go on holiday in the name of Gaia. But there have always been two kinds of environmentalism: the deep green vision and its shallow cousin. The former sees the global ecological crisis as a symptom of humanity's isolation from the rest of the natural world, and of the gigantism and materialism of the industrial civilisation it has built to insulate itself from 'nature'. The latter sees it as a managerial issue, which can be solved by a judicious use of technology and a sprinkling of celebrity endorsements.

It's not hard to see which approach is dominant today, and neither is it surprising. Deep green politics presents a radical challenge to existing mores, which has the disturbing effect of undermining the philosophical basis of human civilisation (indeed, the very *concept* of civilisation: the word stems from the Latin *civilis*, meaning 'townsman' – it is an idea rooted firmly in the urban). Neither James Murdoch nor Keeley Hazell – nor, for that matter, Friends of the Earth – is ever likely to be enamoured with this approach.

The green challenge

Shallow green politics – what we might call managerial environmentalism – is taking over the world. From a conventional standpoint, this is not such a bad thing. It is better to attempt to manage industrial society in a sustainable manner than not to give a stuff about its wider impacts, and it is a good thing that millions of people in the rich world now give greater thought to the impact of their actions on the wider natural world than they ever did before (even if it does not always translate into action). But it is not enough, and neither is it the point. An economic system – now almost universal – which makes paper profits by externalising its real-world costs onto a global ecosystem of limited size and capacity is headed for disaster. Every indicator suggests that that disaster is nearer than ever.

In this context, radical environmentalism – or deep ecology, or whatever you prefer to call it – has a crucial role to play. Humanity's creaking relationship with the rest of the natural world is too important to be left to pop stars and the smooth-tongued pushers of ethical consumption. Managerial environmentalism is too often a fig leaf for business-as-usual, hence its current popularity with everyone from development NGOs to oil company executives. It promises salvation without effort, solutions without pain. It is unlikely to be able to fulfil its promises in the long run – but it can keep people quiet in the present.

The challenge today is to keep that original deep green vision alive in a shallow green world that seems determined to make it look idealistic, naive, misanthropic or simply old-fashioned. In doing so, proponents of that vision need to negotiate two major obstacles to their success.

Challenge 1: green versus Left

The first is the enthusiastic accommodation which green politics has been tempted to make with the political Left. 'Environmentalism' is today widely considered a Left-wing (or 'progressive') position. At least nine out of ten working environmentalists – those employed in green pressure groups, for example, or working for green political parties – are likely to self-identify as Left-wing. They want to prevent 'injustice', whether to other humans or to other species. The motivation is noble, but the result can be that green politics ends up looking less like a radical challenge to industrial society and more like soft-focus socialism fitted with a catalytic converter.

From the point of view of *realpolitik*, this is a problem because it confines the greens to the overcrowded ghetto in which the radical Left has been penned for decades without ever breaking out, and greatly limits its appeal to those (inevitably, most people) for whom that ghetto contains little or nothing of interest. But there is also a more important consideration.

The original aim of green politics was to rise above the Left/Right dichotomy – to speak up for the wider world, for its own sake, because no other ideology would. An accommodation with the conventional Left undermines the entire point of green politics: ecocentrism. The Left, though it likes to lay claim to the 'green' mantle, has no interest in ecocentrism. By definition it cannot have, for the point of the Left is to struggle for social justice for human beings. The environment will always come a poor second to the achievement of this historical mission. In this context, greens who see themselves as part of 'the Left' are effectively surrendering the fundamental point and purpose of deep green politics; they are accepting that human interests, as ever, will always come first.

The point is not that greens should instead make an accommodation with the political Right. The point is that any such accommodation on either side of the traditional spectrum will limit, if not destroy, the eco-centric vision. There is a tension between the political Left and political ecology which will occasionally require a green to choose sides.

The common response to this is to claim, as many environmentalists do, that 'environmental justice and social justice go hand in hand' – or even that 'you cannot have environmental justice without social justice'. Both such claims make explicit the Left-wing nature of mainstream green politics today. Both claims are also patently false. While there is certainly often a connection between poverty and social exclusion on the one hand and environmental degradation on the other (toxic waste dumps, polluting factories and the like have long been shown to impact much more heavily on the poor than the rich; meanwhile, wealthy societies and individuals have a much better chance of adapting to climate change than poor ones) there is also an obvious tension at the very core of any claim that the environment is, at heart, an issue of human social justice.

For a start, social justice is a contested term (everyone has a view on what is just and unjust, and those views differ widely). More importantly though, looked at from a deep ecological perspective it is impossible to get away from the fact that the interests of human beings – or at least, the interests of human industrial society – will often conflict with the interests of the wider natural world. If that were not the case, we would not now be bogged down in the greatest ecological crisis in millions of years.

The most obvious example of this potential clash is the elephant in the room at all environmental gatherings – human numbers. The Earth's human population has grown from 2.5 billion in 1950 to almost 7 billion today, and is expected to reach 9 billion by 2050. The equivalent of the population of London is added to the Earth's already-teeming human melting pot every year, with the obvious consequent impact on every-thing from water supplies to wilderness to carbon dioxide emissions. Yet population growth is an issue which no mainstream environmental organisation will touch with a sustainably-sourced bargepole.

Why? Because any efforts to reduce population growth may have a negative impact on social justice. China, for example, saved itself from possible environmental meltdown by enforcing a one-child policy on its citizens. Democracy, social justice and human rights took a backseat to wider concerns. This is not something that we in the West would want enforced upon us, nor would most of us want to impose it upon others. Yet if some form of action is needed to prevent human population numbers from reaching the point where the impact on both the natural environment and human misery becomes irreversible, that action is likely to clash with our cherished notions of human rights, social justice and individual freedom of choice. This is why environmental groups and political parties, which rely on wide public support, square the circle by simply refusing to talk about population growth at all.

A second example of the tension between people and planet comes not from population growth but economic growth. Mainstream environmentalists, politicians and business leaders regularly insist that there is no tension between economic growth and environmental health. We can have both, they say; hence the eager adoption of the currently fashionable notion of 'sustainable development', which might be better described as 'having your cake and eating it'. Tory leader David Cameron (2006) exemplifies this view, common now to both Left and Right, when he exhorts us to:

> put to bed the notion that the environment and economic growth are somehow necessarily at odds. It is a view that belongs to the last century. What we need now is green growth.

Unfortunately, there is precisely zero evidence that a growth-based economy, in which profit is predicated upon the ability to externalise costs onto the natural world, can ever be sustainable in an ecological sense. We may wish to believe it is so, but there is no obvious path to it becoming so. In fact, all the evidence we have points in precisely the opposite direction. In the meantime, improving material living standards for many human beings often depends directly on destroying ecosystems.

When settlers pan for gold in the Amazon or hack into virgin rainforest to create farms they are doing so to improve life for their families – something we all do; the most basic human instinct. When hunters in the Congo shoot endangered gorillas for bushmeat or trawlermen in northern Europe overfish the seas, they are doing so to make a living; to improve their lot, to pay the rent. Often they have no choice. But the conflict is clear: human need or ecological integrity. Given the choice, every human will meet their own and their family's needs before anything else. To prevent them from doing so is an affront to social justice and to basic human rights. To allow them to do so is often an affront to the global ecosystem. Sometimes the circle is hard, if not impossible, to square; and this is when deep ecology and shallow environmentalism often find themselves in direct conflict.

Challenge 2: heart versus head

In 1798, William Wordsworth and Samuel Taylor Coleridge published *Lyrical Ballads*. A bomb thrown into the heart of the literary establishment, *Ballads*, though slow-selling at first, was to begin a revolution in English poetry. It was to begin another revolution as well, for it was in the *Ballads* that William Wordsworth and Coleridge's (2005: 19) deep green vision was first on display. Perhaps this was seen most clearly in the last three verses of a poem entitled 'The Tables Turned':

> One impulse from a vernal wood
> May teach you more of man,
> Of moral evil and of good,
> Than all the sages can.
>
> Sweet is the lore which Nature brings;
> Our meddling intellect
> Mis-shapes the beauteous forms of things –
> We murder to dissect.
>
> Enough of Science and of Art;
> Close up these barren leaves;
> Come forth, and bring with you a heart
> That watches and receives.

What does this 'Romantic' vision have to do with today's environmentalism? Many greens would probably hurriedly insist that the answer is 'nothing at all'. For in 'The Tables Turned', as in his later writings, Wordsworth was laying down an explicit challenge to the Enlightenment legacy of which he, as a keen supporter of the French Revolution, was himself a product. He talked, unashamedly, of 'Nature' as a living entity. He saw 'our meddling intellect' as the problem rather than the solution. He blasted both human science and human art as being too distanced from the real world of mud, grass and sky to be able to see that world as it really was. Wordsworth lived during the age of industrialisation. The year of his death, 1850, was also the year in which Britain's urban population exceeded its rural population for the first time. He could see what was coming, and his solution was a re-engagement of the human senses with the non-human world.

Try explaining that to many of today's environmentalists. Today's environmental debate is technocratic, scientific, economic; entirely focused on 'realistic solutions'. Politicians, businesspeople and professional sustainability junkies get on with the sombre business of greening modern life, and the undertone is clear: we are serious people now, and environmentalism is a serious business. Ecosystem collapse threatens our economic competitiveness. There is no time for romance. We are not interested in nature. We have a ten-point plan. We have 'solutions.'

The technocratic takeover of modern environmentalism is almost complete, and those who do not buy into it are left with nowhere to turn but the fringes: well-meaning hippy eco-settlements or the self-defeating identity politics of protest. Managerial environmentalism is a matter of the head and not the heart. As such, however, it has bypassed another of the main drivers of the original green movement – the need to reconnect emotionally with the real world outside the cities and the motorway junctions. The need to feel; the need to belong.

By way of example, consider the mainstream green narrative on the most obvious ecological story of our age: climate change. Managerial environmentalism sees climate change as a problem to be solved. The challenge is how to keep the level of carbon in the atmosphere below 350 parts per million, for example; or to prevent warming climbing above two degrees by reducing global emissions by 80 per cent within fifteen years. We know what to do – we now need to do it. We have the technology. The urgency is apparent.

This narrative ignores many wider issues. How much, for example, do we actually know about how the climate works? (very little judging by the rate of change, which has already moved way beyond most predictions). What are we saving, and for whom? If we did, by some miracle, prevent climate change, would it simply empower us to continue destroying the ecosystem as before? As a society, does climate change not tell us something deeper about where we are going? Is it really just a matter of parts per million – or is it something that goes to the heart of the world we have built?

Deep green politics would want to explore these questions; managerial environmentalism to dismiss them and get on with saving the planet – which really means saving human civilisation. What matters in the latter world view is that the myth of human progress should remain unsullied. And if, in order to do this, we need to industrialise the world's remaining wild lands – layer the mountains and oceans with giant wind farms, cover the deserts with solar 'factories', grow biofuels on the prairies, harvest every river – then this is a price worth paying in order to protect civilisation from the results of its own actions. The only impulse from a vernal wood that we can realistically afford to think about is one which provides zero-carbon electricity for our ever-growing economies.

Green politics has become, at once, the most successful and the most threatened contemporary political movement. Managerial environmentalism is late capitalism's last-ditch effort to save itself from what it has done to what we still insist on calling our 'resource base'. It is likely that it will fail. When it does, this may cause those greens who have made an accommodation with it, in order to save civilisation from itself, to question both their motives and their effectiveness.

Alternatively, of course, it may not. Deep green politics may be relegated to history: just another naive radical movement done down by reality. But I suspect that its time is yet to come. Because what happens next is – and how we hate to admit it – probably now entirely beyond human control.

References

Cameron, D. (2006) 'Planet First, Politics Second', *Independent on Sunday*, 3 September.

Independent on Sunday (2008) 'The *IoS* Green List: Britain's Top 100 Environmentalists', 12 October.

Porritt, J. (1984) *Seeing Green* (Oxford: Blackwell).

Wordsworth, W. (1888) *The Complete Poetical Works* (London: Macmillan), http://www.bartleby.com/145/wordchrono.html

Wordsworth, W. and Coleridge, S. T. (2005) *The Lyrical Ballads* (London: Routledge Classics).

4
Radicalism Against the Masses

James Heartfield

For two centuries, to be on the Left meant to be on the side of the people, against the powers-that-be. But today what counts as radicalism is more likely to take the people as the problem than the solution.

Samuel Gompers (1890) said that the whole of trade unionism could be boiled down to the single demand: more! 'We do want more, and when it becomes more, we shall still want more. And we shall never cease to demand more until we have received the results of our labor.' By contrast, the latter-day radical George Monbiot (2006: 215) ends his book on climate change *Heat*: 'It is a campaign not for abundance but for austerity. It is a campaign not for more freedom but for less. Strangest of all, it is a campaign not just against other people, but against ourselves.'

Radicals used to be champions of mass consumption. They marched against hunger, and for increased living standards. They fought for higher wages, for more and better housing and against austerity. 'Our demands most moderate are,' sang James Connolly (1907), 'we only want the earth.' But one, small, insistent voice has come to dominate the Left, and that is the voice of environmentalism, with its hostility to mass consumption. Tentatively at first, the greens reversed the Left discourse on consumption.

Just before the 1997 election in Britain, the Fabian Society secretary summed up the argument, writing that it cannot 'be expected that the disposable incomes of ordinary, reasonably comfortable households in Britain will rise significantly year on year as the political system has come to expect' (Jacobs, 1996: 35). Back then, that was still a surprising thing for someone on the Left to say. Up until then, the people who thought we should cut back were Right-wingers. We have to start living within our means, Ronald Reagan told Congress in 1981, echoing a speech of Margaret Thatcher's to the Shipley Conservative Association. Back then it was the free market economist Frederick Hayek who wanted to curb excessive demand. Nowadays, though, it is the radicals, not the free market economists who are more likely to be found calling on people to live within their means, or to curb their excessive demands.

Training their sights on the growth of budget airlines, the protest group Plane Stupid pour their scorn on working-class travellers: 'There's been an enormous growth in binge-flying with the proliferation of stag and hen nights to Eastern European destinations chosen not for their architecture or culture but because people can fly there for 99p and get loaded for a tenner' (Garman, 2007). Who cannot hear the snobbery in these words? Pointedly, Plane Stupid targeted the airport, Stansted, whose low-cost airlines drew the least well-off travellers.

The name-calling 'Stupid' is a strong theme in the green outlook (a new film on climate change is called *The Age of Stupid*). 'Stupid' is how greens look upon those who do not share their preoccupation with climate change. The fault could not be their message, still less that anyone might dare to disagree with it, but only that many people are too stupid to understand the importance of the environmentalist programme. The radical environmentalists are clear that working-class claims on resources must give way to the greater good. According to Mark Lynas (2004) 'the struggle for equity within the human species must take second place to the struggle for the survival of an intact and functioning biosphere'. Those commentators who embrace the green message know that a campaign to hold down mass consumption will need government force to back it up.

George Monbiot (2008), calling for government repression to prevent the 'perpetual increase in the supply of goods and services', wrote that 'I don't know how to solve the problem of capitalism without resorting to totalitarianism.' We should understand that what Monbiot means by 'the problem of capitalism' is not the limits it puts on working-class living standards, but rather the growth in those living standards.

Climate change: the elephant in the room

What, then? Storm-troopers raiding your fridge? Ration-books? How could radical people get here? Of course, the extreme language of the environmentalists seems wholly unexceptional because of the moral imperative that stands behind it: catastrophic climate change. Because of the threat posed by industry's carbon emissions, acting as greenhouse gases, the globe will warm up to the point that the polar ice caps melt, crops will fail and the world will be plunged into famine, floods and other extreme weather events that will make all of our ambitions for betterment seem pointless. If the scientific models of man-made climate change justified these doomsday scenarios, then of course, not just emancipatory politics, but all politics would be useless. No debate would be necessary. All effort must be bent to the one goal of reducing carbon emissions, and the mass consumption that demands them.

It is a sorry state of affairs, though, for radical politics to reach the point where all decision-making is given up to scientific experts. When we think of the way that supposedly scientific theories have been offered up as justifications for the status quo – and just how critical of those the Left was – it is surprising how insistently today's green radicals embrace what they call 'The Science'. 'Science' it was that told us the Irish famine was unavoidable in 1845; that inferior races had to be weeded out, as all biologists agreed at the 1932 International Eugenics Conference; that planned growth would solve the problems of the Third World in the 1960s; that trade unionists were disturbing the natural equilibrium of the market in the 1980s.

It is not that radicals ought to distrust science – on the contrary, science is inherently democratic, since it takes authority out of the hands of priests and kings, and puts it out into nature, open to be tested and questioned. But what ought to give us pause for thought is the idea that scientific truths are so unassailable that they close off the discussion. At that point, we ought to ask whether these really are scientific truths, or just political ends, masquerading as scientific truths.

It would be a terrible burden if only those with doctorates in climate science were entitled to a political opinion on questions as wide-ranging as whether to build a third runway at Heathrow, whether the Chinese should be allowed to develop their industry or whether mothers should be allowed to drive their children to school. Luckily, the science of climate change is quite distinct from the claims of catastrophic climate change that are driving the green agenda. But what we find is that in most discussion of climate change in the press and public debate, a histrionic spasm of doom-mongering drowns out any real scientific reflection.

The Intergovernmental Panel on Climate Change presents a sober and clear argument. It says that 'Most of the observed increase in globally averaged temperatures since the mid-twentieth century is very likely due to the observed increase in anthropogenic greenhouse gas concentrations' (Intergovernmental Panel on Climate Change, 2007: 10). Those increases are around one degree centigrade. By 2100, according to the IPCC's various models, the best estimate of temperature increase is between 1.8 and 4 degrees centigrade. Their estimate of sea-level rises is between 18 and 59 centimetres. All of those predicted climate changes present a challenge to human ingenuity, but none of them remotely resembles the apocalyptic nightmares that the green scaremongers put before us. The IPCC reports the possibility of sea-level rises between 18 and 59 centimetres, and in his 2006 film *An Inconvenient Truth*, Al Gore tells it back to us as a rise of *six metres*; Mark Lynas claims that the report says that the seas will rise by 70 metres, more than a hundred times greater than the worst rise the IPCC anticipates (Lynas, 2007).Will the Antarctic melt, as greens claim?

The gap between the peer-reviewed science and the hysterical scare-mongering tells us that the attempt to force all political debate into the straitjacket of climate change is thoroughly ideological. There is an unhealthy relationship where green advocates command attention in proportion to the depth of the problem they warn us of. When the IPCC published its report in 2007, environmentalists claimed that the debate was over, and now everyone had to accept what 'The Science' was telling us. Today, environmentalists complain that the IPCC report understates the problem.

In 1962 Rachel Carson warned of a *Silent Spring* of pollution due to DDT (Carson, 1962). In 1972 Donella and Dennis Meadows (1972) predicted that world tin reserves will run out in 1985, zinc in 1988, petroleum in 1990, natural gas in 1992. In 1998, Mae Wan Ho (1998) told us that genetic engineering would lead to a critical genetic meltdown more dangerous than nuclear weapons. These doomsday scenarios are an essential part of the green ideology. Environmentalists needed to believe that the end of the world was nigh, long before the process of global warming was theorised.

An elitist movement

Despite its radical credentials, environmentalist activism is a deeply elitist movement. It is not just that its main activists are overwhelmingly middle or even upper class, though that is indeed remarkable. There are Etonians, Zac Goldsmith, Lord Peter Melchett, Jonathon Porritt, heir to the Baronet Porrit, Tory Chairman's son George Monbiot (Stowe and Oxford) and Charles Secrett (Cranleigh), executive director of Friends of the Earth. Among the younger activists in Plane Stupid there is Tamsin Omond (Westminster and Trinity, Cambridge), the granddaughter of a Dorset baronet and wealthy landowner (Knight, 2008). A movement that so forcefully attacks mass consumption is open to the objection that it stands for minority privilege.

The small-group character of the environmental movement is credited with enhancing the openness of the movement, though it can also tend to cliquishness. As journalist Andy Beckett (2002) reports, 'people who are prepared to take risks, or possess useful skills, can come to dominate, or even have contempt for, the more cautious and amateurish participants'. This is closer to what Max Weber (1947) called charismatic leadership. American labour researcher Stephanie Ross (2003: 294) argues that the 'uncompromising ideological rejection of leadership tout court, results in leadership unbound by structures of accountability'. Greenpeace, the group from which many of the Plane Stupid activists learned their tactical skills, made a virtue of unaccountability. It has a tiny staff, and an unelected board. The millions of Greenpeace subscribers who pay standing orders to Greenpeace have no rights over policy.

Plane Stupid's actions are mostly stunts, on the Greenpeace model, like climbing onto the House of Commons, a sit-down protest on a runway, or throwing green goo over Industry Minister Peter Mandelson. Stunts can play an important part in any campaign. Bernadette Devlin (now McAliskey) punched Home Secretary Reginald Maudling in the House of Commons when he said that the demonstrators killed on Bloody Sunday were armed. Anti-airport protesters rightly argued that direct action was at the heart of the Suffragette movement. But the difference is that the Suffragettes and the Irish Civil Rights movement had a great base of popular support. Devlin was an elected MP. The Women's Social and Political Union was a mass campaign with hundreds of thousands of supporters. Sylvia Pankhurst (1923: 1) in particular would have had no truck with a campaign in favour of cutting living standards: 'We do not call for limitation of births, for penurious thrift, and self-denial', she wrote. 'We call for a great production that will supply all, and more than all the people can consume.'

With Plane Stupid the stunts are not an add-on, but a substitute for a mass campaign. Its staged events reduce the rest of us to onlookers marvelling at their bravery. And in the end it all comes down to Leila Deen throwing green custard over Peter Mandelson in a car park – so what? With hostility to mass consumption as environmentalism's goal, all kinds of reactionary ideas follow. Many green campaigners, like Jonathon Porritt, think that the world would be a better place with less people in it. Where Left-wing radicals used to be in favour of internationalism, Plane Stupid's campaign against international travel smacks of Little Englandism. Greens are to be found campaigning against new homes being built, and pillorying women for driving their children to school.

What is remarkable is that the mass movement of socialism has given way to an elite and anti-mass environmental movement. It was not always so. In 1980, Tony Benn (1996: 502–3) thought Friends of the Earth was 'the middle class expressing its dislike of the horrors of industrialisation – keeping Hampstead free from the whiff of diesel smoke sort of thing'. But in more recent times the Left lost ground as a mass movement, suffering from the limitations of state socialism, and after a decade-long employers' offensive against organised labour.

The disaggregation of mass working-class movements in the 1980s was the condition for the rise of radical environmentalism. That radicalism takes strength from the demobilisation of mass political movements, and the greater opportunities for elite activism. The Left accommodated to the green movement in a bid to overcome its image problem after 1989.

Hostility to mass consumption, though, is not a political outlook that is readily generalisable among the masses. Telling working-class people that their greed is the problem is not an obvious route to popular support. The contradiction was played out in London on 28 March 2009 at the demonstrations against the G20 summit: greens marched against growth, and trade unionists for more jobs under the 'square-the-circle' demand for a Green New Deal. Terrifying the public about disasters to come will not move them to act, but only intensify the fatalism, and promote withdrawal from political life. The Left, as long as it ties itself to radical elitism, will not excite mass interest, but only indifference. It is time to reconnect with people's proper, and ennobling, aspirations to self-betterment. People are not the problem, they are the solution. The earth is there for us, not we for it.

References

Beckett, A. (2002) 'When Capitalism Calls', *London Review of Books*, 4 April, http://www.lrb.co.uk/v24/n07/beck01_.html

Benn, A. (1996) *Diaries* (London: Arrow).

Carson, R. (1962) *Silent Spring* (Boston: Houghton Mifflin).

Connolly, J. (1907) *We Only Want the Earth*, http://www.marxists.org/archive/connolly/1907/xx/wewnerth.htm

Garman, J. (2007) *Plane Speaking*, http://www.planestupid.com/?q=blogs/2007/01/11/plane-speaking-response-brendan-oneill

Gompers, S. (1890) 'We Want Eight Hours and Nothing Less', *Louisville Courier Journal*, 2 May, http://www.history.umd.edu/Gompers/quotes.htm

Ho, M. W. (1998) *Genetic Engineering: Dream or Nightmare* (Bath: Gateway Books).

Intergovernmental Panel on Climate Change (2007) *Climate Change 2007*, Fourth Assessment Report, Summary for Policy Makers, http://www.ipcc.ch/pdf/assessment-report/ar4/wg1/ar4-wg1-spm.pdf

Jacobs, M. (1996) *The Politics of the Real World* (London: Earthscan).

Knight, K. (2008) 'Posh Protesters: How the anti-Heathrow Commons Invaders Included a Baronet's Granddaughter and an MP's Grandson', *Daily Mail*, 29 February, http://www.dailymail.co.uk/news/article-523220/Posh-protesters-How-anti-Heathrow-Commons-invaders-included-Baronets-granddaughter-MPs-grandson.html

Lynas, M. (2004) *Interview*, http://www.redpepper.org.uk/Interview-with-Mark-Lynas-author

Lynas, M. (2007) 'Global Warming: the Final Warning', *Independent*, 3 February, http://www.independent.co.uk/environment/climate-change/global-warming-the-final-warning-434807.html

Meadows D. and D. Meadows (1972) *The Limits to Growth* (New York: Universe).

Monbiot, G. (2006) *Heat* (London: Allen Lane).

Monbiot, G. (2008) 'Climate Change is Not Anarchy's Football', http://www.guardian.co.uk/commentisfree/2008/aug/22/climatechange.kingsnorthclimatecamp

Pankhurst, S. (1923) 'Socialism', *Workers' Dreadnought*, 28 July.

Ross, S. (2003) 'Is This What Democracy Looks Like?', *Socialist Register* (London: Merlin).

Weber, M. (1947) *The Theory of Social and Economic Organisation* (London: William Hodge and Co.).

5
Moving Targets and Political Judgements

Terrell Carver

My primary aim in this chapter is to dissociate radical politics from the Left–Right political axis. This division has been commonplace since the French Revolution. Yet it is very unsteady and prone to ambiguity. I will argue that it is unhelpful to align one moving target, such as 'radical', with another, such as 'Left–Right'. This is illustrated by the fact that radical politics has most recently been dominated by neo-conservatism.

Backdrops and scene-shifting

It would seem that political backdrop is perhaps the greatest determinant in producing a politics that qualifies as 'radical'. That is, if the backdrop is an established order – resistant to change, exclusionary, uninventive, possibly oppressive – then this is probably a good starting point for understanding how radicalism arises. But there are no guarantees that that radicalism is necessarily of the people, divorced from authoritarianism, and interestingly intellectualised, as many on the Left tend to assume. There are many examples of this.

Against a backdrop of Communist, one-party oppression, and subservience to a foreign power, Polish Catholicism was radical in the 1980s, and performed as a radical politics. But the Church and its doctrines are not models of democratic organisation or of social progress, defined in terms of secular notions of equal citizenship that liberals endorse. Nor was the integral practice of nationalism democratic in any challenging way, other than as a form of national liberation from an occupying and bullying superpower. What made this practice radical was thus not so much its inherent doctrines as its positioning against an 'Other', and its uncompromisingly clear goals of self-rule via representative and responsible government. While widespread popular courage should have its due, the ultimate victory of the movement owed considerably to a collapse of the will to rule among local elites of state, party and military bureaucracies, and particularly on the part of the occupying power from the east. But radical politics is not always the property of an insurgency.

Arguably the most successful radical political movement of the later twentieth century was neo-liberalism, perhaps loosely defined as an economic individualism that demonised the state, regulation, redistribution and welfare, deifying instead the market, entrepreneurs, for-profit provision of goods and services, and economic rationality *tout court*. This was a radicalism of elites, albeit one that in many cases enlisted voters. However, the *modus operandi* in this case was to gain the heights of power via universities and business schools, newspaper and media commentary, and of course through conventional political structures, especially those at party-level. While Reagan and Thatcher may – in their inconsistent and mercurial ways – have been prime movers and examples, the neo-liberal attack on the settled certainties of social democracy and welfare-state consensus touched billions when it became orthodoxy at the World Bank, World Trade Organization and International Monetary Fund. These agencies were in a position to dictate political terms to borrower-countries, a mechanism of drastic change for large populations far more thoroughgoing and effective than guns and bombs. Local elites then proved, in many cases, to be avid recruits to the cause of elite radicalism. This form of radical politics was neither Left wing, nor popular, nor liberatory from foreign oppression. However, it was doctrinaire, simplistic, sweeping and aggressive – qualities often associated for better or worse with 'the Left', which is more usually identified as radical, not least by 'Leftwingers' themselves.

The association between radical politics and populist anti-elitism probably has its roots in the anti-Roman Catholic or Protestant agitations of the late middle ages and early modern period. While there has been a major focus on the individualism involved in these ideological and institutional struggles – the primacy of individual judgement in matters of conscience and of individual freedom to choose one collective practice rather than another – there has perhaps been rather less attention given to the mass character of the protests and to the enduring changes this brought to politics in its very definition and scope. What were at the outset yet more forms of heresy and hysteria amongst 'the people' were linked not only to changes in individual subjectivities but – eventually via the printing press – to wider intellectual practices of judgement, debate and choice. While the radicalism obviously lies in resistance to the oppressive 'Other' in religious matters, and in widespread mass refusals to cooperate any longer with those structures, it grew into a wider project to topple elites of the state, not just the Church (in so far as these were distinguishable). Doctrine fitted action, and the 'Other' – Catholic Church and authoritarian state – obliged by resisting, as indeed they still do, notwithstanding considerable 'climbing-down' and retreating to non-violence (as a rule).

Given that the 'Other' of today is oftentimes a self-styled democratic but capitalist state and supposedly meritocratic social system (or at least some gestures and pretences in this direction are maintained), the familiar attributes of radical politics – mass participation, demonstrations, revolutionary violence and doctrinaire goals – are perhaps surprisingly still in evidence, much as they were – repeatedly – as the French Revolution unfolded in the 1790s. Parliaments in Buenos Aires and Belgrade have been stormed in recent scenes harking back to the 'rose revolution' in Portugal of the 1970s, and there are doubtless others on the cards. My point is that radical politics is standardly identified with these scenarios of popular causes and populist methods, and with good reason. Of course the near-failures and utter failures count, too. Tiananmen Square lives on in infamy, and Les événements of '68 produced remarkable regime change in France but certainly no social or political revolution as such.

So what counts as radical politics today? This depends on what your backdrop is. If it is 'the infidel' or atheists, then any number of militant religious movements would count as radical. Perhaps the Iranian revolution is a good place to start here, along with the Taliban era in Afghanistan. Much of the activity was specifically targeted to change subjectivities, or at least outward behaviour, and ruling elites were ruthlessly supplanted and restructured. However, there is nothing that says that radicalism must always proceed in public and be non-secretive. Lenin's *What is to be done?* was certainly radical, given a backdrop of Marxist political organisers resistant to secret cells, clandestine activities and military-style obedience to orders. Nor is terrorism necessarily ruled out, because, like radicalism, the descriptive and judgemental qualities wrapped up in the term require a backdrop and observer, and so are relational, too. Anything attempting to be radical could hardly proceed if its effective modes were limited to non-violent means within legal terms set and operated by the 'Other'. While there are obvious questions about discrimination in the use of violence, and the relation between risk and moral worth, it is remarkable that in recent years suicide bombing has altered risk factors for certain political actors to 100 per cent, and is generally characterised by a studied lack of discrimination in terms of who gets killed or maimed. This does not make the politics more radical, nor does it count as a more radical method. But it is a notable form of contemporary difference.

If one's backdrop is an occupying power – overtly in military terms, or rather more covertly in terms of economic control and influence – then national liberation will appear radical, and this has not gone away. It may be separatist (South Ossetia, Muslim provinces of Thailand, Tibet, East Timor etc.), or a mobilisation against neo-colonialism (Philippine guerrillas, Zapatistas, Sandanistas etc.). States themselves are not ruled out as actors, though this is frequently belittled as posturing or rogue behaviour (Venezuela, Bolivia, Cuba). It follows that state-level diplomatic and military actions can be as radical as anything else, and have considerable symbolic as well as physical clout (e.g. Hugo Chavez's offer of foreign aid to the Bronx). Perhaps some of this might not be construed as properly diplomatic, but then that merely reproduces the highly problematic dichotomy between what is military and what is terrorist, other than wearing uniforms (sometimes) and (generally) high tech weaponry for the military, and the opposite for terrorists or insurgents, as they are externally denominated.

If one's backdrop is global warming, then it becomes difficult to judge what is radical at all. This is because both judgements are scalar, that is, global warming as a concept involves contested notions of how much, how quickly, and with what effects, which are themselves hypothetical and can be rank-ordered in terms of catastrophic (or merely inconvenient) impacts. It follows that responses are more or less radical, that is, thoroughgoing and dramatic, in relation to wherever one sets the preceding measures and timescales. Thus, however radical-looking the Puerto Alegre or Gothenburg or Seattle 'anti-globalisation' demonstrations and running battles, and however much one is willing to condense the varied protesters and their varied targets into some coherent if rather hypothetical coalition, the lack of firm parameters in the backdrop conditions rather disarms any firm judgements about radicalism. While fighting with the police is hardly new, the use of wireless technologies (e.g. cell phones, internet, YouTube) and media-grabbing protest tactics (e.g. mass nudity) are not radical in themselves. Rather they represent an elision between the radical and the new that can be misleading, and of course therefore turned to political advantage from either 'Right' or 'Left' (e.g. anti-globalisation protesters are said to be crazed or insufficiently serious). Certainly, though, these events have had a radical effect, namely that high-level, high-profile meetings of heads of state and world leaders who meet to consider and negotiate profoundly important issues (or sometimes, of course, merely to appear to do so) are now often held in much more remote locations that are more easily secured – typically mountain and seaside resorts formerly known more for their seclusion than for their celebrity-appeal or convenience to international airports.

Radical politics today and tomorrow

My candidate for the most radical – if not the only – radical politics of the first decade of the new millennium is the neo-conservative response to the events of 11 September 2001, which involved terrorist attacks on high-profile US targets using hijacked domestic airliners. Those neo-cons involved were clearly the US President, Vice-President, Secretary of State, and various advisers such as Paul Wolfowitz and Donald Rumsfeld, who were already identified with neo-conservative thinking on American foreign policy. Against a backdrop of liberal policies based on multi-lateralism, international cooperation, arms reduction and treaty-based institutions, neo-cons had argued for what they characterised as moral clarity, backed up with aggressive interventionism in securing US interests. This is thus a case of elite and oxymoronic radicalism, according to my schema. What makes it a prize-winner is the small size of the elite, the use of 9/11 as a pretext for implementing policies and practices that were extremely radical in numerous areas, and the hugely important national and international consequences that followed, especially those that challenged the boundary lines that most international actors and indeed ordinary citizens had presumed to be irrevocably in place.

The Bush doctrine and subsequently published 'National Security Strategy of the United States' (2002) took neo-con principles to specific conclusions, namely justification for pre-emptive strikes and regime change on ideological grounds, declaring that it is the mission of the USA to spread democracy and therefore eliminate terrorism. This is to be achieved through unilateralism in the first instance, rather than through multilateral coalitions and cooperative decision-making, which might of course result in a somewhat different outcome. While the obvious consequences of this doctrine were invasions of Afghanistan and Iraq, pursued by using NATO forces or shaky 'coalitions of the willing', these could possibly count as mere further instances of US adventurism and aggression dating back to the Spanish-American War of 1898. However, the radicalism of the neo-con enterprise shows through in a number of novel ways: the intensive securitisation of air travel, not merely in the USA but throughout the world, with a considerable apparatus of compulsory inspections and information surveillance, backed up with clear sanctions for those countries or entities (such as the EU) that fail to comply. On a more voluntary basis, a number of countries have used this apparatus to institute their own mirroring of American security concerns in counter-terrorism legislation, security practices, identity and other information requirements, and numerous areas of inspection, control and surveillance.

However, the most radical and perhaps under-appreciated consequences of neo-con radicalism have been the brutal erasure in practice of some of the boundary lines that have demarcated democratic from authoritarian politics since the promulgation of the Rights of Man and the Citizen in 1793. These boundary lines – however they are drawn in detail – include the civil/military distinction (when a US citizen was incarcerated in a US Navy prison), habeas corpus/incarceration without charge or legal redress (as in Guantanamo Bay and numerous other secret gulags overseas), interrogation/torture (as against unconvincing defences that this distinction is still in place), war within international law and legal frameworks/lawless barbarous conduct in war (again, with reference to bizarre ways out of the Geneva Conventions and even more bizarre invocations of them), and flagrant disregard for any consistent and defensible conception of logic or evidence relating to the relationship between terrorism and Iraq, and the (non-)existence of weapons of mass destruction there. While it is amazing that so few have achieved so much that is so different and destructive, it is perhaps far more sobering to consider the decidedly non-radical reasoning of those who voted them the money (as in the US Congress), mirrored the policies and practices elsewhere (as in the UK), and in general normalised an enormous revolution in how the international politics of the world is discursively and practically pursued.

My candidate for the radical politics of the future is the one that will respond to the global challenge of planetary catastrophe. Taking the worst-case scenarios for climate change as our backdrop, what would qualify as a radical response? It would have to be radical in the sense of thoroughgoing and dramatic in order to be effective. On the plausible assumptions that the catastrophe could be prevented by drastic cuts in greenhouse gas emissions, that these emissions come from the processes of production through which contemporary consumer populations are sustained (in their bubbles of confidence), and that even a shift to more efficient and less polluting forms of energy would itself require current or even increased levels of carbon-based energy consumption, it follows that only an internationally negotiated cut in production, and hence in living standards, could possibly have the desired effect. This sets the logic of capitalist commodity production against itself, in that the competitive pursuit of profit only works on expectations of expanding economic activity and prospects. And it also sets the logic of international competition for power and resource security against itself, in that nations generally try to move their populations (or at least some of their inhabitants) both absolutely and relatively up the league tables of capitalist economic achievement. In a democratising world, where more politicians chase more voters every year, and where more voters are connected to the internet and other media and thus have easy access to comparisons, it is a fair assumption that this international dynamic of competition has been accelerating, especially when viewed against perceptions that access to scarce resources in water, fuels and minerals will become more competitive as well.

At the moment there are only deep greens who advocate deindustrialisation. But on the foregoing view of the backdrop, radical politics would have to be much more specific than this. In particular it would need to develop and defend a sliding scale that would adjust resources and hence living standards throughout the world, and effectively require the largest absolute and per capita generators of greenhouse gases to deindustrialise the most. A non-dystopic work of science fiction along these lines could be quite useful and perhaps yet another Michael Moore movie. Elite economists and geographers could also be helpful, especially as they easily grab the headlines in quality media. There is perhaps a role, regrettably, for eco-warriors, in constructing events that provide politicians with ironclad excuses for assembling new regimes of control that would – as opposed to 9/11 – enforce planetary ecological security (rather than, for example, neo-con conceptions of US security as an end in itself). My scenario would effectively reproduce the Marxist analysis of class struggle, but on a global scale, and with a compelling reason for the majority (who are far from wealthy) to internationalise control of the production process itself, and thus plan for consumption levels, broadly construed. Perhaps as Marx and Engels argued, the commanding heights of capitalist production could be identified and stormed, rather than hypostasised as the market and worshipped as a fetish god. Besides saving the planet, we could take the tradeoffs from capitalist production as welcome leisure time. Obviously I am not saying that this would be an easy process, achieved through consensus and compromise. But then what makes politics radical is precisely what precludes its opposite – muddling through to we know not where.

Reference

'National Security Strategy of the United States' (2002),   http://www.commondreams.org/headlines02/0920-05.htm, 20 September.

6
The Forces Shaping Radical Politics Today

Clare Short

It is often assumed that radical politics is progressive and Left wing. But it also comes from the Right and is regressive. For example, Mrs Thatcher was radical, the British National Party is radical and Hitler was radical. Extreme Right-wing movements have been increasing in strength in Europe, even before the recent economic crisis. Although driven by a small group of elites, neo-conservatism has been radical in its global impact. On the other hand, when we think about Left-wing and progressive radical politics today, in the OECD countries this includes the green parties and environmental, anti-war and peace activists. It also includes many development NGOs who advocate a more equitable world order. These are largely ineffective. Nowhere have they managed to break through to achieve significant political progress. They are mostly dependent on government funding and charitable status, therefore unable to act as radical forces for change. In fact, progressive radical politics is as yet to emerge strongly in the OECD countries.

However, there are other radical forces at work globally. These are driving major change. Progressive and Left-wing radical politics will need to respond to them more effectively than at present. In what follows I will discuss these forces shaping radical politics, concluding on a note of caution for those concerned with progressive and Left-wing radical politics today.

Developments in China

The first major driver of radical change is China's incredible economic development. This has helped drive the global boom which is now coming to an end. That country of 1.3 billion people has been undergoing its own industrial revolution and providing the post-industrial OECD countries with a flood of increasingly sophisticated, low-cost consumer goods. China has created a new model of authoritarian capitalism which is stirring increasing interest in the poorer countries of the world as they hope to emulate the speed of China's development. China's massive dollar holdings, alongside those of the rest of Asia and the Middle East, have also helped to keep the global boom going by financing the USA's deficits, enabling American consumers to live beyond their means and to act as consumers of last resort for the global economy.

But this arrangement cannot be sustained in the long term. It is not widely reported how much dissent and agitation is bubbling away in China. Workers and peasants are protesting, just as they did when Western Europe and North America were undergoing their industrial revolutions. It seems inevitable that organisation and agitation amongst the low-paid factory workers of China will inevitably intensify as they demand better treatment at work and greater social benefits from the great wealth that they are generating. This is one of the major forces of radical politics today which is unleashed alongside a deeply polluting industrialisation at a time of global environmental strain. The Chinese people deserve to enjoy more of the wealth they are creating. They also deserve a decent health service. History tells us that their consumption will increase as will their agitation. This implies a big change in the nature of the Chinese regime and a shock the USA's consumption patterns, the ramifications of which are likely to be deep and complicated. But the prospect of Chinese people demanding a bigger share in the proceeds of their economic development has wider consequences.

According to Lester Brown of the Earth Policy Institute in Washington DC, who is one of the leading American environmental analysts, if growth in China continues at 8 per cent a year, by 2031 China's income per head for its 1.45 billion people will be equal to that of the USA today. He said:

China's grain consumption will then be two thirds of the current grain consumption of the entire world. If it consumes oil at the same rate as the US today, the Chinese will be consuming 99 billion barrels a day – and the whole world is currently producing 84 billion barrels a day, and will probably not produce much more. If it consumes paper at the same rate that we do, it will consume twice as much paper as the world is now producing. There go the world's forests. If the Chinese then have three cars for every four people – as the US does today – they would have a fleet of 1.1 billion cars compared to the current world fleet of 800 million. They would have to pave over an area equivalent to the area they have planted with rice today, just to drive and park them. (Quoted in McCarthy, 2005)

Lester Brown, who has been tracking and documenting the world's major environmental trends for thirty years said:

> The point of these conclusions is simply to demonstrate that the western economic model is not going to work for China. All they're doing is what we've already done, so you can't criticise them for that. But what you can say is it's not going to work. And if it does not work for China, by 2031 it won't work for India, which by then will have an even larger population, or for the other three billion people in the developing countries. And in some way it will not work for the industrialised countries either, because in the incredibly integrated world economy, we all depend on the same oil and the same grain. (Quoted in McCarthy, 2005)

The bottom line of this analysis is that we're going to have to develop a new economic model. Instead of a fossil-fuel based, automobile-centred, throwaway economy, we will have to have a renewable energy-based, diversified transport system, and comprehensive reuse and recycle economies. If we want civilisation to survive, we will have to do that. Otherwise civilisation will collapse.

Our conclusion has to be that if the OECD countries are entitled to enjoy their current way of life then the people of China and India, as well as Africa and Latin America, are entitled to the same. And the future will be catastrophic. The planet simply cannot cope with its entire people living in this consumerist and greedy way.

This means that the old model that saw the developing world becoming like the OECD countries is neither desirable nor possible. And the inequality of the world, with 20 per cent of people living with material plenty in a world in which a billion people remain abjectly poor, is also unsustainable. As the poor of the world urbanise and see very clearly how others live they will not be willing to tolerate the suffering and poverty they currently endure. Thus if we want our civilisation to survive we have to learn better to share our knowledge, technology and capital to make the world more equitable both between and within nations. All people have to have access to the basics that they need and to education and health care and the freedom to be themselves, express their ideas and be treated with respect. Within such a world order we have to evolve a new way of living that ceases to make economic growth the purpose of politics and instead looks for genuine sustainable development and find satisfaction in our lives without the expectation of increasing economic consumption. Within such a world order, we are more likely to be able to reach agreements on curbing carbon dioxide emissions so that over a number of years we converge on an equal entitlement per head to a share of what our planet can bear.

Anger in the Middle East

The second major force for radical change that is at work is the widespread and deep anger amongst the people of the Middle East and the wider Muslim world. This is the intensified polarisation which has been used to justify massive increases in defence spending, which in the USA constitutes half of global defence spending and is now in excess of American spending at the height of the Cold War. It was President Eisenhower who warned the American people in his retiring address as President that they should 'guard against the acquisition of unwarranted influence . . . by the military-industrial complex'. It is impossible to explain the USA's counter-productive response to the attack on the Twin Towers without taking account of the influence of the military-industrial complex. It is also rationally impossible to explain the quantity and quality of the USA's military spending and the conduct of the wars in Iraq and Afghanistan through a calm consideration of the USA's legitimate and important interest in countering the ideas of Al-Qaeda.

One consequence of the USA's policy towards the Middle East (which is so abjectly supported by the UK and, post Iraq, by the EU), is that the military power of the biggest economy on earth, the Rome of our era, has been shown to be vulnerable. The USA has been unable to defeat the resistance in Iraq. NATO is in considerable difficulty in Afghanistan and Hezbollah has shown that it cannot be controlled by the military power of Israel, the USA's major ally and greatest armed power in the Middle East.

The Middle East is the source of most of the world's oil at a time when we are massively increasing our levels of oil consumption and are also approaching peak oil when half of the available oil reserves of the world have already been used. This implies a long-term growth in the price of oil and as bio-fuels are increasingly used to create substitutes for oil, a long-term growth in the price of food, which means continuing food shortages in the poorer countries. This nexus of forces has produced two sources of radical political energy. The first is the anger of the people of the Middle East which could easily topple one or more of the pro-American dictatorships of the region. Few people expected the fall of the Shah of Iran; the turbulence and anger of the Middle East could easily produce similar regime change. In addition, the forces of resistance, which are increasingly critical of the sectarian attacks on civilians justified by Al-Qaeda's ideology, are strengthening in Palestine, Egypt, Afghanistan, Pakistan and elsewhere. Some of these forces are progressive in that they seek to resist occupation and dictatorship. Others are reactionary and oppressive, but they are powerful and radical forces, and without a major change in the USA's and general Western policy towards the Middle East are likely to be radical political forces able to bring about major change in the existing global order with potential consequences for oil prices and the global economy.

To settle the conflicts in the Middle East will require a return by the USA and its allies to a system of international law and strengthened multilateral institutions. Western support for Israel's grave breaches of international law in the Occupied Territories undermines the authority of international law more generally. The inability of the UN to enforce adherence to international law undermines its moral authority. In order to create a more peaceful, just and equitable international order, we will need to build a stronger United Nations that reflects the current balance of population in the world and is capable of deploying force effectively to deal with the growing problem of weak and failing states. In order to uphold the authority of international law, we will need all states, including the USA, to accept the authority of the International Court and the International Criminal Court. We are a long way from American acceptance of these realities, but we must hope that the failings of its unipolar moment and the coming turbulence will lead the USA back to a belief in multilateralism and international law.

Population growth

The third major radical force at work in the world is the combination of population growth and urbanisation in the poorest countries. In 1800 there were fewer than 1 billion people in the world. By 1960, it was 3 billion. It is now nearly 7 billion and the projection is that we will reach 9 billion by 2040. At least 1 billion of the new people will be born in the poorest countries. In addition, in Africa and more generally in the poorer countries, urbanisation is intensifying. Humanity has reached the point where more than half of us are urban dwellers. In fifteen years' time this is projected to reach 65 per cent. The poorest countries have seen improved economic growth in the last decade, but there are still 1.2 billion people desperately poor, ill educated, malnourished, lacking health care and suffering shortages of water and sanitation. They are about to be joined by another billion people living alongside them and imposing further strain on land, water and other resources. In addition, the effects of climate change will hit the poorest countries hardest because they have such weak capacity to adapt. They will experience more floods, agricultural disruption and the likelihood of more conflict caused by shortage of basic resources. In addition they are urbanising. The history of Western Europe and North America suggests that urban populations are likely to be less passive than the rural poor. The prospect of political protest, riot and disorder is great. There is a risk that this protest will conflate with the resistance to the 'war on terror' which is spreading through Somalia into Africa. Such protest could be captured by political movements of Right or Left, or simply lead to a spread of massive disorder.

Climate change

My view is that humanity now faces a greater challenge than we have ever faced since *Homo sapiens* evolved 160,000 years ago. There have in those years been natural disasters, terrible wars, plagues, flood and famine and more recently the threat of nuclear annihilation. But never before have groups of intelligent and well-informed people contemplated, within the foreseeable future, the possibility of a complete collapse of human civilisation, with all the terrible conflict and suffering that would accompany that process. The greatest risk we face now is runaway climate change

It is now widely accepted that global warming is a reality and an enormous threat. The consensus of climate change scientists is stark and authoritative. There will always be some who deny any changing reality but, even in the USA, it is now accepted that climate change caused by human use of fossil fuels is a serious threat to the future. However, although the problem is increasingly widely acknowledged there is not as yet a sufficient sense of urgency. Johann Hari summarised the danger in *The Independent* on 20 October 2008. By 2013, the Arctic will be free of ice. The last time greenhouse gases were at rates equivalent to those of today, was 50 million years ago. The last ice age was only six degrees colder than today. Soon, our emissions will make a two degree rise in temperature inevitable. This means countries like Bangladesh and the islands of the South Pacific will be inundated and hundreds of millions of people displaced. This is a terrible prospect, but if we cooperate to deal with this crisis, we could stop the warming rising further and stabilise our climate at a higher temperature. But if we go beyond two degrees, we will create the real danger of an unstoppable escalation. At three degrees, almost all our ice will have melted. This means that the ice will cease to reflect a third of the sun's rays back into space as it does now. At three degrees of warming, the Amazon will burn and release more carbon and the Siberian peat bogs will release vast quantities of methane. Very soon, human civilisation will collapse and human life become unliveable.

Radical politics has to deal with this prospect. It means that we need unprecedented global cooperation to limit carbon dioxide emissions. We also need to create a new, more sustainable way of living on our planet. Instead, the world is led by foolish elites, fixated on controlling the Middle East and therefore causing bitter division. They are also tied to an economic model of unsustainable consumption that is incompatible with long-term sustainability.

A word of caution about radical politics today

More immediately, we are living through a major crisis in the international financial system and belatedly, governments have started to take coordinated action to avoid the financial meltdown that would throw the world into a deep and long depression. So far, they have acted to prop up otherwise bankrupt banks by injecting taxpayers' capital. This is by no means the end of the story. There are still dangerous assets on many banks' balance sheets and the worldwide recession will mean further mortgage and credit card defaults and corporate bankruptcies. This will impose greater strain on the solvency of the banks.

There is suddenly more talk of what we have learned from Keynes and even Marx, but as yet no agreement on coordinated international action to help the less well off to weather the crisis. In addition, much of the commentary assumes that all that is needed is better bank regulation so that we can get back to the globalising boom. But clearly an economic system that pumps out credit so that the same old houses treble in price and encourage people to take on unrepayable levels of debt, inevitably leads to bust. Seventy-two per cent of the USA's economy is consumption, and it is two-thirds of the UK economy. The boom years were built on sand. Underneath the constant shopping was massive production of consumer goods in China and a greedy, wasteful way of life that was completely unsustainable financially and environmentally. This era was also accompanied by an increase in inequality and an increase in family breakdown, addiction, obesity and mental health problems.

My conclusion is that the highest priority for radical politics is to generate an international commitment to halt global warming and develop a more sustainable way of living. To achieve this, we need to end the current conflicts that are undermining the prospects of international cooperation and to create a more equitable world order. This means that we have to build a less consumerist, throwaway style of life. This would be a massive but achievable challenge, which can only be met by reducing inequality within and between countries. The promise of constant growth and consumption will have to be replaced by a commitment to adequacy for all, more frugality and human satisfaction achieved less through consumption and more through scholarship, the arts and altruism. We need a system capable of major technological innovation and progress that is not based on unsustainable consumption. This is the kind of civilisation that religious leaders, moral philosophers and political idealists have dreamed of. It has now become a necessity for our survival.

As we experience the mounting economic crisis and the growing environmental crisis, it is easy to spot major historical forces of resistance and protest that are evolving across the world. What is less easy to know is how the people of the OECD countries will respond to the downturn. The movements that are organised around the values that could carry the world through the coming crisis – a belief in equity, internationalism and regulation of markets – were built in the nineteenth century. The labour and social democratic parties were built on the democratic and human rights values of the French Revolution, to which were added the nineteenth-century socialist movements, values of solidarity and equality, internationalism and market regulation. Almost all of these parties have weakened during the last two decades and absorbed the values of neo-liberalism and to varying extents neo-conservatism which originate with the radical Right. They have experienced a general weakening electorally and/or a movement to the Right when in power. The new consumerist, post-industrial economy has weakened the trade union movement. The membership base of all parties, but particularly the parties of the Left, has weakened and crumbled. In addition, there has been a move to the Right in Europe in response to the growth in the number of asylum seekers that result from post-Cold War disorder, aspirations for a better life amongst the displaced and rising environmental strains.

It is very easy to see where forces of radical resistance to current global trends will arise. I have attempted to draw an outline of these forces in this chapter. It is also easy to see how forces of the radical Right might strengthen in response to economic recession, government rhetoric on terrorism and the growing movement of people across the globalising world. The 'war on terror' and its erosion of the rule of law and basic civil liberties, demonstrates a movement to the Right by those in power. One response to uncertainty which we have already seen displayed is to foster a sense of fear and hatred of the 'Other'. Given the likelihood of displacement of hundreds of millions of people as a consequence of global warming, there is a high likelihood that governments in the OECD countries will become more fascistic in their response.

The big question we are left with is where and how the political forces that can organise a solution to the growing crisis can gather. The values of the Right are incapable of mobilising the spirit of international cooperation and equity necessary to carry the world forward. The forces of the social democratic Left are gravely weakened. Many people put their faith in civil society and look to the development and environmental NGOs to create new political movements.

I have no faith that development NGOs will help to create a new political movement. They depend on charitable giving and government grants. They tend to speak on behalf of the poor of the world, but not be of them. The mobilisation known as 'Make Poverty History' which organised around the G7 meeting in Gleneagles demonstrates their frailty. They want to sound radical, but stay on good terms with governments and keep issues of global poverty separate from contentious arguments about foreign policy. The environmental NGOs are mobilising for a more radical agenda. In their early days, they were seen to care more for trees and animals than human beings and to be opposed to development in the poorest countries. Their arguments have become more inclusive and concerned for suffering humanity. But pressure groups, no matter how popular and radical, are not a political movement. They work to try to shift public opinion and the political system but not to take power. The green parties have tried to make the move into the political mainstream, but with very limited success so far.

My conclusion then to the question 'What *is* radical politics today?' is that it has to be internationalist, committed to global equity and reduced inequality at home. There is an obvious conflation of green and social democratic forces that might be able to create a global movement capable of carrying these values into effect. But currently the social democratic forces are in decline, green political movements are weak and movements of the Right in the ascendancy. In the fog of the future, I see a rise of fascistic movements. It is worth reminding ourselves, as did Edward Nugee in a letter to the *Financial Times* on 16 October 2008, of the effects of the 1929 crisis on Germany. Gustav Stresemann, who was Chancellor and Foreign Minister during the Weimar Republic, did much to stabilise the German economy between 1923 and 1929. But the New York stock market crash of 29 September 1929 brought a halt to American loans which had largely underpinned the rebuilding of the German economy.

Unemployment soared and Hitler was the only one seeming to promise a way out of the crisis. In the election of May 1928, the Nazi party had won 810,000 votes and 12 seats in the Reichstag. In the election of September 1930, it won 6,409,000 votes and 107 seats, and in July 1932, 13,745,800 votes and 230 seats. Hitler did seem to restore Germany's economy in his first eighteen months in power, so that Winston Churchill said in 1935 'One may dislike Hitler's system and yet admire his patriotic achievement. If our country were defeated, I hope that we should find a champion as indomitable to restore our courage and lead us back to our place among the nations.'

Churchill changed his view of Hitler the following year. Obviously, history never exactly repeats itself and the fascistic forces of the future will look different from those of Nazi Germany, but they will contain the same politics of division, hatred and national aggrandisement that cannot solve the problems that we face. I have no doubt that in response to the rise of such ugly forces there will be a gathering of the forces of generosity, capable of mobilising the world to deal with the coming crisis. I am afraid it will all get nastier before we see a rise in generous, radical politics, but I suspect that history is about to speed up in front of our eyes and all who oppose the radicalisation of fear, ethnic hatred, racialism and division have to be ready to create a new movement that contains the solutions to the monumental historical problems we currently face.

References

Hari, J. (2008) 'Don't Kill the Planet in the Name of Saving the Economy', *The Independent*, 20 October.

McCarthy, M. (2005) 'China Crisis: Threat to the Global Environment', *The Independent*, 19 October.

Nugee, E. (2008) Letter in the *Financial Times*, 16 October.

7
Resistance after the Spatial Turn

Edward W. Soja

Radical politics changed dramatically in 2009. No matter what Barack Obama does in office, his election removed the easy target supplied by the arrogant imperialism and neo-conservative excesses of the Bush-Cheney regime, while the global financial meltdown that helped Obama win provided a new easy target, the possibility that the end of capitalism, or at the very least of its neo-liberal variant, is near. Whatever happens in the aftermath of these epochal events, radical politics today is shifting its focus, moving away from an all-embracing anti-neo-liberalism towards a renewed hope that radical change is possible.

Although they have been around a long time, two diverging streams of radical political thought are becoming more clearly defined in these changing times. One tends to see the events of 2008 as a confirmation of core Marxist theories of the anarchy of capitalist production, the destructive consequences of greed-driven competitive behaviour, and the almost inevitable tendency for crises to emerge after long periods of expansive and super-exploitative growth. Believing that these persistent continuities with the past significantly outweigh all that is new and different in the present, the resurgent traditionalists see radical anti-capitalist politics as usual, modified perhaps to give greater emphasis to environmental and a few other issues, as the obvious and necessary response. Reinforcing this reaction is an undercurrent of I-told-you-so confidence.

A different political stream, one that I will follow more closely here, calls for greater flexibility, openness to diverse views, and cautious optimism. For this group, the events of 2008 do not affirm traditional Marxist arguments as much as they demand innovative departures, a search for new modes of radical political action that can more effectively take advantage of the opportunities the current situation provides. Continuities with the past persist, but the contemporary capitalist world economy is so different from what it was just twenty years ago that to react as if conditions are the same as they were is not likely to lead to significant results.

Backing this view is the unusual nature and timing of the current financial crisis. It is not the familiar crisis of capitalism that follows a long period of expansionary boom, as happened in the Great Depression and after the series of urban, oil, and other crises in the 1960s and early 1970s. It is much more like the period of intense instability and unpredictable change that have marked the end of a prolonged period of restructuring and reconfiguration. Over-accumulation, under-consumption, or simple falling rate of profit models do not get us very far into what is happening today. The crisis now is a product of a very different kind of capitalism than existed thirty years ago, a new variant of capitalism that has taken shape from the accelerated globalisation of capital, labour, and urban industrial culture; and the new technology-fed transition from Fordist mass production and mass consumerism to more flexible, post-Fordist, and information-intensive economic systems.

This suggests that radical politics, rather than smugly speaking of some culminating last stage of capitalist development, needs to build upon a deeper understanding of the current restructuring-generated crisis and its distinctive and different dynamics and contradictions, many of which do not fit powerful Marxist orthodoxies. Particularly unusual today is the behaviour of finance capital. Throughout the history of urban industrial capitalism, finance capital working with the state has served a disciplinary and regulatory function, reacting to problems of over-production, under-consumption and inefficiency. Over the past thirty years, with the rise of neo-liberal states and policies, it has not just lost much of its traditional regulatory function, it has formed itself into a propulsive and profitable centre.

What happened in 2008 revolved around the breakdown of this enormously expanded and distorted version of finance capital, defined best in the widely used acronym of FIRE, Financial services, Insurance and Real Estate. The FIRE sector's contribution to the gross national product and to overall employment grew at an extraordinary rate in the past three decades, but what developed outside the normal limits of the real economy was even more amazing. A ballooning credit economy became bloated with trillions of dollars' worth of fictitious exchange value in the form of hedge funds, credit default swaps, private equity funds and other electronically recycled forms of money and credit. The traditional banking industry, which had been so drastically restructured and reorganised over the previous twenty years as to be almost unrecognisable, was absorbed into the expansive balloon which came to be worth much more than the combined gross national product of every country on earth.

Sucked up into this virtually unregulated FIRE-fed super-bubble were worker pension funds, household savings, first and second mortgages and bank reserves – any source of capital not yet absorbed into high-risk investments. Neo-liberal ideology, pushed forward initially in the Reagan–Thatcher years and accelerating over the past two decades, spread a gospel of privatisation, deregulation, devolutionary 'small' government and the magic of the market nearly everywhere in the world, facilitated by the revolution in information and communications technology, broadcast via the globalisation of capital, labour and culture, and maintained by armies of ideological spin doctors. Nearly everyone believed. After all, the word 'credit' is derived from the Latin *credo*, I believe.

While statistical averages appeared to indicate overall growth in the world economy, wealth became more polarised than perhaps ever before in the history of capitalism. Even in those countries where strong welfare states tempered growing income inequalities, enormous wealth, both real and fictitious, became concentrated in the upper 1 per cent of the income ladder, the so-called super-rich, while the bottom 40 per cent often experienced decades of declining real income and relative wealth. Billionaires abounded as never before and the earth simultaneously became a planet of slums, with now well more than a billion forming a vast reserve army of still disunited workers for the hungry global economy.

There are many continuities with the past that can be found in the restructuring-generated crises that began in the late 1980s, multiplied in the 1990s anti-globalisation riots, exploded in frustration on 11 September 2001 and crashed contagiously in 2008, but the main point I am making here is that the accumulated differences have become much greater than the continuities today. One might have understood a great deal of what was happening in the world thirty years ago by recalling Marx's inspiring critiques of capitalism and insightful explanations of why capitalism globalises, but to depend heavily upon them today would be much less helpful and potentially misleading. This magnifies the need for innovative new forms of radical politics.

Developing these new forms needs to begin with a depolarisation of radical theories and practices, especially those that revolve around an absolute or categorical choice, such as that between capitalism and socialism. More than ever before, this is not a simple either/or choice, but is increasingly a matter of combining both and demanding something more. Expressed differently, the primary focus of radical politics today is to make capitalism as socialist as we can rather than demanding pure socialism or, for that matter, pure capitalism (neither of which is ever likely to work). Pushing radical politics further in this combinatorial direction is the demand that the mixture of socialist capitalism creates new hybrid forms that even more vigorously promote social, economic, and, as I will explain below, spatial justice and democracy. Depolarisation also opens up the possibility if not the necessity of being only partially Marxist in one's political perspective. To insist on either 100 per cent allegiance or total rejection of Marxism is to strangle nearly all possibilities for radical change today.

Focusing further on what is different and distinctive about the present-day situation, two particular developments come to mind, and each is likely to influence radical politics well into the twenty-first century. The first is the extraordinary expansion of China and its continuing role in defining the future of both capitalism and socialism. China must not be submitted to the outdated either/or choice of being labelled communist or capitalist in any holistic sense. China not only exemplifies a highly advanced form of socialist capitalism, it demonstrates that urban industrial capitalist development can be achieved more quickly under socialist than under capitalist guidance, democratic or otherwise. As might be expected, very little is written about this socialist road to capitalism.

Even more startling, Chinese leaders seem better informed than Western critical scholars and policy-makers about the double dynamics of capitalist development, that it is both creative and destructive, driven by innovative forces as well as by forces fostering inequality and polarisation, and that it tends to plunge into crisis after periods of rapid growth, requiring new and different economic policies aimed at achieving greater social justice and equality rather than simply faster accumulation. The Chinese experiment that continues today is no longer about maximising the speed of capitalist development but addressing its expected negative urban and rural consequences through effective social and spatial planning.

The second influential force affecting the future of radical politics is what some refer to as the 'spatial turn', the growing recognition in nearly every field of the usefulness and creative power of a critical spatial perspective. As I see it, the spatial turn and the new spatial politics that is emerging from it represent more than a passing academic fad. Nor can the resurgent interest in spatial thinking be reduced merely to an acknowledgement of what the traditionally spatial disciplines such as geography and architecture have been doing for years. The spatial turn is signalling a sea-change in intellectual and political thought and practice and has the potential to be the driving force behind a new radical politics.

Radical politics for the past century or more has been rooted in the triumph of a historicist and socialist materialism that was promulgated by Marx and others against any suggestion of a spatial, geographical or environmental causality shaping human social relations. Nearly every social movement in the past, whether based on class, race, gender or any other axis of discriminatory power, defined itself around taking control over the making of history, based on the belief that the contested differential power relations have been historically constituted or created and therefore need to be similarly redefined. Remaking history has accordingly been the foundational objective for mobilisation and strategic action.

Something quite remarkable, however, started to happen in the last decade of the twentieth century. Scholars and others, in a wide variety of fields, began to think seriously and critically about space and the spatiality of human life in much the same way they thought about time and the historical nature of human life. Over the last 150 years, as I just discussed, we have grown accustomed to seeing the world through historical lenses, much more than through a critical spatial perspective. Today, however, the spatial or geographical imagination has been reawakened and has taken on a new significance in making practical and theoretical sense of the present. Just think about how the contemporary economic crisis is dominated by discussion of complex geographical conditions relating to the globalisation of capital, labour and culture; the changing role of the territorial state; the emerging problems of regulating inter-urban and inter-regional as well as international flows of capital investment, credit and currency; and the spreading crisis of territorial governance and regulation at multiple scales, from the global to the local and at every scale in between.

As the privileging of time and history (socially transformed time) over space and geography (socially transformed space) is being rethought, a new awareness is developing that we all share to some degree a sense of being negatively affected (exploited, dominated, oppressed) by the spatially unjust geographies which we have constructed and in which we live. This shared consciousness of the geography of injustice and the injustices embedded in our geographies can add significantly not just to the empowerment of particular social movements but even more so to making connections between them. Seeking spatial justice and such related objectives as regional democracy and the right to the city can provide, not as a substitute for but an addition to historical conscious-ness, a more effective way of connecting radical social movements and building new cross-cutting and inclusive coalitions aimed not just at remaking history but remaking geography as well.

Perhaps never before has the spatial organisation of human soci-ety, particularly as it takes shape in the modern metropolis, in the regional makeup of the sovereign state, and in the expansive global economy, been as widely recognised as an influential force shaping human behaviour, political action and societal development. A critical spatial perspective has become increasingly relevant to understanding the contemporary condition, whether we are pondering the increasing intervention of electronic media in our daily routines, trying to under-stand the multiplying geopolitical conflicts around the globe, or seeking ways to act politically to reduce poverty, racism, sexual discrimination and environmental degradation.

The growing interest in the spatial turn was clearly illustrated to me at an event organised through 'The *Spaces of* Democracy and the *Democracy of* Space' network, directed by the editor of this book. At that event held in Long Beach, California in early August 2008, I was struck in particu-lar by the large numbers of younger people who turned up, interested in how our understanding of 'the spatial' can be rethought and strate-gically utilised in radical politics today (for more on this meeting see http://www.spaceofdemocracy.org).

Several conclusions emerge from these observations. First, radical pol-itics today and in the future will be more specifically urban than ever before, focusing on the poverty, inequality and injustice embedded in the 'megacity regions' that now contain close to a majority of the world's population and an even greater proportion of its wealth, power, slums and poverty. Second, radical politics will revolve increasingly around spa-tialised concepts of justice, democracy, citizenship, human rights and especially the more concretised and grounded rights of residents to a fair share of the resources and services that agglomerations generate and provide. Third, geographically uneven development at multiple scales, from the global to the local and at the many regional scales in between, will become the target for new cross-scalar connections that will inform and invigorate a radical politics aimed at seeking spatial justice, creating non-discriminatory geographies, and opening new spaces of democracy.

Part II
New Forms of Radical Politics

8
Questioning Global Political Activism

David Chandler

For many people the fact that politics has become global – that politics is no longer restricted to narrow questions and institutions at a national level, or mainly contested in territorial boxes of the nation state – demonstrates that the stakes are much higher today. On the one hand, it appears that Western powers have carte blanche for the assertion of power in the war on terror or new rights of preventive or humanitarian intervention; on the other, it appears that there are new forms of global opposition in global civic movements and radical campaigns. The sense of global struggle is well summed up in radical theorists Michael Hardt and Antonio Negri's (2001, 2006) view of a struggle between 'Empire' and the 'Multitude' – where every struggle and protest becomes a direct struggle against the Empire of global capital serviced under the USA's leadership. I think that the stakes are indeed high in the new global ethics and activism, but that the stakes are somewhat different to those laid out above. I want to discuss what I think these stakes are by drawing out the reasons for the shift in politics to the global level and the consequences of this process.

The demand for global politics

The stakes seem to exist largely at a global level at the same time as what is at stake in domestic politics seems to be increasingly diminished. However, politics is no less important to many of us today. It is just that the nature and practices of this politics are different. We are less likely to engage in the formal politics of representation – of elections and governments – but in post-territorial or global politics, a politics where there is much less division between the private sphere and the public one. This type of politics is on the one hand 'global' but, on the other, highly individualised: it is very much the politics of our everyday lives – the sense of meaning we get from thinking about global warming when we turn off the taps when we brush our teeth, take our rubbish out for recycling or cut back on our car use. We might also do global politics in deriving meaning from the ethical or social value of our work, or in our subscription or support for good causes from Oxfam to Greenpeace and Christian Aid.

I want to suggest that when we do politics nowadays it is less the old politics, of self-interest, political parties and concern for governmental power, than the new politics of global ethical concerns. I further want to suggest that the forms and content of this new global approach to the political are more akin to religious beliefs and practices, than to the forms of our social political engagement in the past. Global politics is similar to religious approaches in three vital respects: (1) global post-territorial politics is no longer concerned with power: the concerns are free-floating and in many ways, existential, about how we live our lives; (2) global politics revolves around practices that are private and individualised: they are about us as individuals and our ethical choices; (3) the practice of global politics tends to be non-instrumental: we do not subordinate ourselves to collective associations or parties and are more likely to give value to our aspirations, acts or the fact of our awareness of an issue, as an end in-itself. It is as if we are upholding our goodness or ethicality in the face of an increasingly confusing, problematic and alienating world – our politics in this sense is an expression or voice, in Karl Marx's (1975: 244) words, of 'the heart in a heartless world' or 'the soul of a soulless condition'.

The practice of politics as a form of religiosity may seem radical but could also be understood to be highly conservative. As Marx argued, religion was the 'opium of the people' – this is politics as a sedative or pacifier: it feeds an illusory view of change at the expense of genuine social engagement and transformation. I want to argue that global ethical politics reflects and institutionalises our sense of disconnection and social atomisation and results in irrational and unaccountable government policy-making. I want to illustrate my points by looking briefly at the practices of global ethics in three spheres: those of radical political activism, government policy-making and academia.

Radical activism

People often argue that there is nothing passive or conservative about radical political activist protests, such as the 2003 anti-war march, anti-capitalism and anti-globalisation protests, the huge march to Make Poverty History at the end of 2005, involvement in the World Social Forums or the radical jihad of Al-Qaeda. I disagree; these new forms of protest are highly individualised and personal ones – there is no attempt to build a social or collective movement. It appears that theatrical suicide, demonstrating, badge and bracelet wearing are ethical acts in themselves: personal statements of awareness, rather than attempts to engage politically with society.

This is illustrated by the 'celebration of differences' at marches, protests and social forums. It is as if people are more concerned with the creation of a sense of community through differences than with any political debate, shared agreement or collective purpose. It seems to me that if someone was really concerned with ending war or with ending poverty or with overthrowing capitalism, political views and political differences would be quite important. Is war caused by capitalism, by human nature, or by the existence of guns and other weapons? It would seem important to debate reasons, causes and solutions; it would also seem necessary to give those political differences an organisational expression if there was a serious project of social change.

Rather than a political engagement with the world, it seems that radical political activism today is a form of *social* disengagement – expressed in the anti-war marchers' slogan of 'Not in My Name', or the assumption that wearing a plastic bracelet or setting up an internet blog diary is the same as engaging in political debate. In fact, it seems that political activism is a practice which isolates individuals who think that demonstrating a personal commitment or awareness of problems is preferable to engaging with other people who are often dismissed as uncaring or brainwashed by consumerism. The narcissistic aspects of the practice of this type of global politics are expressed clearly by individuals who are obsessed with reducing their carbon footprint, deriving their idealised sense of social connection from an ever-increasing awareness of themselves and by giving political meaning to every personal action.

Global ethics appear to be in demand because they offer us a sense of social connection and meaning, while at the same time giving us the freedom to construct the meaning for ourselves, to pick our causes of concern, and enabling us to be free of responsibilities for acting as part of a collective association, for winning an argument or for success at the ballot-box. While the appeal of global ethical politics is an individualistic one, the lack of success or impact of radical activism is also reflected in its rejection of any form of social movement or organisation.

Governments

Strange as it may seem, the only people who are keener on global ethics than radical activists are political elites. Since the end of the Cold War, global ethics have formed the core of foreign policy and foreign policy has tended to dominate domestic politics. Global ethics are at the centre of debates and discussion over humanitarian intervention, 'healing the scar of Africa', the war on terror and the 'war against climate insecurity'. Traditional foreign policy, based on strategic geopolitical interests with a clear framework for policy-making, no longer seems so important.

The government is downsizing the old Foreign and Commonwealth Office where people were regional experts, spoke the languages and were engaged for the long term, and provides more resources to the Department for International Development where its staff are experts in good causes. This shift was clear in the UK's attempt to develop an 'ethical foreign policy' in the 1990s – an approach which openly claimed to have rejected strategic interests for values and the promotion of Britain's caring and sharing identity. Clearly, the projection of foreign policy on the basis of demonstrations of values and identity, rather than an understanding of the needs and interests of people on the ground, leads to ill thought-through and short-term policy-making.

Governments have been more than happy to put global ethics at the top of the political agenda for the same reasons that radical activists have been eager to shift to the global sphere: namely, the freedom from political responsibility that it affords them. Every government and international institution has shifted from strategic and instrumental policy-making, based on a clear political programme, to the ambitious assertion of global causes – saving the planet, ending poverty, saving Africa, not just ending war but solving the causes of conflict, etc. Of course, the more ambitious the aim the less anyone can be held to account for success and failure. In fact, the more global the problem is, the more responsibility can be shifted to blame the USA or the UN for the failure to translate ethical claims into concrete results. Ethical global questions, where the alleged values of the UN, the UK, the civilised world, NATO or the EU are on the line in wars of choice (from the war on terror to the war on global warming) lack traditional instrumentality because they are driven less by the traditional interests of *realpolitik* than the narcissistic search for meaning or identity.

Governments feel the consequences of their lack of social connection, even more than we do as individuals; it undermines any attempt to represent shared interests or coherent political programmes. As Jean

Baudrillard (1983) suggests, without a connection to the represented masses, political leaders are as open to ridicule and exposure as the 'Emperor with no clothes'. It is this lack of shared social goals which makes instrumental policy-making increasingly problematic. Donald Rumsfeld (2003) said that there are no metrics to help assess whether the war on terror is being won or lost. These wars and campaigns, often alleged to be based on the altruistic claim of the needs and interests of others, are demonstrations and performances, based on ethical claims rather than responsible practices and policies. Max Weber (2004) once counter-posed this type of politics – the ethics of conviction – to the ethics of responsibility in his lecture on 'Politics as a Vocation'. The desire to act on the international scene without a clear strategy or purpose has led to highly destabilising interventions from the Balkans to Iraq, and to the moralisation of a wide range of issues, from war crimes to EU membership requirements.

Academia

Today more and more people are 'doing politics' in their academic work. This is the reason for the boom in International Relations (IR) study and the attraction of other social sciences to the global sphere. I would argue that the attraction of IR for many people has not been IR theory but the desire to practise global ethics. The boom in the IR discipline has coincided with a rejection of Realist theoretical frameworks of power and interests and the sovereignty/anarchy problematic. However, I would argue that this rejection has not been a product of theoretical engagement with Realism but an ethical act of rejection of Realism's ontological focus.

It seems that our ideas and our theories say much more about us than the world we live in. Normative theorists and Constructivists tend to support the global ethical turn arguing that we should not be as concerned with 'what is' as with the potential for the emergence of a global ethical community. Constructivists, in particular, focus upon the ethical language which political elites espouse rather than the practices of power. But the most dangerous trends in the discipline today are those frameworks which have taken up Critical Theory and argue that focusing on the world as it exists is conservative problem-solving while the task for critical theorists is to focus on emancipatory alternative forms of living or of thinking about the world. Critical thought then becomes a process of wishful thinking rather than one of engagement, with its advocates arguing that we need to focus on clarifying our own ethical frameworks and biases and positionality, before thinking about or teaching on world affairs. This becomes 'me-search' rather than research. We have moved a long way from Hedley Bull's (1995) perspective that, for academic research to be truly radical, we had to put our values to the side to follow where the question or inquiry might lead.

The inward-looking and narcissistic trends in academia, where we are more concerned with our reflectivity – the awareness of our own ethics and values – than with engaging with the world, was brought home to me when I asked my IR students which theoretical frameworks they agreed with most. They mostly replied Critical Theory and Constructivism. This is despite the fact that the students thought that states operated on the basis of power and self-interest in a world of anarchy. Their theoretical preferences were based more on what their choices said about them as ethical individuals, than about how theory might be used to understand and engage with the world.

Conclusion

I have attempted to argue that there is a lot at stake in the radical understanding of engagement in global politics. Politics has become a religious activity, an activity which is no longer socially mediated; it is less and less an activity based on social engagement and the testing of ideas in public debate or in the academy. Doing politics today, whether in radical activism, government policy-making or in academia, seems to bring people into a one-to-one relationship with global issues in the same way religious people have a one-to-one relationship with their God.

Politics is increasingly like religion because when we look for meaning we find it inside ourselves rather than in the external consequences of our 'political' acts. What matters is the conviction or the act in itself: its connection to the global sphere is one that we increasingly tend to provide idealistically. Another way of expressing this limited sense of our subjectivity is in the popularity of globalisation theory – the idea that instrumentality is no longer possible today because the world is such a complex and interconnected place and therefore there is no way of knowing the consequences of our actions. The more we engage in the new politics where there is an unmediated relationship between us as individuals and global issues, the less we engage instrumentally with the outside world, and the less we engage with our peers and colleagues at the level of political or intellectual debate and organisation.

You may be thinking that I have gone some way to describing or identifying what the problems might be but I have not mentioned anything about a solution. I won't dodge the issue. One thing that is clear is that the solution is not purely an intellectual or academic one; the demand for global ethics is generated by our social reality and social experiences. Marx spent some time considering a similar crisis of political subjectivity in 1840s Germany and in his writings – *The German Ideology, Introduction to the Critique of Hegel's Philosophy of Right, Theses on Feuerbach*, and elsewhere – he raged against the idealism of contemporary thought and argued that the criticism of religion needed to be replaced by the criticism of politics – by political activism and social change based on the emerging proletariat (see Marx, 1975, for example). Nearly two centuries later it is more difficult to see an emerging political subject which can fulfil the task of 'changing the world' rather than merely 'reinterpreting it' through philosophy.

I have two suggestions. Firstly, that there is a pressing need for an intellectual struggle against the idealism of global ethics. The point needs to be emphasised that our freedom to engage in politics, to choose our identities and political campaigns, as well as governments' freedom to choose their ethical campaigns and wars of choice, reflects a lack of social ties and social engagement. There is no global political struggle between 'Empire' and its 'Radical Discontents'; the Foucauldian temptation to see power and resistance everywhere is a product of wishful or lazy thinking dominated by the social categories of the past. The stakes are not in the global stratosphere but much closer to home. Politics appears to have gone global because there is a breakdown of genuine community and the construction of fantasy communities and fantasy connections in global space. Unless we bring politics back down to earth from heaven, our critical, social and intellectual lives will continue to be diminished ones.

Secondly, on the basis that the political freedom of our social atomisation leads us into increasingly idealised approaches to the world we live in, we should take more seriously Hedley Bull's (1995) injunction to pursue the question, or in Alain Badiou's (2004: 237–8) words subordinate ourselves to the 'discipline of the real'. Subordination to the world outside us is a powerful factor that can bind those interested in critical research, whereas the turn away from the world and the focus on our personal values can ultimately only be divisive. To facilitate external engagement and external judgement, I suggest we experiment with ways to build up social bonds with our peers that can limit our freedoms and develop our sense of responsibility and accountability to others. We may have to construct these social connections artificially but their value and instrumentality will have to be proven through our ability to engage with, understand, critique and ultimately overcome the practices and subjectivities of our time.

References

Badiou, A. (2004) 'Fragments of a Public Diary on the American War against Iraq', *Contemporary French and Francophone Studies*, 8(3): 223–38.

Baudrillard, J. (1983) *In the Shadow of the Silent Majorities* (New York: Semiotext(e)).

Bull, H. (1995) *The Anarchical Society: a Study of Order in World Politics*, 2nd edn (Basingstoke: Palgrave Macmillan).

Hardt, M. and A. Negri (2001) *Empire* (New York: Harvard University Press).

Hardt, M. and A. Negri (2006) *Multitude: War and Democracy in the Age of Empire* (London: Penguin).

Marx, K. (1975) 'A Contribution to the Critique of Hegel's Philosophy of Right', in L. Colleti (ed.), *Karl Marx: Early Writings* (Harmondsworth: Penguin), pp. 243–58.

Rumsfeld, D. (2003) 'Rumsfeld's War-on-Terror Memo: the full text of Defense Secretary Donald Rumsfeld's memo on the war on terror', 16 October, http://www.usatoday.com/news/washington/executive/rumsfeld-memo.htm (accessed 23 May 2006).

Weber, M. (2004) 'Politics as a Vocation', in D. Owen and T. B. Strong (eds), *Max Weber: the Vocation Lectures* (Indianapolis: Hackett), pp. 32–94.

9
Rethinking Political Organisation
Hilary Wainwright

The membership and influence of political parties is declining through-out the Western world, and most quickly in Britain. Traditionally, political parties have been the means of giving shape, leadership and coherence to radical politics. But in present circumstances they are sim-ply not up to the task. There's never been a golden age for parties of the Left, but there have been periods – the 1920s up till the late 1960s – when the majority of people desiring change in a broadly socialist direction would be members or supporters of mass socialist or communist parties. The situation now is that by far the majority of people actively pursuing goals of social justice, equality, deeper democracy, demilitarised poli-tics, and social and environmental sustainability, do so without being members of political parties. I am one of them.

Like many others, I'm not anti-party. If I lived in Norway or Germany, for instance, I might join the Socialist Left Party (SV) or Die Linke or in Greece, Synaspismos. But I would not see party activity – at any rate not in the forms that it conventionally takes – as my main focus. I would instead join those searching and experimenting with new forms of transformative organisation, especially those involving means of com-munication. Yet the sum of extra-party, movement-oriented activity does not somehow add up to political change, even if it were more adequately coordinated. We cannot look to social movements to get us out of a tight spot. It should be clear by now that movements come and go and can-not be invoked as some self-evident answer to the problem of creating effective agencies of social change.

At their most effective, progressive social movements radicalise pub-lic consciousness. Generally, however, they are unable to give these shifts in consciousness a wider political coherence. This limit means that the desire for change that such movements stimulate can be politically ambivalent. It can be tapped by the Right if there is no possibility of these hopes gaining political expression and developing coherent alternatives through the Left.

Perhaps we therefore need to experiment with hybrid forms of 'movement party' organisation, especially in a context in which the nation state, the traditional focus of political parties, can only be one of many focuses of political struggle. It is clear from experience, however, that so-called 'movement parties' provide no simple answer. We've watched in dismay the movement dynamic behind parties such as the German Greens, and more significantly the Brazilian Workers Party at a federal level, acquiescing to the conservative pressures of conventional electoral politics, state institutions and the financial markets. Or we've seen them split and in all likelihood doom the fragments to marginality; like Rifondazione Communista in Italy, the Scottish Socialist Party and Respect in England. This frustration prompts me to stand back and investigate some of the basic concepts involved in our thinking about radical change. Consider, for example, concepts of knowledge and its social organisation, of power and its plural sources, of representation and alternative models. Also consider the question of how we should interpret Marx's famous remark about men making history, but not in conditions of their own choosing . . . but for our own times.

Rethinking power

The political thinking in many contemporary movements distinguishes between two radically distinct meanings of power: on the one hand, *power as transformative capacity* and on the other hand *power as domination*, as involving an asymmetry between those with power and those over whom power is exercised.

Historically, the major parties of the Left have tended to be built around a benevolent version of the second understanding of power: that is, around winning the power to govern and using it paternalistically to meet the needs of the people. This has shaped the nature of politics, concentrating it around legislation and state action. It has underpinned the position and self-conception of the political party as having a monopoly over political transformation. This, in turn, has meant that parties have tended to see the political role of movements as subordinate to the party, as a matter of lobbying, support, and mobilising supportive pressure behind legislative, parliamentary action spearheaded by the party. The assertion of power as transformative capacity, first by the student, feminist, radical trade union and community movements of the late 1960s and 1970s, and more recently by the global justice movement of the late

1990s, produced a break with this narrow definition of politics. It led to a far wider understanding of the scope of politics, that is of conscious efforts to end injustice and to realise the dignity and potential of all; a scope way beyond the traditional focus on state, government and legislation, pervading all the relationships and institutions of our daily lives. The other side of this opening and deepening of the definition of politics has been an effective challenge to the party's monopoly of the leadership of social change.

This understanding of power as transformative capacity is related to a distinct understanding of social change, implicit in the practice of the movements. Particularly crucial here is the way that we started from our own circumstances and took personal responsibility for change by directly refusing to reproduce relations of oppression and exploitation. This applied both to our own lives and to our implicit complicity with it elsewhere, especially in the global South. Our aim has been to create spaces for transformation and to at least illustrate alternative values in practice. This understanding was evident vividly in the women's liberation movement, which quickly directed its energies towards mobilising whatever resources it could, material or cultural, to bring about change in the present, both in personal relationships and, closely connected, in the social and cultural environment that had reinforced women's subordination. It made demands on the state for support, but on the basis of its own alternatives and self-organisation. Similarly in the workplace, for a brief but revealing and inspirational period in the 1970s, the shopfloor organisations that had developed since the 1950s became the basis for real shifts in the balance of power in the management of factories and for alternative plans for industrial policy and reorganisation. I've only briefly highlighted here the radical dynamic of this transformative approach to power. This approach can of course also stop at the level of personal change without making the wider connections that require a collective exercise of transformative power. This is now clearly a central issue for addressing the causes of the major issues of the day, such as climate change.

As we know, the Labour Party in Britain rarely took up these opportunities for radical social change at a national level. Local attempts to experiment with this new politics in the 1980s, most notably with the Greater London Council, were also swept aside. But this was not simply a matter of political ill will or reasoned disagreement; it was more fundamentally the result of complete incomprehension of a fundamentally different understanding of politics. The assumption that underpinned traditional parties of the Left was that the state, government or party – the social subject – acted on the rest of society – the social object. This traditional but still influential model took insufficient account of the way in which change is coming from *within* society, the way in which those who were previously considered the objects of change *are themselves* actors for change, including self-change.

Changed understandings of knowledge

Closely associated with an understanding of transformative power are the distinctive understandings of knowledge influenced by the movement-based politics of recent decades. In good part as a result of this politics and – not unrelated – developments in the philosophy of science, we are increasingly aware of the plural sources of knowledge: as tacit, practical and experiential as well as scientific. We are working increasingly with complexity, ambivalence and uncertainty.

This does not imply a postmodern, relativistic notion that anything goes, that there are no independent grounds for judging arguments. On the contrary, it implies that supposedly postmodern concepts like 'deconstruction', and a recognition of the many perspectives from which a single phenomenon can be understood, must be reclaimed as tools for analysing and changing a complex and differentiated real world. These new understandings of knowledge point towards an emphasis on the horizontal sharing and exchange of knowledge and collaborative attempts to build connected alternatives and shared memories. They stress the gaining of knowledge as a process of discovery and therefore see political action, the exercise of transformative power, as itself a source of knowledge, revealing unpredicted problems or opportunities. This implies a self-consciousness of the sense in which actions are also experiments and therefore the need for spaces and times for open reflection and synthesis of different experiences.

This recognition of the importance of experiential and practical knowledge does not do away with the importance of debate and argument; in effect it extends it. It implies the importance of debate driven not so much by the struggle for positions of power exemplified in many of the traditional factional struggles in political parties as we have so far known them, as by a search for truth about the complexity of social change, a collaborative knowledge which itself becomes a source of power. The Social Forum process, globally and at continental level is perhaps the most important and appropriately transnational experiment so far in finding ways of sharing ideas rooted in both experience and different political traditions. Like any experiment it is messy and uneven but contains crucial lessons from which any rethinking of the party and the development of political programmes must learn.

New models of political representation – examples from Latin America

Where do these notes on rethinking power and knowledge lead in terms of rethinking of political parties whose distinctive role concerns institutions of state and government? Here all that I can do is to note some pointers and ask some questions.

A first implication of the analysis of power as transformative capacity is that action in and around political institutions is but one – albeit crucial – sphere of action and struggle for fundamental change. But are there any implications for the direction and content of such action? In general terms one can say that the goal must move from winning the power to govern *for* the people paternalistically to meet their needs, to being a struggle *in collaboration with* organised citizens to change political institutions from sources of domination, to resources for transformation. What does this mean in practice?

It is an approach that is best illustrated by experiments in Latin America: some of the local authorities controlled by the Workers Party in Brazil, the MAS government in Bolivia and the Bolivarian process in Venezuela, where parties (or, in the latter case, a leader) winning elections have then used their democratic legitimacy to attempt to reach out beyond parliamentary institutions and strengthen popular control over the state institutions. The declared goal – not always the reality – has been to turn them into public resources for change controlled by a combination of participatory democracy and elected politicians. These experiences are exploring anew the role for political representation where political parties do not have a monopoly over the leadership of social and political change. These Latin American experiences have their roots in struggles against dictatorship or extreme forms of corruption and oligarchic rule. They take elections and representative democracy seriously; not as a sufficient definition of democracy, but rather as one part of a strategy for more radical democratic – including economic – transformation. A key element in making this possible has been the existence in most parts of Latin America of strong and often highly politically conscious forms of popular democracy or non-state sources of democratic power – in neighbourhood organisations, movements of the landless and indigenous people, and radical trade union organisations. (This is one reason why the commercial media have much less effective political influence in these countries than in the global North, in spite of their best and most insidious efforts to influence hearts and minds.)

In these circumstances the distinctive contribution of radical Left political parties, at their most innovative, has been to open up the institutions, to redistribute power, to facilitate a sharing of power with organised citizens, to stimulate and support new institutions of public participation in control over state power. They have sought to straddle the political institutions on the one hand and the conflicts and emergent sources of power in society on the other. The logic is to work both in and against the institutions and with autonomous movements and social conflicts to open up and democratise the institutions. Encouraging non-state sources of democratic power has been a necessary part of this process.

The changing politics of communications

A distinctive aspect of this organising at the base, in Europe as well as in Latin America, is a shifting understanding of the relationship between political organisation and the means of communication. It is noticeable that those organising to change the world increasingly put their energies into developing independent means of communication. This is often a response to experience of the exhaustion or plain uselessness of political parties as we know them. Certainly that has been my experience and that of many of my – 1968 – generation. We founded magazines or radio stations or quickly responded to the possibilities of the new information technologies, not so much because we were journalists or media people by trade, but because developing a strong movement-based infrastructure of communications seemed instinctively the way to move forward. It is striking that many of the post-Seattle generation(s) put much of their organising energy into developing new means of communication using the new information technologies and have generally, with a few exceptions, stayed clear of political parties.

João Pedro Stedile, a leader of the Brazilian movement of landless people (MST), one of the most powerful and innovative movements in Latin America, stresses the importance of developing the alternative media. He sees this as an essential part of developing autonomous sources of power, which in the case of the MST are both a basis of bargaining power with the Lula government and protection against being incorporated and compromised by over-dependence on the government. This pervasive emphasis on communication amongst those organising to achieve radical transformation is in part a product of the shifting understandings of knowledge I discussed earlier in this chapter.

As I noted, the shift from political parties is associated with profound shifts in the understanding of knowledge. This is the move away from a hierarchical view, with knowledge being the exclusive privilege of a few, to a capacity of all and therefore to an understanding of diverse and plural sources of knowledge. In other words, our forms of organisation, from the '68 student movements and the 1970s women's movement to most of the networks at the Social Forum, are at the same time forms of inter-communication. And self-consciously so.

We have created organisational forms and chosen tools of organisation with considerations of communication at the centre of our thinking. From the consciousness raising groups of the women's movement, through to the networks of the struggles over globalisation, we have built ways of organising in which there is a continuing interconnection between processes of action, struggle and experience and processes of reflection; the continuing generation of knowledge through sharing what knowledge we have: a collaborative and experimental search sharing what we know to reach what is still unknown. The shift is profound; so it is taking time to work its way through.

Underlying this shift to means of intercommunication is also the shift we referred to earlier in our understanding of the process of transformation away from the notion of a political actor – party or state – acting on society, as if from the outside, towards a recognition of the transformative capacities of the oppressed and exploited themselves as knowing and creative subjects. In other words, an emphasis on acting to transform the relationships which existing society depends upon. This is another aspect of the break from a narrow, one-way, instrumental idea of communication as mobilisation or persuasion. Instead it implies a close relation between communication and a Paolo Freirean idea of education as empowerment, as enabling people to gain confidence and realise their power and their potential.

How do the rapid developments of horizontal, potentially egalitarian forms of communication stimulated by the new information technology impact on electoral politics? It's too early to see but the experience of Moveon.Org, a political networking initiative founded by Howard Dean but then having a major influence on the Obama campaign, opens up new possibilities for movement politics to enter electoral politics without losing its autonomy. Any attempt to engage in electoral politics faces all kinds of pitfalls, but also imposes disciplines and provides the stimuli of translating transformative politics into practical and widely accessible alternatives. The conditions may not be of our choosing. But through a collaborative and engaged rethinking, inspired by a wide range of historical and present-day experiences, we can indeed still make history.

10
Iraq, Trauma and Dissent in Visual Culture

Dora Apel

In my contribution to the 'What *is* radical politics today?' project, I think it is important to highlight the nature and character of radical art through three case studies. These are a work on paper, a new media sculpture and a guerrilla theatre performance. In doing so, I describe and reflect upon different ways of being political within the public sphere of visual culture, specifically in relation to the inequities of capitalist culture, abuses of human rights and investments in anti-war activism, in relation to the American wars in Iraq and Afghanistan.

Since television first transformed the home from sanctuary and retreat, from the threat of the world, into a zone easily entered by war, the internet and global blogosphere have extended the integration of the domestic and the military, further dissolving the divide between public and private (Colomina, 2007). In response to the ongoing wars of occupation in the Middle East, artists have also mobilised media and military technologies, but for the purposes of making visible what is often oblique, slowing down the consumption of atrocity images, creating more critically aware relationships to the real, through imaginative forms of representation, and actively protesting American foreign and domestic policy. Three projects related to the wars in Iraq and Afghanistan by politically engaged visual artists and activists examine social and political issues largely opaque to the American public. The first is a photomontage by Martha Rosler, which looks at causes and connections between the domestic and the military (Figure 10.1). The second is a video projection by Krzysztof Wodiczko, which focuses on US veterans and the traumatic psychological effects of war that lead to social isolation and homelessness (Figure 10.2). The third is the guerrilla street performances by Iraq Veterans Against the War, which demonstrate some of the devastating impacts of the American occupation on Iraqi civilians (Figure 10.3).

These projects also raise larger questions about perpetrators and victims, patriotism and dissent, justice and democratic rights, and highlight the importance of representation on perception. Engaging viewers by deploying familiar images from print and television media in unexpected and imaginative ways, each project plays an activist role in the heightened anti-war discourse following eight years of an increasingly reviled war in Iraq initiated by the government of George W. Bush, who sank to the lowest level of popularity of any American president in decades.

Martha Rosler first visualised the militarisation of domestic space during the Vietnam War in her images, *Bringing the War Back Home: House Beautiful*, a series of photomontages produced between 1967 and 1972. In these works, Rosler combined photos of the suburban home from *House Beautiful* with images from the battlefields of Vietnam taken from *Life* magazine. Her images evoke the highly politicised, sardonic photomontages of Weimar-era Dada artists Raoul Hausmann and Hannah Höch, who used montage as a new visual language to produce anti-war images in the face of continuing militarisation, despite Germany's catastrophic losses in the First World War, and John Heartfield, who produced powerfully satirical anti-Nazi montages in the 1920s and 1930s. Like those works, Rosler's montages are meant to outrage the audience, as Walter Benjamin once described Berlin Dada, and to provoke the viewer through the uncanny juxtapositions that make visible the dissolving divide between war and the domestic. In Rosler's images, war not only enters the home through every visible window and screen, but its presence suggests that middle-class privilege in America precisely depends on American imperialism abroad.

Rosler revives *Bringing the War Back Home* in a new series begun in 2004 in response to the USA's invasions of Iraq and Afghanistan, continuing her critique of capitalist war culture and globalisation by combining war imagery with glossy fashion imagery. Unlike the Vietnam War series, which was originally produced in colour, but photocopied in black and white for distribution at demonstrations and in the underground press, these new photomontages are colour cut-and-paste images produced as larger digital prints that are shown in commercial galleries, print media reproduction, and small posters, taking advantage of the publicity and distribution networks of the art world. Commenting on her trepidation about reviving the series, Rosler (cited in Kino, 2008: 76) observed, 'The downside was that people could say, "She's revisiting something she did 30 years ago", but I thought that actually was a plus, because I wanted to make the point that with all the differences, this is exactly the same scenario. We haven't advanced at all in the way we go to war.' Technology may be updated in war as in art, but Rosler's revived series recalls a history of US military arrogance and aggression that has not changed at all from then to now. The new series again focuses on the militarisation of everyday life, the violence and chaos of war, and the traumatic effects on soldiers, even as it shows how these conditions are obscured by a streaming consumer culture.

Rosler's image *Invasion* (2008) serves as a good illustration of her radical critique of capitalism and American foreign policy. Part of the exhibition *Martha Rosler: Great Power* shown in September and October 2008 at the Chelsea gallery Mitchell-Innes & Nash in New York City, it pictures several small tanks on burning streets, the entire area aflame in red and yellow explosions (Figure 10.1). A small sign in Arabic, which stands at the lower left, positions us in Iraq and/or Afghanistan. Invading the scene is an army of young men identically uniformed in black suits. Their hair is carefully parted and pomaded into pompadours, their mien is unswervingly intent. They wear skinny pencil ties and their shoes are shiny lizard or snakeskin, with three of them ending in sinister points like metal blades. The men are like replicants or apparatchiks but sleekly outfitted in Dolce & Gabbana couture (Rosler, 2008). The West prides itself on its fashion sense but the irony is that they all look the same, like an army of Harvard lawyers or investment bankers, upper class playboys and privileged sons, the newly romanticised admen of the fifties, or new

Figure 10.1   Invasion, 2008, Photomontage, 77.2 by 137.2 cm, by Martha Rosler (Photo: Mitchell-Innes & Nash Gallery)

Young Republicans in sixties' Beatles suits. They are the next generation of the corporate elite, the drones of capitalism, the occupying army that stands behind the working-class grunts in fatigues.

Rosler gives us a surreal vision of a higher reality, in which corporate aspirations at home and the war abroad are creepily conjoined. Rather than picturing the domestic invaded by war, here Rosler brings the home-front to the battlefront. In the process she creates a seamless cinematic space that aligns fantasies of American military power and world dominance, with popular military and sci-fi films that pit good against evil in ways that usually have satisfying endings. The portents of this scenario, however, are both faintly ridiculous and weirdly chilling, as we gaze at these baby-faced masters of the universe, or Manchurian candidates whose personas, defined first and foremost by class, seem to remain unchanged through decades of neo-colonialist wars. If military technology can be domesticated, like Humvees that became a vehicle of choice for the wealthy, the domestic can also be weaponised. These unarmed corporate soldiers, still shiny with certainty in their values, seem dangerously oblivious to the missiles exploding behind them, or worse, they emerge from that inferno eerily unscathed by the destruction they wreak as though blissfully protected by a greater controlling power they never imagine may one day crack. Rosler's image thus attends to the way the corporate elite profits from the suffering and destruction it produces, even as the USA's government is at pains to efface it.

Krzysztof Wodiczko's project addresses the traumatic effect of war on soldiers from a psychological perspective. His work often takes the form of public projections in which real people who have suffered various forms of trauma tell their stories. The projects offer a therapeutic pathway to healing by providing a public platform for those whose voices would otherwise be silent. In *If You See Something . . .* (2005), for example, a quartet of videos projects the life-size figures and traumatic stories of real immigrants in the wake of government repression following 11 September 2001. They act out their private dramas of pain behind projected frosted glass windows on gallery walls as though they have been under surveillance (Apel, 2008). In his *Veteran Vehicle Project*, premiered in the week before and during the 2008 Democratic National Convention in Denver, Wodiczko appropriated the trappings of war technology to produce a critical intervention about the effects of war on returning veterans. A new media sculpture that transforms a military Humvee into a travelling media and sound projection vehicle, the *Veteran Vehicle Project* makes public the stories of Denver homeless veterans in their own words and voices (Figure 10.2). Left to assimilate as best they can without

Figure 10.2   Veteran Vehicle Project, Denver, August 2008, by Krzysztof Wodiczko
(Photo: Krzysztof Wodiczko)

adequate federal social support, there is an unprecedented incidence
of homelessness among veterans, who are damaged and traumatised
through repeated tours of duty in ways that make their reintegration
into civil society and their own families a daunting task.

Creating an electrifying three-dimensional soundscape with four-
horned speakers, like a battlefield under bombardment, the Humvee
mounted projector, the most powerful of its kind, shoots out words that
seemingly explode towards the viewer when projected on a wall, with
each speech act ending in a repeated phrase to the sound of rapid gun-
fire, 'to really blast home the message', as one observer noted on the
blog *MegofMegs*. Difficult to recognise out of context, the sound script is
taken from electronic war games on the internet, in which all the details
of gun operation, from the reloading mechanism to shells falling on the
ground, can be heard. This is a level of sophistication more convincing
than sound used in the movies (the seven and a half minute video is
available online at http://kwodiczko.com/WarVeteranVehicle/).

The video text is culled from collaborative sessions over the course of
seven months with more than forty Denver-based veterans. In short narratives, it offers intimate portraits of the veterans' experiences through

audio and text projected onto the wall of the Aromor building in a central part of Denver, which is undergoing renovation by Mercy Housing Colorado as permanent supportive housing for homeless veterans. The project was presented at dusk from 22 August to 26 August 2008, and included a one-night projection on a wall of the Performing Arts Center next to the convention centre. Proceeds from a private VIP event went to the non-profit organisations America's Road Home and their Denver partner, Denver's Road Home, which focus on ending family homelessness.

Wodiczko's project therapeutically addresses traumatic injury and healing by attempting to construct a radically democratic space that reconnects the individual with his or her community. In her landmark study, *Trauma and Recovery*, Judith Herman (1997) established the central dialectic of psychological trauma as the conflict between the will to deny terrible events and the need to proclaim them and have them heard. The truth of trauma, once spoken aloud and witnessed, is the first step towards repair and recovery; thus it is imperative for the larger society in which the trauma resides, and in which secondary trauma ripples outward through the families of victims, to act as civic witness and take responsibility for acknowledging and addressing the effects of trauma on its citizens. During World War One, the medical establishment considered traumatised soldiers weaklings or cowards, hysterics or moral invalids. Although in World War Two, 'shell shock' was recognised as a psychological injury that could happen to any man in combat, especially if exposure was intense and prolonged, it was not until Vietnam that the diagnosis of PTSD (post-traumatic stress disorder) gained legitimacy and was later extended by theorists such as Herman to include other traumatised groups, such as the victims of sexual abuse and rape.

One goal of the veterans who participated in Wodiczko's project was the desire to dispel the fantasies of heroic deeds, the imprimatur of manliness that war experience allegedly produces, and the promise of a better life propagated by military recruiters. As one veteran comments in the video, 'Recruiters lie; if his mouth is moving he's lying' (http://kwodiczko.com/WarVeteranVehicle/). The *Veteran Vehicle Project* thus becomes a critical examination of the rhetoric that constructs patriotism.

Wodiczko also emphasises the lack of awareness regarding secondary trauma. 'Veterans often destroy family life to protect their families from themselves', he notes (Wodiczko, 2008). 'They refuse help because they are "warriors", until they are picked up by ambulances' (Wodiczko, 2008). One moving outcome of the project was the response of a son to the plea of his veteran father who had walked away from his family nine years earlier. The appeal from the father to his son (just before the son's eighteenth birthday) asks for forgiveness and implores the son to break his long refusal 'to have anything to do with me'. The sound clip from the video featuring the father's plea was aired on the local NPR station and Wodiczko independently called the son and left a message inviting him to the projection, as part of his routine telephone invitations and announcements made to the families of the homeless veterans. After the first projection night, the father called Wodiczko and tearfully announced that his son had called and was planning to attend the next night's projection. 'But', warns Wodiczko, 'one problem will be replaced by ten' (Wodiczko, 2008). There are many social and cultural support projects needed to respond to the crises in which veterans find themselves.

This is not Wodiczko's first project with war veterans. His *War Veteran Vehicle Project*, designed in collaboration with Theodore Spyropoulos (and still under production), is a specially designed vehicle that functions as a kind of protective staging platform and sanctuary for its prospective war veteran occupant. Equipped with video screens and speakers for the transmission of memories and images of war without direct exposure of the veteran's face, the vehicle also has mechanical wings that serve as 'communicative shields' that open and close as needed by the emotionally vulnerable veteran. Physically manifesting the numbing emotional shields necessarily developed by soldiers, the vehicle operates as a metaphor for the emotional armour of traumatised veterans that must be dealt with by veterans themselves and their families, as well as the larger public (Apel, 2008). Wodiczko's projects allow the marginalised to develop a civic voice in the public sphere, externalising the interiority of trauma by making what is functionally private and effectively invisible into something highly public.

The most theatrical response to the Iraq War is the guerrilla theatre squad sponsored by the group Iraq Veterans Against the War (IVAW), which includes veterans from Iraq and Afghanistan, active duty servicemen and women from all branches of military service, and National Guard members and reservists who have served since 9/11, all of whom are opposed to the USA's occupation of Iraq. Their goal is to raise public consciousness by re-enacting terror raids on the streets of American cities. IVAW advocates three principled political demands: (1) the immediate withdrawal of all occupying forces in Iraq, (2) full benefits, more healthcare benefits (including mental health), and other support for returning servicemen and women, and (3) reparations to the Iraq people (see http://ivaw.org/).

The group has performed in New York, Washington, Chicago and Denver. In Washington DC in March 2008, a guerrilla theatre group of twelve men and one woman performed sweeps and raids in camouflage to mark the fourth anniversary of the war in Iraq. *Washington Post* reporter David Montgomery (2008: CO1) noted that they crept down streets in formation, 'detained' suspected hostile individuals (played by volunteers), and 'generally shocked, frightened and delighted tourists and office workers'. The *Washington Post* website, which includes a video clip, reports that the Marines are investigating two reservists who participated in the event. A similar performance took place in Denver, first on 4 July and again during the Democratic National Convention in August 2008, with fully uniformed veterans in camouflage who mimed holding guns while stopping and subduing suspects face down on the pavement with cuffs and hoods. Called *Operation First Casualty*, participant Geoff Milliard (2008) explained, 'We're performing our guerrilla street theatre called "Operation First Casualty", or OFC, because the first casualty in war is truth, and we're going to bring some of that truth here to Denver for the delegates to see.' Lasting about two hours, the veterans effectively recreated an atmosphere of trauma and terror (videos are available at YouTube – see Operation First Casualty). Like Rosler's updated edition of *Bringing the War Back Home*, the IVAW street theatre is modelled after a Vietnam-era protest action, in this case Operation Rapid American Withdrawal, which took place in Pennsylvania, in the summer of 1970. Other artists groups such as Northern Arts Tactical Offensive (NATO) and the performance works of Guillermo Gómez-Peña and his collaborators also address issues of war and the effects of capitalism in radically political and emotionally powerful ways.

The IVAW protest performances were perhaps most shocking on the busy urban streets of New York City during Memorial Day (Figure 10.3). The IVAW members performed searches, detentions, squad patrol, and crowd control operations in locations that included Central Park, Times Square, Union Square and Grand Army Plaza. Described by James David (2008) on *The Grounswell Blog* as 'alarming and powerful', he advised viewers of the 'shock value' of the online video he posted, in which the simulated military operations involved much shouting by soldiers and distress among bystanders. B. Colby Hamilton also described the scene in *The Brooklyn Rail*:

> Out of nowhere and without provocation, nine soldiers in full-desert fatigues appeared and screamed at the group in white to 'get on the fucking ground ...' The soldiers pinned people to the pavement and began bagging and tagging, using zip-ties on their wrists and stuffing

Figure 10.3 Iraq Veterans Against the War: *Operation First Casualty*, New York City, 27 May 2007, by Lovella Calica (Photo: Lovella Calica)

bags over their heads. People ran to get out of the way. The crowd pushed back to create a wall of wide eyes and open mouths around the soldiers.

In Iraq a truck would have pulled up to haul people off to detention centres. Instead IVAW members in black T-shirts distributed flyers after performances. As terrifying as they are, it is safe to assume that these re-enactments offer only a glimpse of the daily traumatic experiences of Iraqi civilians, whose deaths in the tens of thousands remain officially uncounted, whose injuries are unattended by the mainstream Western media, and whose broken lives after five years of war exist on an unimaginable scale of chaos, fear and deprivation.

Though protest actions, performative artworks and images by themselves arguably have limited ability to effect direct political change, their power should not be underestimated, as may be seen in the attempts by the USA's government to harass protesters and to limit, censor and ban images, such as the American war dead or the photos of Abu Ghraib. The artistic works produced by Rosler and Wodiczko, and the street theatre of the IVAW perform valuable political interventions into public discourse today, which can stimulate political thinking towards socially transformative effects. As Rosler notes, 'Social change depends on social movements, and all that artists can do is be a partner to a kind of concentrator of ideological currents' (Rosler and Blazwick, 2008: 7). With irony, humour, pathos and passion, the power of these projects resides in their ability to trouble, disturb, outrage or shock, maintaining an immanent critique as they enter visual culture in ways that are visually and sensually powerful, conceptually arresting, and inescapably visceral in their effects.

References

Apel, D. (2008) 'Technologies of War, Media, and Dissent in the Post 9/11 Work of Krzysztof Wodiczko', *Oxford Art Journal*, 31(2): 261–80.

Colomina, B. (2007) *Domesticity at War* (Cambridge, MA: MIT Press).

David, J. (2008) 'Operation First Casualty Street Theatre (The Groundswell Blog)', http://blog.groundswellcollective.com/2008/08/25/operation-first-casualty-street-theatre/

Goodman, A. (2008) 'Operation First Casualty': Outside Democratic Convention, Iraq Veterans Against the War Re-Enact Raids on Iraqi Civilians (Democracy Now: The War and Peace Report), http://www.democracynow.org/2008/8/27/operation_first_casualty_outside_democratic_convention

Hamilton, B. C. (2007) 'Bringing the War Home', *The Brooklyn Rail*, http://www.brooklynrail.org/2007/6/express/bringing-the-war-home

Herman, J. (1997) *Trauma and Recovery: the Aftermath of Violence – From Domestic Abuse to Political Terror*, 2nd edition (New York: Basic Books).

Iraqi Veterans Against the War, http://ivaw.org/

Kino, C. (2008) 'Glossy Idealism on the Front Lines', *New York Times*, 7 September, p. AR76.

MegofMegs (2008) 'Get Yer Art Here! (Denver Connects)', http://dencx.com/?p=27219

Milliard, G. (2008) http://www.youtube.com/watch?v=vbSXKSKQ-DI

Montgomery, D. (2007) 'Far From Iraq, A Demonstration of a War Zone', *Washington Post*, 20 March, p. CO1.

Rosler, M. (2008) [Email] Personal communication, 21 September.

Rosler, M. and I. Blazwick (2008) 'Taking Responsibility: Martha Rosler Interviewed by Iwona Blazwick', *Art Monthly*, 3(314): 29–31, http://www.artmonthly.co.uk/rosler.htm

War Veteran Projection Vehicle, Denver, CO, 22–25 August (Democratic National Convention), http://kwodiczko.com/WarVeteranVehicle/

Wodiczko, K. (2008) [Telephone conversation] Personal communication, 30 August.

11
Radicalism, Writ Large and Small
Michael J. Watts

I want to begin with the law but that is not where I shall end. Hailing the juridical sphere – more precisely the USA's federal judiciary – is not everyone's idea of a good time. Nor for that matter is it widely held to be a productive starting point for a discussion of contemporary radicalism. Is there another profession, populated by its massive armies of legal practitioners, subject to greater popular scorn and comedic abuse? I suspect not. Nevertheless, even from within the deepest and darkest recesses of the belly of the beast there are shafts of light to be found. One at least became clear to me recently in providing expert testimony in an interminably protracted piece of litigation heard in October and November 2008 in the northern California District Court, finally coming to trial after nine years of baroque legal wrangling (http://ccrjustice.org/ourcases/current-cases/bowoto-v.-chevron). Chevron v. Bowoto et al. pitted the unimaginably poor and disenfranchised against the unthinkably rich and powerful; the wretched of the earth against the Olympian powers of the corporate behemoths, the biggest of Big Oil. Fourteen villagers from some of the most isolated and desperate communities on the Nigerian oilfields brought a class action lawsuit charging Chevron/Texaco Corporation (as it then was) with gross violations of human rights including extra-judicial killings, crimes against humanity, and cruel, inhuman and degrading treatment.

In May 1998, roughly 150 Ilaje villagers occupied Chevron's Parabe Platform eight miles offshore, demanding to meet with senior executives of the corporation to discuss resources for community development and compensation for environmental destruction associated with oil and gas exploration and production along the Atlantic coastal littoral and especially across the deltaic creeks from which most Ilaje eke a miserable existence. The occupation of a barge and platform – populated by a rainbow coalition of a hundred or so expatriate and Nigerian oil-workers – came on the back of what the Ilaje saw as a history of serial neglect and abuse. A deep well of local resentment and frustration seeded, inevitably, an unstoppable surge of political energy. Direct action against oil installations was a way of drawing the attention of senior oil executives, a class holed up in their corporate compounds in Port Harcourt and Lagos for whom the only Nigerian constituency to appear on their Blackberries was a venal and corrupt political class presided over by President Sani Abacha. Even though negotiations between the protesters' leaders and representations of Chevron Nigeria Ltd (the local subsidiary of Chevron Corporation) appeared to be making headway and a tentative agreement reached, on the morning of 28 May, a group of the protesters were shot (some in the back) and killed by Nigerian government security forces and Chevron security personnel transported to the platform on Chevron-leased helicopters. The plaintiffs sought compensation injunctive and other relief under the federal Alien Tort Claims Act (ATCA, 28 USC 1350) – a statute two centuries old, framed as part of the original Judiciary Act – which provides a sort of testing ground within the federal court system on which victims against individuals or corporations that commit human rights violations outside of the USA's territorial jurisdiction can have their day in court. In this particular case, Chevron won, fully exonerated on all claims in a unanimous jury verdict rendered on 1 December 2008 after barely one day of deliberation.

All of this took me back two decades and more to E. P. Thompson, *Whigs and Hunters* and the Black Acts, and to a debate, conducted among and across broad swathes of the British Left, over matters of law, state, power and ideology. At the centre of this dispute stood two great public intellectuals, arguably the finest socialist intellectuals of their generation, quite specifically Perry Anderson's (1980) ferocious, and ferociously intelligent, engagement with Edward Thompson's *Poverty of Theory* (1978) and his account of English Marxism. One thread running across the often heated rhetoric was something called 'the rule of law' and whether the judicial sphere was anything more than 'an instrument of class power *tout court*' (Thompson, 1975: 262). Reading now through this magnificent corpus of political writing – drafted, one needs to say, at a moment when talk of 'proletarian democracy embodying a new and insurgent sovereignty' would solicit no fear of embarrassment – is a salutary exercise. We can now see clearly with the powers of hindsight that operating behind the backs of those who fought over Marxist rectitude lay an insurgent radical Right, whose long ascent subsequently came to include Mrs Thatcher's authoritarian populism, the crushing of the miners' strike, the privatisation of collective assets and the gradual evisceration of the institutions of parliamentary democracy. The long march of what we now call neo-liberalism – from the founding of Friedrich von Hayek's chummy club of free-market utopians at Mont Pelerin, to the collapse of the Berlin Wall – took about forty years, by way of the Chicago Boys in Chile, the IMF–IBRD–Treasury complex, and the Reagan–Thatcher–Kohl dispensations. As the Italian Marxist Antonio Gramsci might have put it, there has been a free-market (Hayekian) 'passive revolution' from above. We have witnessed what the Left's great pessimist Perry Anderson (2002) has dubbed a 'neoliberal grand slam': the 'fluent vision' of the Right has no equivalent on the Left he concluded, and embedded liberalism (let alone something called socialism) is, we are told, as remote as 'Arian bishops'. Neo-liberalism rules undivided across the globe and is the most successful ideology in world history. Resistances are like 'chaff in the wind', and the Left can only 'shelter under the skies of infinite justice'. The goonsquads and salesforces of neo-liberalism had taken, one might say, the commanding heights. Well perhaps, or perhaps not.

But before I return to Anderson's account of the irresistible rise of a radical *Right* – and what this might imply for being radical today – let me dwell for a moment on the law and what the 1970s Marxists had to say about it. Thompson's (1975) magisterial examination of the Black Acts – an omnibus statute passed over four weeks in 1723 which in defending the rights of the propertied classes contained a criminal code with an unprecedented scope and breadth of capital provision – argued that its very hegemony depended upon the credibility of rules, which in turn imposed limits and restraints on its manipulability by the dominant classes. The dialectics of class and law – there was no simple predetermined relations between the operations of the law and those in and with power – made the juridical sphere a 'genuine forum within which certain kinds of class conflict were fought out' (Thompson, 1975: 265), even producing reversals and interruptions in the operations of state power. The rule of law imposed 'effective inhibitions upon power and the defense of the citizen from power's all intrusive claims' (Thompson, 1975: 266). Law provided some sort of defence for those who sought to protect, as commoners, the rights and privileges over the commons – to resist enclosure. Anderson's (1980) defence was that the rule of law did not perform such work, but rather the popular defence of specific civil liberties as part of a wider set of quite different juridical rules and processes (constitutional and criminal law for example). The procedures for the substantive codes of legal conduct – applied differentially over time and space – were drawn together in common institutions, not the least of which was jury by trial. And it was here in the jury, a custom that predated the feudal epoch in England, that resided, said Thompson, a 'stubbornly maintained democratic practice . . . a lingering paradigm of an alternative mode of participatory self government, a nucleus around which analogous modes might grow' (Thompson, 1978; cited in Anderson, 1980: 202).

Thompson's central claim was that 'the immense capital of human struggles over the previous two centuries' was, as he put it, 'passed down as a legacy to the eighteenth century . . . where it gave rise to a vision, in the minds of some men, of an ideal aspiration toward the universal values of law' (Thompson, 1975: 269). The Chevron case stands surely as part of this inheritance, passed down as the accumulated capital of human struggles over several centuries. The Alien Tort Claims Act – the legal vehicle for bringing transnational corporations to account – was after all signed by George Washington in 1789, now put to the service of addressing the contradictions of making contemporary law congruent with the realities of a gentry, class power and a state that operate with and through a lethal mix of transnational capital flows, 'poor governance', privatised security forces, and military neo-liberalism.

Construed in this way – that is to say as a bequest which speaks to the positive and popular inheritance of struggles for civil liberties – Chevron v. Bowoto represents a radicalism (for my purposes I shall call it radicalism writ small), which places its feet at the confluence of two streams of political practice. One returns us to the original definition of radical as root invoked by Raymond Williams (1976). It speaks to an enduring sense of civil liberty and the preservation of civil liberties, a longue durée of human struggles now confronting the class prerogatives of a different cast of oligarchs and great gentry: a set of corporate personalities equally 'content to be subject to the rule of law only because this law was serviceable and afforded to their hegemony the rhetoric of legitimacy' (Thompson, 1975: 269). The Chevron case represents, at risk of universalising a precedent-setting but nevertheless tightly circumscribed case of human rights violations and torture, an exemplar of a radical politics placing the defence of civil liberties as a bulwark against the relentless march of the commodity in its various guises.

The other stream discloses the potentiality for alternative modes of participatory self-government in the town halls, factories, villages and streets (what I shall call radicalism writ large). The untold story of the plaintiffs in the Chevron litigation was that, under conditions of extraordinary differences in class power and among dispersed and isolated villages located in some senses at the margins of the modern world-system, they forged a robust solidarity spanning forty-three communities (the Concerned Ilaje Citizens). To suggest that the Ilaje plaintiffs were marginals brought to the juridical centre ignores, of course, the central fact that the enclosure of *their* commons by a non-local gentry and oligarchy – Big Oil and a military *junta* – was preceded by two *other* rounds of primitive accumulation: three centuries of the slavery trade, followed by another lubricant of industrial capitalism, palm oil (RETORT, 2005). What matters surely is that across the great arch of what my friend Iain Boal has called 'the long theft', the vast capital of human exploitation and struggle broke into the judicial hallways of the federal courts standing at the heart of American empire.

The cynic may say, of course, that they *only* reached the hallways of the federal chambers. After all, the jury, confronted with sixty pages of jury instructions of mind-numbing complexity, rendered a decision based on, at best, a parsimonious account of Nigerian political economy and a defence pandering to the basest sorts of white fears, racial violence and African primitivism ('juju' was the term of art). The villagers lost and the gentry won. Class power was expressed, registered and executed through forms of law. And yet there is a sort of residue, a legacy at work, because the law is, as Thompson reminded us, not merely fraud or force by another name. Quite critically, the case *was* heard and more will follow in its wake – another case opened in the New York federal court on 27 April 2009, and other cases are lined up waiting on judges' dockets. What links radicalism writ small with radicalism writ large is a politics of scaling-up – through a raft of modalities, the law being only one element within the arsenal – producing an alternative practice, a radicalism, which turns for want of a better word on enclosure, or resisting enclosure, and protecting other commoning activities from the depredations of corporate capital (Linebaugh, 2008).

What is the genealogy of this notion of radicalism? Here I want to start with the observation that we are living through a counter-revolution on the backs of a free-market revolution. To appreciate the character and depth of this struggle we can return to World War Two and two towering figures in the study of economics. Karl Polanyi's *The Great Transformation* and Friedrich Hayek's *The Road to Serfdom* were both published in 1944. Hayek, an Austrian economist trained at the feet of Ludwig von Mises, but forever associated with a largely non-economic corpus produced at the London School of Economics and the universities of Chicago and Freiburg between 1940 and 1980, is widely recognised as one of the leading intellectual architects of the neo-liberal counter-revolution (Harvey, 2005).[1] Hayek's critique of socialism – that it destroys morals, personal freedom and responsibility, impedes the production of wealth and sooner or later leads to totalitarianism – is the founding text for market utopians. In the Hayekian universe, collectivism was constructivist rather than evolutionary, organised not spontaneous, a *'taxis'* (a made order) rather than a *'cosmos'* (a spontaneous order), coerced and concrete rather than free and abstract (see Gamble, 1996: 31–2). From Hayek's perch, socialism's (and social democracy for that matter) fatal conceit was that it admitted the 'reckless trespass of *taxis* onto the proper ground of *cosmos'* (Anderson, 2005: 16). To roll back the incursions of *taxis* required a total redesign of the state. A powerful chamber was to serve guardian of the rule of law (striking all under the age of 45 off the voting roll), protecting the law of liberty from the logic, indeed the dangers, of popular sovereignty. As Anderson (2005: 17) notes, the correct Hayekian formula was 'demarchy without democracy'.

Polanyi conversely was a Hungarian economic historian and socialist who believed that the nineteenth-century liberal order had died, never to be revived. In the Polanyian account, by 1940 'every vestige' of the international liberal order had disappeared, the product of the necessary adoption of measures designed to hold off the ravages of the self-regulating market. The market left to its own devices produced disorder, chaos and social collapse. It was the conflict between the market and the elementary requirements of an organised social life that made some form of collectivism or planning inevitable. The liberal market order was, in sharp contrast to Hayek, not spontaneous at all but rather a planned development, and its demise was the product of the market order itself. A market order could just as well produce the freedom to exploit as it could the freedom of association. The grave danger, in Polanyi's view, was that liberal utopianism (free market fundamentalism) would endorse the idea of freedom as nothing more than the advocacy of free enterprise, that the notion that planning was nothing more than 'the denial of freedom' and that the justice and liberty offered by regulation or control became nothing more than 'a camouflage of slavery' (Polanyi, 1944: 258).

Liberalism in this reading will always degenerate, ultimately compromised by an authoritarianism that will be invoked as a counter-weight to the threat of mass democracy. Modern capitalism contained the famous 'double-movement' in which markets were serially and coextensively 'disembedded' from, and necessarily re-embedded in, social institutions and relations, a process Polanyi called the 'discovery of society'. In particular, a refusal of the self-regulating market could be located in resistance to the commodification of the three 'fictitious commodities' (land, labour and money), commodities that entered the marketplace with their respective price tags and yet were not produced as commodities (hence their fictive nature). The buying and selling of labour, land and money could only produce crisis and anarchy. Reactions to the consequences of virtually everything being bought and sold *without limits* represented what Polanyi saw as a spontaneous defence of society. In this Polanyian world, a crisis arises necessarily because the logic of commoditisation and a fully realised market utopia would eviscerate and dissolve all forms of sociability (Williams, 2005).

A textbook case of spontaneous defence to commodification gone utterly awry is the spectacle of the Wall Street – and now mainstreet – crisis of American finance capitalism. The chicanery of the credit-default swaps, the Potemkin villages otherwise know as investment banks, Ponzi schemes run by small armies of physicists and mathematicians turned money managers, the organised fraud perpetrated by derivative traders, and the depravity of CEOs going cap in hand to Washington to defend not just their salaries but the next *tranche* of government bailouts, can only be read as the excretions of the sort that Polanyi predicted. From the ashes of the USA's ruined investment banks – and with Barack Obama now in possession of the White House – calls for state regulation, for more robust forms of fiscal governance and a deep suspicion of new forms of financial commodification (credit default swaps, collateralised debt obligations and so on) are now heard and discussed among the Washington chattering classes, to the point that some within the Democratic party have uttered the words: New Deal.

All of which is to say that what we blithely call modernity is the business of continually and simultaneously creating real and fictive commodities and their negation (the ugly words de-commodification or re-embedding will have to suffice). What distinguishes and marks off the uneven displacements and disjunctures of capitalist development – what we call economic history – is the relative and defining weight of this two-pronged process of creation and destruction. Sometimes they occur concurrently in an implosion, a sort of upending of the world as we know it. Joseph Schumpeter (1975) called it creative destruction.

Resisting the deadly solicitations of the market is to assert or reassert a commons, that is to say to resist enclosure (RETORT, 2005), and to claim a space in which the logic of commodification is circumscribed. Indian peasants resist the state-backed takeover of land for export processing zones or massive highway construction; governments renationalise banks (albeit in a variety of ways and forms); the global commons are defended by a multiplicity of state and non-state actors in the name of human survival; workers contest the privatisation of public pension funds; and yes the Ilaje struggle to retain customary control of coastal lands appropriated by fiat, through powers vested in the Nigerian state and ecologically obliterated by its joint venture corporate oil partners.

To assume that anti-enclosure politics are all of a piece or indeed are necessarily Left or anti-capitalist would be to fall prey to the same logic that all anti-imperialist movements (Al-Qaeda, the quit-India movement, Mr Chavez and his happy band of 'chavistas') are somehow an unqualified good. My point is rather different. It is to suggest that a radicalism with credible claims to be representative of the Left must have as a reference point a critical stance towards capital, a formulation which sees a resistance to the commodity world as a refusal of capitalism's basic most primitive impulses. The fronts along which contemporary enclosures now proceed are multiple and often synergistically related, encompassing the proprietorship of the human genome, the privatisation of airwaves, the annexation and plundering of the Arctic and much more. But they *are* resisted. Whether these radicalisms writ small, often geographically dispersed and fragmented, can amount to radicalism writ large (an organised and perhaps global politics of anti-enclosure) remains a very big question. They might at least be profitably understood in the same terms that Edward Thompson invoked the jury as a harbinger of self-government. Resisting and transforming the logic of the competitively produced commodity is to endorse a certain sort of collectively; therein lies a politics of what we might call 'commoning'.

Anti-enclosure holds out the prospect of breaking through the barrier of what Roberto Unger (2005) calls 'the dictatorship of no alternatives' and a proclivity to be wary of proposals to reorganise society. It may prefer to resign itself to small victories in the defense of old rights . . . 'The discipline of ruling interests and ideas has allied itself with a skepticism that masquerades as realism . . . creating a sense of closure' (Unger, 2005: 169). The Left, says Unger, has no central agent. He proposes a prophetic project to democratise the logic of the market, to deepen democracy through a high-energy deliberative politics, each of which contributes towards a cumulative reorganisation of economy and state (see also Fong and Wright, 2003). I believe that the prospect of resisting enclosure presents an opportunity not, as we are seeing currently, to rehabilitate J. M. Keynes, but to endorse a project worthy of the appellation 'alternative'. Resistance to neo-liberalism is heterogeneous and worldwide. The revolts in France, the factory occupations in Argentina, the oil nationalisation in Bolivia and the insurgencies in Iraq are all symptomatic, even if the national and local dynamics differ greatly. Here there is perhaps reason to be less gloomy than Anderson's prognosis might suggest.

Note

1. Margaret Thatcher famously pronounced that 'This is what we believe' as she slammed a copy of Hayek's *The Constitution of Liberty* onto the table at Number 10, Downing Street during a Tory Cabinet meeting.

References

Anderson, P. (1980) *Arguments Within English Marxism* (London: Verso).

Anderson, P. (2002) 'Internationalism: a Breviary', *New Left Review*, 14: 5–25.

Anderson, P. (2005) *Spectrum* (London: Verso).

Bowoto v. Chevron, http://ccrjustice.org/ourcases/current-cases/bowoto-v.-chevron

Fong, A. and E. Wright (eds) (2003) *Deepening Democracy* (London: Verso).

Gamble, A. (1996) *Hayek: the Iron Cage of Liberty* (Boulder: Westview).

Harvey, D. (2005) *A Brief History of Neoliberalism* (Oxford: Clarendon Press).

Hayek, F. (1944) *The Road to Serfdom* (Chicago: University of Chicago Press).

Linebaugh, P. (2008) *The Magna Carta Manifesto* (Berkeley: University of California Press).

Polanyi, K. (1944) *The Great Transformation* (Boston: Beacon).

RETORT (2005) *Afflicted Powers* (London: Verso).

Schumpeter, J. A. (1975) *Capitalism, Socialism and Democracy* (New York: Harper & Row).

Thompson, E. P. (1975) *Whigs and Hunters* (London: Allen).

Thompson, E. P. (1978) *The Poverty of Theory and Other Essays* (London: Merlin Press).

Unger, R. M. (2005) *What Should the Left Propose?* (London: Verso).

Williams, C. A. (2005) *A Commodified World?* (London: Zed Books).

Williams, R. (1976) *Keywords* (New York: Oxford University Press).

12
Continuing the Struggle in Hard Times

Jason Toynbee

I take a grey October walk through a slice of the city near my home. There are Edwardian brick terraces and, further out, semis from between the wars. On the footprint of a factory I see a clump of freshly built, toy town houses. Strangely, a few engineering workshops linger on here and there – ghosts of the industrial past. But the big plants have all gone, and with them the militant labour movement that fired up the city and made it a centre of radical politics during much of the twentieth century. Nostalgia threatens to overwhelm me as I think about this. It's a perversely pleasurable feeling: melancholia mixed up with memories of my own arrival here as a student years ago. Of course it's an utterly self-indulgent sentiment too. For radical politics means nothing unless it confronts 'now'.

Same but different

And now is the neo-liberal moment which shapes not only how we carry on our everyday lives, but also how we fight for change. Crucially, thirty years of neo-liberalism have curbed the power of radicals while at the same time encouraging a new diversity among them. Where there used to be an identifiable Left, ranging from pale pink to deep crimson, there is now a bewildering multiplicity of issues and campaigns. So, if we're going to do a survey of radical politics I'd say the first task is to try and assess precisely how neo-liberalism has impacted on it.

The main way is through brute power. The coup of Thatcher and Reagan, followed by a host of other governments around the world, was to enable capitalism to operate 'as itself' – red in tooth and claw – and then present the barbarous consequences as the effect of a rational mechanism called the market. Above all, neo-liberalism has delivered inequality.

As UN figures show, 'the income gap between the richest 20 percent and the poorest 20 percent in the world rose from 30:1 in 1960, to 60:1 in 1990, and to 74:1 in 1999, and is projected to reach 100:1 in 2015' (Li, 2004: 21). In short, neo-liberalism means redistribution of wealth in favour of the capitalists and their retainers.

That the working-class movement has not been able to fight back against this renewal of class power has to do with a powerful combination of worsening conditions of work, authoritarian control and insidious ideology. To take the first point first, a key part of the offensive during the early 1980s was the generation of unemployment. In Britain, the laboratory of neo-liberalism, high interest rates and a restricted money supply forced millions of people on to the dole, especially in manufacturing. This sector was increasingly transferred to the developing world where labour was much cheaper. As employment rates began to climb again in the 1990s the new jobs came in services, and here wages were lower and traditions of unionisation much weaker. Meanwhile, cowed by defeats early on in the offensive, and then grown comfortable collaborating with employers, union leaders became less militant. As a result the difference between wages in unionised and non-unionised workplaces declined. The effect on levels of unionisation has been stark. By 2002 only 31 per cent of employees were union members compared to 49 per cent in 1983. In the private sector in Britain today union membership stands at a mere 17 per cent.

The second factor has been authoritarian control. So, while labour rights, for instance the right to picket, have been cut back, corporate power has been enshrined by the state. In particular, privatisation and 'public–private partnerships' have massively expanded the control of capital over working life, and increasingly over civil society too. On the international stage organisations such as the IMF and WTO have forced governments around the world into acceding to the neo-liberal regime. As a result poorer states have become the victims of corporate pillage. Everywhere, though, the lobbyists of big business are hugely influential, ensuring that new legislation reflects business interests while restricting the scope of labour to act in its own defence. It seems that the state, with all its powers of doing and not-doing, has been returned to the service of capitalism.

A third factor undermining resistance is the development of new ideologies. Margaret Thatcher's 'there is no alternative' (TINA) doctrine has been highly effective here – the assertion that private ownership is right, markets are good and that history shows socialism to be dangerous and unworkable. Formerly social democratic parties which embrace this view such as New Labour in Britain have been especially persuasive. Who could have learned the truth of TINA better than the party which presided over the failure of state intervention? Another neo-liberal ideology is fed by a rather surprising stream. As Ian MacDonald (1995) suggests, the 'revolution in the head' of the 1960s counter-culture has degenerated into a narcissistic project for individual self-realisation. Tony Blair and Bill Gates, from the youth generation of the 1960s and 1970s, represent a polite version of this. Another, populist variant can be found in celebrity culture, and especially 'reality' TV where ordinary people are transformed into giants of the ego. The effect of the new individualism is to undermine collective action and divert attention from social reality.

To sum up: what I've been proposing so far is that neo-liberalism is actually an old structure of domination – capitalism – which now appears in a new, adaptive form. Same but different. The differences are what have weakened the labour movement, and make it difficult for traditional radicals to fight back today.

New radicals

For new radicals, on the other hand, neo-liberalism is simply the ground on which politics is conducted. There is no narrative of loss here. Rather the traditional Left itself appears as archaic, and even part of the problem which a modern radical movement has to confront. For most of all, the new politics sees the enemy as universalism – of which there are Left versions as well as Right. Feminism provides the case in point. Launched in the 1960s and 1970s, the 'second wave' of feminism demanded recognition for women as women, not as women who were adjunct members of the working class. The same was true of black power, and the gay, lesbian and bisexual movement. This new type of identity politics asserted the difference of political subjects against monolithic and exclusive definitions of what it is to be human.

Today, politics in the plural has become a radical orthodoxy. And it is found not only in identity politics, but campaigns with broad and diverse constituencies. For instance, the Zapatistas in Mexico represent indigenous peoples (previously ignored by the Left), but also build alliances with other social movements nationally, and, at an international level, through global anti-capitalism (Subcomandante Marcos, 2001). This pluralism, whereby movements are made up of other movements, is partly an effect of the new emphasis on recognition. To call for recognition of oneself implies the mutual recognition of others, and suggests horizontal rather than hierarchical organisation. As such it marks an important libertarian development in radical politics – beyond old-style anarchism towards a new, network-based pluralism.

But this is also a pragmatic politics which has helped to keep the flames of opposition burning during the dark times of neo-liberal ascendancy. New radicals are flexible – quick to respond to new opportunities. And they don't try to take on the system by capturing it, or even going on strike against it. Perhaps the pluralism and the emphasis on democratic process *within* radical politics is actually a response to the immovability of neo-liberalism. At least some kind of change is possible, even if it is only enacted in meetings or forms of direct action.

It is largely for the same reason, however, that the new radicals have never really succeeded in generating a durable movement. Take the World Social Forum. Launched at Porto Allegre in Brazil in 2001, and sponsored by that city's council, the WSF was a meeting of delegates and individuals from around the world. It became an annual event. In 2005 155,000 people attended and, building on discussions there, nineteen participants issued the Porto Allegre Manifesto. With the evocative slogan, 'another world is possible', this called for the reversal of key neo-liberal economic policies, the advancement of 'community life' and information democracy. Significantly, it was not a revolutionary programme; there was no suggestion that the demands represented a step towards a new kind of post-capitalist global society. Nevertheless, the manifesto was didactic enough to alienate many in the social movements who felt either that it failed to represent their cause, or that it was simply a centralising step too far.

By 2007 the numbers attending the WSF (held in Nairobi that year) had fallen to 66,000. The event was notable for criticism of the growing involvement of NGOs which, it was said, claimed to represent the global poor, yet were in reality compromised though their relationship with neo-liberal governments. For 2008 the WSF took the form of a global day of action around the world. Many have suggested that this low-impact event, geographically dispersed and unevenly implemented, marks the death knell of the Forum.

In a way, the WSF, and the anti-globalisation movement from which it emerged, have failed for the same reasons that they initially succeeded. A coalition of diverse groups and individuals, the movement took off because it offered a seductive vision of democratic process *and* critical mass. People and groups talked to one another in common but loose opposition to neo-liberalism, while at the Forum itself participants got a sense of their power palpably, in the presence of others.

Yet without a programme and organisation to carry on agitation on the ground the movement has faltered. The contrast then is with neo-liberalism itself. Far from being laissez-faire as it likes to suggest, this political project actually involves the concerted prosecution of the interests of capitalism in a systematic way; via governments and intergovernmental organisations, but also through the transnational corporation – a world-spanning apparatus which exploits and transforms people's lives without any reference to their needs or desires.

This is a depressing analysis for any radical. Neo-liberalism smashes the traditional Left, while the new social movements, despite being intermittently vibrant, are incapable of mounting a challenge to the system they oppose.

Crash, bang

And yet . . . it is too bleak a conclusion to reach, because it is too Romantic. It implies that radical movements have to deliver their promise of radical change right now simply because 'we have waited long enough'. This is petulance masquerading as politics. In fact what's called for, and I'll attempt it in what follows, is a more sober assessment of where we are today – something as banal as a balance sheet of radicalism.

First of all, we need to credit the simple survival of activists and ideas. Consider those I have been calling the traditional Left. In fact the socialists never went away. While labour movements have been weakened as we have seen, and social democratic parties have shifted to the Right, the independent Left has continued to organise and has even won some victories. In Britain, for example, the anti-Poll Tax campaign of the early 1990s not only stopped the imposition of this regressive tax, but also brought down Margaret Thatcher. Socialist supporters of the *Militant* newspaper played a key role in it, mobilising hundreds of thousands of people who demonstrated and refused to pay. Today in Britain, there are still perhaps five thousand members of a few Left groups who keep alive the idea of the revolutionary socialist transformation of the world.

Secondly, structures of power, just like the radical political movements which struggle to overcome or supersede them, are historical. So while neo-liberalism has been presented as a permanent solution to the instability of capitalism, it turns out that this economic regime has actually been built on over-accumulation, and dangerously uneven development across the world (Harvey, 2006). Since the mid-1990s there has also been massive 'financialisation' – the expansion of capital way beyond the functional requirements of international trade and investment.

The credit crunch which has followed, and now a recession, suggests that the neo-liberal bubble is bursting on its own. This certainly makes it easier for radicals to find some space. Most important perhaps, current events undermine the TINA doctrine. So the quasi-nationalisation of banks gives the lie to free market dogma, while the crisis as a whole is rightly seen as a challenge to the long historical reign of neo-liberal ideas. After all, these were supposed to provide the remedy to capitalist crises. The opportunities here for making the case for radical system change seem clear enough.

Nevertheless, the Romantic impulse is to be avoided. There's no guarantee, or even likelihood, that recession and the more intense poverty it brings will lead to a resurgence of working-class consciousness and resistance. As the 1980s showed all too well, recessions can weaken resistance by making solidarity more difficult to build. And there is something else here. If economic crisis does indeed contribute to radicalisation it may not be of the kind I've been discussing. The assumption so far has been that radical politics is located outside the centrist parties and political system. But the first political beneficiary of the economic downturn was an American presidential candidate for a mainstream party, namely Barack Obama. Backed by Wall Street, Obama has nevertheless posed a mildly interventionist economic agenda to great effect. Indeed his popularity took off in early September 2008 just at the moment that the credit crunch bit hard. This was enough to win him the election. Thus, paradoxically, the most radical aspect of the Obama campaign – the way that he became the emblem of a resurgent politics of black identity and recognition – was achieved on the back of quite contingent support for his come-little, come-lately policies of redistribution.

The third item to draw attention to in this balance sheet of radical politics is looming environmental catastrophe. It's the most Romantically radical issue of all: the threat of the end of the world wrought by the drive to accumulate that pumps through the heart of the capitalist system, combined with a corrupt form of governance which is barely capable of planning two years ahead. Still, it can't be ducked. There is no way of watching and waiting to see how an intervention might best be made. Climate change demands radical action now and on a concerted basis.

Yet as the urgent need for this has become starkly clear, in terms of electoral politics at least, the environmental movement has hardly grown in commensurate strength. Ten years ago it appeared that the Green Party in Germany was about to become a major political player. Now it is split and much reduced in influence while elsewhere, in first-past-the-post electoral systems like Britain, Green politicians are confined to a handful of town councils. Outside party politics there is a good deal more vigour. Direct action campaigns like those of Greenpeace continue to have a high impact and have helped push the issue of climate change on to the agenda of mainstream parties, but this is happening agonisingly slowly.

Saturday morning

I'm standing in front of the Party stall in the shopping precinct, shouting for socialism. I try to break it up with some humour. 'It'll only take you nine point three five seconds to sign this petition.' Or, 'It's pouring with rain and you've got a large soft toy under your arm, but you *have* got time to stop for a chat about the Post Office closure.' This is one of the oldest forms of political communication there is – engaging people face to face on the street. It can be extraordinarily effective. Quite a few people just sail on. Occasionally you get a 'piss off'. But depending on the issue and the 'objective situation' (i.e. how well/badly things are going for capitalism) it is possible for five of us to have a decent political discussion with a couple of hundred people in the course of a Saturday morning.

The hardest issues are the wars in Iraq and Afghanistan, and immigration. With the wars you often encounter someone who has a relative or friend in the forces. I've talked to soldiers about it too, and this can be tricky. But the thing is to be sensitive while keeping on with rational criticism. 'The war against terror isn't working, and it's not about betraying the lads – we ought to bring them home where they won't get killed in a fight for oil and US prestige.' Immigration is even harder because it's true that some working-class people really are suffering as a result. Pious talk about saying no to racism or advocating compassion for people less fortunate than ourselves won't wash. You have to go in quite deep and talk about capitalism, the global division of labour, and the way that people get shunted around the world in the pursuit of profit. It's the bosses and grotesque inequality which are to blame for bad conditions, not immigrants.

I think the point I'm trying to make is that if radical politics is about changing the world (and not merely yourself) then engaging in it today is remarkably timeless. Historical analysis is supposed to give you strategy. And maybe a 'balance sheet' can give you a sense of the pressure points, a feel for where change is likely to come or not. But the task on the ground is always about getting radical politics and its truths across to people: arguing, cajoling and getting wet.

References

Harvey, D. (2006) *Spaces of Global Capitalism: Towards a Theory of Uneven Geographical Development* (London: Verso).

Li, M. (2004) 'After Neoliberalism: Empire, Social Democracy, or Socialism?' *Monthly Review*, January.

MacDonald, I. (1995) *Revolution in the Head* (London: Pimlico).

Porto Allegre Manifesto, http://www.openspaceforum.net/twiki/tiki-read_article.php?articleId=276

Subcomandante Marcos (2001) 'The Punch Card and the Hourglass' [interview by García Márquez and Roberto Pombo], *New Left Review*, 9 (May–June): 68–79.

13
A Politics of Commitment

James Martin

Radical politics demands commitment. This much seems obvious. All politics, surely, is a commitment to something, to achieve one end or another, and a 'radical' politics is a commitment to radical change. But can commitment itself be radical? Do we need to radicalise commitment to make politics radical? In the age of new media, it has become possible to sign up and pledge ourselves to a variety of causes with surprising ease, to attach our names to web petitions, to email our subscriptions, and to blog and paste in our views on numerous issues of the day. But with this proliferation and pluralisation of politics, commitment itself flattens out. To support a radical politics is, for many, more a lifestyle choice in keeping with a consumer identity than a risky personal transformation. Commitments hang on principles, certainly, but if all it takes to show commitment is a demonstration of principle then we lose sight of the politics that commitment is able to engage. Nor is the answer to go to the other extreme and make personal sacrifice the only marker of authentic radical political engagement. I want to underscore the importance of a politics of commitment, as opposed to its mere display.

It's no surprise, I think, that we are often uncertain as to how we respond to the political commitments of others. They come in increasingly new and unfamiliar forms: the commitment of activist movements, community organisations, pressure groups, politico-religious organisations, or just individuals with personal preferences they are prepared to defend to the hilt; all projected and circulated through an enormous range of media that don't always lead back to an identifiable source. Other people's commitments are on show everywhere. Such a bewildering array of public commitments can be tough to fathom. Of varying degrees of scope (from the local to the global) and intensity, each declares itself committed to its cause, each pledges to change, transform, revolutionise, improve or modernise the world. A proclamation of commitment is the badge of intent, the self-attached seal of approval that testifies to a desire to give oneself over to the cause.

But in all the heat and light of committed politics, it is easy to feel overwhelmed and, consequently, to withdraw from the energies that flicker before us. This has certainly been the case after major military conflagrations, when the old order seems bankrupt and exhausted and the new is yet to be defined. As Yeats (1919) put it in his poem 'The Second Coming', written after World War Two: 'The best lack all conviction, while the worst / Are full of passionate intensity'. At such moments, one person's commitment is, to another, the deranged enthusiasm or self-affirming righteousness of the narrow-minded or personally ambitious. How on earth can we judge one commitment from another? How do we know whether we can trust anyone's commitments? Perhaps these are perennial problems in political life. In the twentieth century, political parties were the key organisation for channelling political commitments of various sorts, for discriminating and tempering them, providing them platforms and shaping their public expression. But the party form now struggles to fulfil these roles. In part this is because political parties have sacrificed their function for the purposes of short-term advantage and a narrow but slick mode of market campaigning that personalises politics and reduces it to certain kinds of (media-friendly) performance. But it is also because, in a diverse society, no party system can ever monopolise control of political commitment. Those that do seek control – and the Left has more than a few examples here – can seem narrow, deeply cynical or plain sectarian.

As social diversity increases, so party politics will seem inadequate to the task, even if it remains the dominant model of political organisation. Nevertheless, while we continue to hear of the Western public's alienation from parliamentary politics, there is no lack of enthusiasm for myriad other forms of political engagement: street campaigns, petitions, referenda, global forms of solidarity and action, and so on. Politicians and governments make desperate efforts to latch on to new forms of popular politics but none manage fully to seize it. Passions for the various issues and causes exceed the grip of party advantage, sometimes because they are just so fleeting and ephemeral and sometimes because governments and institutionalised politics simply cannot satisfy demand. 'Passionate intensity' all around us but, at the same time, a widespread lack of conviction holds sway when no obvious single alternative emerges to parliamentary politics. As Yeats indicated in his poem, written in the explosive disorientation of post-war conditions, this is a perilous situation where 'the centre cannot hold'.

To escape Yeats' dilemma, we need not go in the other direction and substitute commitment simply with organisation. As New Labour (like other parties of the centre-Left in Europe) is discovering to its great cost, adapting the party machine to a semi-presidential form of politics sacrifices too much in the way of popular commitments to maintain a sufficient support base. Instead, we ought to avoid the twin extremes of romantic radicalism that speaks primarily to itself and cynical party advantage that speaks in once voice only. This means thinking of commitment as itself a kind of political responsibility and not merely a badge of attachment and identification.

But in what way is commitment itself political? What responsibilities ensue from the claim to hold a commitment? In an obvious sense, commitment entails a politics of the self. When we commit to something we pledge or promise ourselves to a cause or to some specific end. We do not just express desire about that cause, as though we were choosing from a restaurant menu. Rather, we stage inside ourselves the breach between the world as it is and how it ought to be. We make the resolution of that breach integral to our personal identity. The term 'commitment' derives from the Latin for 'bringing' or 'sending' together (the root *mittere*, to send, also relates to 'mission'). When we express commitment, we dispatch ourselves towards this goal. Thus commitment is a statement of direction, of conviction to achieve an end that is not yet before us.

Of course this sense of conviction need not be overtly political in its content. We can be committed to all sorts of things: to pursue the contemplative life, to impart the divine message, to protect our children, or merely to excel in our chosen employment, sport or hobby. But this choice can nevertheless be a profound and powerful contortion within the self, one that does not always manifest itself in a complex belief or an attachment to a doctrine. Its force stems from a demand, as Simon Critchley (2007) puts it, made on us by the other; a demand that feels unlimited in its scope. It is precisely this combined experience of division and calling that makes commitment akin to a religious experience. Like the committed individual, the divided soul is a subject that seeks healing. Commitment is rarely just about personal self-motivation and drive. Often it involves the practical organisation and disciplining of one's life around a search for redemption. In this sense, it has a 'biopolitics' of its own, intertwining politics and life in the striving for a goal. Urgent devotion, personal privation and the careful control of desire are common in all forms of seriously committed activity, be it political or religious. Indeed, although Critchley quite reasonably prefers to keep the religious and the political forms of commitment separate, it is not wholly clear what it is that divides them. At the level of the self, perhaps there is very little to tell apart.

But political commitment is not simply a private journey. Promising one's self to another is a public act that invokes, and usually speaks to, a community of like-minded selves. This is where the seriously committed often differ from those who simply sign up to any cause going. A politics of community is often the flipside of the politics of the self. In giving ourselves to the cause, we give ourselves to a fate shared with others. We make our promises through – and sometimes to – these others. As any activist knows, doing committed politics is often as much about supporting, arguing with and, frankly, tolerating others as it is about the cause itself.

In pledging one's self and in forming a community through which to enact this pledge we enter into a world of choices about who we are and how we relate to others. Whilst our commitments may often seem natural and instinctive, invariably they require us to make decisions concerning how to conduct our relations with others (our friends and families), our values, the things to which we are prepared to listen and respond, with what and to whom we feel some proximity. All commitment involves building a filter through which such things are either brought into view or excluded. And it is in this filtering of our selves through commitment that a danger also arises. For commitments can sometimes seal us off from the choices that we make in order to fulfil them. I do not mean simply that we might ignore our families or fail to be sufficiently attentive to others because we feel the force of our pledges so intensely. Such is the danger of any kind of association. More importantly, commitments can be experienced as though they entail no politics at all, as if the choices we make are incontestable judgements that align us smoothly with ourselves and the communities with which we share common space. Curiously, what is shared by both the flimsy attachments to any cause going and the total commitment of fundamentalism is this sense of the metaphysical ease of being committed. Whilst undoubtedly they differ in the intensity of their commitments, neither is exposed (or not for long) to the troubling undecidability that aligning oneself with a cause necessarily involves. Indeed, making a commitment can often seem like a way of 'immunising' oneself from such exposure (Esposito, 2008).

Feeling protected by the certainty of our beliefs may feel personally satisfying, deeply motivating and yield a sense of intense solidarity with others but it can also support the most dogmatic forms of enclosure and outward contempt that, in effect, undermine the political dimension of our commitments. Too often, commitment is measured in terms of its intensity, the degree to which we devote ourselves to it, or sacrifice our personal choices for its strictures. The deeper our identification, the more radical and more authentic our commitment is thought to be. But this is a partial sense of the term 'radical'. For commitment to be deeply rooted (as 'radical' implies) is not for it to be so embedded in our daily lives we cannot see where it begins or admit of any part of our lives that escapes it. That, simply, is an entrenched commitment that obscures the decisions we made in order to hold it. But roots also remind us where our limits are; they are not anchors that disappear into the murk, attaching us to some unshakeable earth. However far they reach into our sense of identity, roots also remind us that we are not yet at one with it; that we are 'rooting around' for some kind of connection. This latter sense of 'radical' demands some awareness of how we remain exposed to others that do not share in our pledge, not an immunising form of commitment that seals us off from them. Not a smooth, contained sense of self, but an incomplete one; not a certainty born of communal identification, but the uncertainty of simultaneously not sharing-with, but still living among, others.

The proof of commitment, I am suggesting, lies not in the purity and all-encompassing character of some total experience but, rather, in its capacity to engage in dialogue with those who do not share it; working at its own limits, not at its centre. Commitment is not an interior state whose worth is validated only by intransigent forms of outward display, however important it is from time to time to make a show of principle. Passionate intensity is a phase, not the culmination, of commitment.

When engaged with its own limits, commitment accedes to its own politics of self and community, inviting others to question them and call them to account rather than take them as given. To be committed, in this sense, is continually to expose ourselves to the uncertainty of the pledges we make, exploring their boundaries and blind spots as well as their more comforting principles. This does not mean weakening our principles but, rather, acknowledging the weaknesses of the traditions we often inherit and repeat without question. Too often radical politics can succumb to a form of self-congratulation: think of the haughty disdain so many on the Left showed for President Bush and his folksy style of leadership; as though all we had to do was point and laugh and everyone would wake up. It just didn't happen. If a radical politics is to succeed, it needs a form of commitment that is political and not just self-righteously principled.

But how do we do this? What does it entail? As I've suggested, it means taking seriously others with whom we disagree. That doesn't mean agreeing with them or desperately seeking the grounds of a new consensus, but it does mean acknowledging the legitimacy of the differences between us. It calls for a kind of commitment that is rhetorically inclined; that is, open to debate with others, being prepared to illuminate the weaknesses of the other's position and to concede where we cannot improve our own. This is the politics of persuasion where we seek not only to inform others of our view but, further, to make them desire the same ends. It means treating our opponent like an 'adversary', as Chantal Mouffe puts it, rather than an 'antagonist' (see Mouffe, 2000). Of course this is something that already occurs in all forms of radical politics (as well as other kinds of politics). But if we are to sustain a radical politics of commitment, we need to make much more of this skill. Radical politics must reach outwards and engage as much as it reaches inward. This is a difficult and humbling task. We have to make our passions into more than declarations of independence, placing us on another shore altogether from those with whom we disagree. A radical political commitment should be a principled, passionate engagement, not a monastic withdrawal. We should be troubled by our beliefs and the seamless affirmation they seem to give us; this calls for us to be responsible for them, to find resolution among others for the rifts they cause, not to hide away from them.

On a whole series of topics – from far Right racism, political Islamicism, to carbon emissions, the defence of public services or debates over military interventions across the globe – radical politics needs to improve its engagement with those with whom there is disagreement. This is not easy, of course, and certainly not simply a matter of will. The Left has never had the resources to operate a powerful stake in the media. But in the absence of platforms to debate and argue, it has often been easier to take up a stance of offence (often on behalf of others) than to contest positions rhetorically. In the current age of the global media, this is perhaps irresolvable. But, at the same time, one of the Left's most powerful weapons has been its capacity to argue and critique, to bring together different voices and make alliances, sometimes solid and sometimes not. It is this tradition of arguing, debating and contesting that ought to be enhanced, if only to stop commitment reducing to a matter of spectacle.

Of course, radical politics cannot be reduced to argument alone. But without argument, and without a style of engagement that rouses friends and foes alike to hear and to respond, there is no politics at all. In a plural society, ideologies have become fragmented and fluid. The premises from which, once, we began to debate don't always end up with the same conclusions; the allies we make are often strange and uncomfortable. The test of commitment in this age is not that of the last century: namely, declaring and demonstrating one's allegiance to a party or social group. Identification now tends to appear as a way of deliberately not hearing others, or refusing to speak and be accountable for what one says to those who do not identify in the same way. When the authority of the position from which we speak and argue cannot be assured, engagement itself must be the source of radical political commitment.

References

Critchley, S. (2007) *Infinitely Demanding: Ethics of Commitment, Politics of Resistance* (London and New York: Verso).

Esposito, R. (2008) *Bios: Biopolitics and Philosophy*, trans. T. Campbell (Minneapolis and London: University of Minnesota Press).

Mouffe, C. (2000) *The Democratic Paradox* (London and New York: Verso).

Yeats, W. B. (1919) *The Second Coming*, http://www.potw.org/archive/potw351.html

14
Beyond Gesture, Beyond Pragmatism

Jeremy Gilbert and Jo Littler

What is radicalism?

In this contribution we will confine ourselves to thinking about 'radicalism' in terms of a commitment to the historic goals of the Left – i.e. the elimination, as far as possible, of fundamental imbalances of power between different communities, classes and individuals – and in terms of a willingness to pursue that objective beyond the limits set by conventional political or cultural practice. This brings us back to the initial idea of 'radicalism'; as a measure of how *fundamental* the change might be that one is willing to pursue.

A problem emerges here already, however. Consider the implications of the word 'fundamental'. It has its origins in the Latin 'fundamen', meaning 'foundation'. In fact, one of the marked tendencies of 'radical' thought in recent decades has been the 'anti-foundationalist' and 'anti-essentialist' turn: the move away from any conception of the social which would identify one element, institution or group as necessarily 'fundamental', determinant or constitutive of all others. What does it mean to retain a conception of 'radicalism' in such a context?

To answer this question, we need to be clear about what is implied by such anti-essentialist conceptions of the social. Such an approach rejects the assumption that one single set of power relationships – such as relationships between classes, between genders, or between the governors and the governed – determines all others. But such an approach does *not* necessarily deny that such different sets of relationships affect each other. Rather, it stresses the *dynamic* and *unpredictable* nature of their mutual influence. Various terminologies have been mobilised in order to capture this quality of interrelation between different sets of dynamic power relations, understanding the social in terms of its 'formations' or 'assemblages', for example.

   One thing these reflections might draw our attention to is that 'radical' does not share the etymology of 'fundamental'. 'Roots', understood literally, are not the same thing as 'foundations'. Roots are organic elements without which a plant cannot survive, but which also cannot survive without the other elements of the plant and of the broader ecosystem in which it is located. Might 'radicalism' then be thought of in terms of a particular attentiveness to the *interrelatedness* of different elements of the social – even to the 'ecological' interaction between those elements and the wider geophysical and technological environment? (Guattari, 1989). Our suggestion here is that this might be a useful way of supplementing the usual understanding of 'radicalism' as a measure of the dramatic and far-reaching ambitions for change registered by a particular political position or project. At the same time, this suggestion itself draws attention to the issue of how, today, we might meaningfully differentiate 'dramatic' and 'far-reaching' ambitions from more limited ones.

Revolution vs. reform?

Within an older paradigm, it might have been possible to differentiate the radical from the non-radical in terms of a relative degree of commitment to revolution. The classic distinction between revolutionary and reformist politics continues to inform much far-Left political discourse to this day. The problems with this distinction are well known. Firstly, many uses of it rely upon a fixed historical narrative according to which revolution is the inevitable destiny of social change if it is not hampered by distracting 'reform' (a hypothesis which has absolutely no historical evidence to support it). Even if such a strict conception of history is not in place, the distinction still assumes that it is possible to plot a straight line from a given present to an imagined future which can be determined as being, or not being, revolutionary in nature. Such a perspective makes no sense in the context of an understanding of the social and its processes which accepts the radical unpredictability of complex ecologies of which any human society is an example. It is simply not possible to predict in advance whether a given course of action will or will not tend towards something like a revolution, unless that action is being taken in an obviously pre-revolutionary situation.

   This is not to say that nothing could remain of the revolutionary spirit within such a perspective. A certain willingness to push change as far as it can go – and to intensify lines of transformation past those tipping points which might alter the dynamics of the entire system – would still be a necessary element of any conceivable 'radicalism'. For example, in a situation such as the UK in 2009, where neo-liberal hegemony has resulted in an almost unquestioned acceptance of the value of privatisation by most of the political class, such radicalism might be registered just as well by local campaigns to democratise public services without handing them to the commercial sector, as by explicit commitments to socialism and class struggle. However, such campaigns would perhaps only deserve the epithet 'radical' if they were unwilling to *limit* their objectives to the mere defence of existing arrangements in a local context, and instead oriented themselves towards a longer-term and permanent intervention in the wider arrangement of power relationships in which they find themselves. The successful campaign against the privatisation of local government IT services in Newcastle a few years ago is one good example.

Strategic orientation

Such an orientation towards long-term and permanent intervention might best be understood as 'strategic' in nature. In our view, the distinction between strategic and tactical interventions is a crucial one. A particular tendency in 'radical' thought – informed by de Certeau, Hakim Bey, certain immature strands of anarchism and some deeply confused misreadings of Deleuze and Guattari – tends to assume that true radicalism can operate on a purely 'tactical' level, and that 'strategy' must always be the property of authoritarian organisations and projects. Such a position inevitably ends up endorsing a range of 'tactical' manoeuvres which give expression to a 'radical' identity but have no apparent impact on power relationships: examples of such ineffectual gestures include 'subvertisements', short-term squatting, conceptual art shows, or spectacular political 'actions' involving large numbers of arrests and no change whatsoever to the policies being protested. In fact, we are highly sympathetic to the creativity and dynamism of such activity, and we would also share this tradition's hostility towards rigid doctrine, party discipline and organisational authoritarianism. As should be clear from our rejection of the revolution/reform distinction, we do not believe that it is possible to formulate all-encompassing 'strategies' with determinate final goals for radical political projects. Any action is without guarantees and can of course have unpredictable effects. But at the same time, there can be no conception of radicalism as tending in the direction of 'tipping points' if there is no attention at all to the wider configurations in which particular actions are taken and no desire to intensify change in the direction of their possible transformation. Such an attention and desire might best be characterised as a 'strategic orientation' (Gilbert, 2008).

A strategic orientation, we suggest, is what characterises genuine radicalism. This is, of course, a perspective very much in the Gramscian tradition. From this point of view, it is possible to be thoroughly militant in one's declared opposition to, say, capitalism, or patriarchy, or imperialism, or whatever; but if that opposition is expressed in terms which have no hope or intention of *persuading others* to engage in similar opposition, no chance whatsoever of *broadening and intensifying* such opposition in the direction of some transformatory tipping point, then it can be at best merely 'tactical' in nature, a mere statement of opposition which makes no impact upon the wider configuration of forces, and so is devoid of any real political efficacy. However, this is not to make a case for mild-mannered pragmatism. The distinction we are making is one which may at times be a very fine one: between, for example, the short-term occupation of a building which there is no hope of holding indefinitely (symbolic tactical gesture) and the establishment of a social centre as a permanent community resource (a clear strategic gain in the struggle for democratic spaces).

Against 'pragmatism'

Our distinction would also be just as critical of an insufficiency of militancy as of an excess of it. For example, one of the chronic problems facing the mainstream Left in Western Europe is the apparent inability of social democrats and their supporters to appreciate the sheer levels of sustained *effort* which would today be required to defend the remnants of the welfare state from creeping privatisation. Under conditions of global neo-liberal hegemony, for example, free universal health care is not the 'reasonable' expectation that it was, but a radical demand only likely to be met by sustained militant action against that hegemony. Few politicians or voters of the 'moderate' European Left have yet grasped this fact.

In fact, the dominant tendency amongst parties and governments of the social democratic Left in Europe, the USA and Australia in recent times has been the embrace of the technocratic programme of the Third Way, which claims to move beyond the political polarities of the modern era, occupying a pragmatic position from which to solve social problems efficiently. In the UK this tendency to take each social issue in turn as a discrete technical problem to be solved is only really a position adopted by think tanks such as Demos and the IPPR (Institute for Public Policy Research). Government may mouth the pragmatist mantra 'what matters is what works', but in practice the commitment of UK governments to neo-liberal programmes has often flown in the face of any objective measures of those programmes' success in generating social benefits. But for the think tanks and the intellectual cadres in their wider orbit, including most professional political commentators, this pragmatist ideology has an absolutely paralysing effect, in effect reducing their policy programmes to a set of tactical proposals which make as little impact on the wider configuration of social forces as do the sermonising and self-publicity of some self-identified 'activists'. In fact, the consequence has been that most think tanks have been quite unable to make any critique of New Labour's ideological conversion to neo-liberalism, and have only seen their policies adopted when they happen to converge with its existing agenda. Without any aspiration to such critique, the think tanks and NGOs have been unable to pull New Labour away from the influence of the corporate lobby and the 'Washington consensus'.

Politics as technocratic tinkering, then, we argue, is no more effective than politics as pseudo-radical posturing. For a politics to be radical involves attacking imbalances and concentrations of power wherever they are found; functioning with a well-developed understanding of the 'ecologies' – the relational contexts – in which such imbalances and concentrations exist; and operating strategically for far-reaching change. We might think about what this means in practice by comparing different agendas in the area of recycling and green energy.

Green gestures

There has been a great deal of innovation in the areas of recycling and green energy over the past decade. This is because they are seen as a way of addressing a number of environmental problems, particularly climate change, pollution and the potential problems generated by 'peak oil'.

Let us take one example: the act of buying a product such as the 'Worn Again' brand of trainer, made with various recycled components. In the UK this product became fairly high profile when it was worn by the leader of the Conservative Party David Cameron as one of a number of attempts to 'green' his image. As a political move this is clearly not very 'radical' for a number of reasons. The production of the shoe does not go very far in reducing power imbalances: whilst it uses recycled components, including London firemen's uniforms, these are shipped to Tangxia in Southern China for production where (as even the Conservative-friendly UK tabloid the *Daily Mail* pointed out) workers are paid little and the local river is black with shoe factory pollution (Daily Mail, 2007).

Terra Plana who produces the expensive high-end shoes is not a cooperative, a means by which wealth could be shared; nor does it use unionised labour. In fact Terra Plana specifies in its ethical policy that whilst it uses recycled materials it 'does not have a code of conduct for its overseas production'. Furthermore, these are expensive shoes, and therefore ones which are predominantly available only to an elite.

Buying the 'Worn Again' shoe as a political gesture is therefore not particularly radical. Whilst wearing the trainer might work as a tactical move to promote recycling and the idea of green politics, then, it exemplifies a politics that offers environmentalism as a shopping option for the relatively privileged (see Littler, 2009). (Here Cameron's wearing of the shoe is significant, as it echoes how the Conservative Party's particular shade of green revolves round an 'eco-aristocracy' of millionaire environmentalists like Zac Goldsmith.) Moreover, wearing 'Worn Again' does not produce many significant moves towards equality because of its environmental effects and relatively elite approach. In ethical shopping terms, a more 'radical' clothing choice would be the USA-based company No Sweat, which uses unionised labour to produce all its products, organic material in the local production of its shoes, and has a very low profit mark-up on its products which are therefore available to a wider segment of the population.

Green strategies

But the purchase of a shoe is still on its own a relatively isolated gesture. We might therefore look elsewhere to find examples of a radical politics of recycling. Consider, for example, the remarkable expansion of household recycling, the growth of which 'has been of a kind that few would have predicted ten years ago' (Murray, 2002: 32). In the UK, recycling has become such a popular practice that it regularly tops the list of green facilities people want to see provided by local government. Household recycling has been described by waste guru Robin Murray as an example of 'productive democracy', because it involves a degree of collective work which members of the public are increasingly willing to engage in for a 'wider good' (Murray, 1999: 70). It has also involved an innovative mobilisation of new constituencies. As Gay Hawkins (2006: 64) puts it, some of the more inventive language around recycling has worked not by addressing a pre-existing public, but by creating a new public that was 'called into being through a vision of a contaminated world'.

The potential seeds of a radical politics exist in these practices of 'productive democracy', which try to move towards creating environmental equalities, and do so on a very participative social basis. They become more pronounced in their radicalism when the sentiments they have mobilised become used as a *resource* to extend further activity. This, in effect, is what many 'zero waste' campaigns are doing, by building on popular enthusiasm for recycling to extend green sensibilities outwards towards 'closed loop' or 'cradle-to-cradle' environmental thinking (see Braungart and McDonough in IPPR and Green Alliance, 2006: 12). Put simply, this emphasises the idea of recycling as a continuous practice taking place across a wide range of interconnected social contexts, rather than imagining recycling as a series of isolated actions or events. It emphasises the value of a 'reduce, re-use, recycling' attitude, of clean production, of atmospheric protection and of resource conservation. Such zero waste strategies have begun to be deployed by a number of areas including San Francisco, Bath and New Zealand (IPPR and Green Alliance, 2006: 6). Zero waste campaigns are radical activities in that they are strategic in their nature whilst mobilising an understanding of the context they work within. Importantly, they also work to publicly politicise previously taken-for-granted areas of social life such as household consumption, retail and small-scale manufacturing.

Energy independence for all?

We might take a different example of radical politics from the area of green energy. Getting a solar panel or wind turbine fitted on the roof of your house might appear to be a radical gesture in the current social and environmental climate. But on its own it is not particularly radical as it is limited to the few people who can afford the cost of fitting solar panels or wind turbines, which at the time of writing in the UK remains prohibitively high.

Of course it would not be helpful to dismiss such activities of middle-class people 'doing what they can' as useless, because as an environmental practice it is more helpful than harmful. But a more radical politics around green energy in the UK would involve campaigning for the government to adopt feed-in tariffs. These are set prices which national and regional energy suppliers are legally *obliged* to pay for the power generated from renewable sources by domestic producers using household wind turbines, solar panels or geothermal systems. Where feed-in tariffs are adopted, generating companies are obliged to pay more for locally produced renewable energies than for 'dirty' fuels. This system has been massively successful in increasing the proportion of renewable energy generated and used in countries like Germany, where the appeal of the extra income is a powerful motivation to householders to generate their own renewable energy. To date, many Western governments have pursued an environmental strategy which mainly seeks to shift the costs of environmentalism on to consumers: an approach that is sometimes termed 'Green Governmentality' (Luke, 1999). By contrast, Germany's use of feed-in tariffs stands out as an approach which tries to solve environmental problems on a collective basis while addressing issues around energy generation at the level of *production*.

Not simply *using* renewable energy, but campaigning so that *everyone* will want to and be able to generate and use it characterises radical politics in this area. This means that paying attention to cultural context is also crucial. In the UK, popular green politics has been hamstrung by its lack of resonance with the deeply individualist political tradition of the country and its appeals to an uninspiring rhetoric of moral responsibility. A far better strategy would be to mobilise a rhetoric of independence and economy around the ideal of giving all householders the *right* to become energy-independent, and hence free from the vagaries of the energy market, which have produced massive, and massively unpopular, rises in household bills in recent years.

Could such a rhetoric be linked successfully to a wider critique of the power relations which underpin our environmentally unsustainable economy? It could through the 'Green New Deal', a package of far-reaching proposals brought together by a group of politicians, journalists, academics and the radical NGO, the New Economics Foundation (2008). The Green New Deal, which suggests ways of tackling the credit, oil and climate crunch simultaneously (for example by creating more 'green collar' jobs) is a good example of a radical green energy politics because it has the potential to mobilise a range of constituencies – from militant eco-activists to bill-conscious suburban householders – around a programme that would actually shift power dramatically away from major corporations (the energy producers), distributing it amongst a much wider population.

We are arguing, then, that for a politics to be radical means that it is a politics which is pushing for redistributions and reconfigurations of power on a number of levels; that it is a politics which is sensitive to its material and cultural environment; and that it works with a sound contextual understanding of the 'ecology' it is part of. We are also arguing that it works on a strategic level; for long-term change, not short-term spectacular effect. It is possible to identify strategies which meet these criteria in contemporary politics, but they are far too often marginalised by a politics of gesture on the one hand, and a technocratic pseudo-pragmatism on the other.

References

The Daily Mail (2007), http://www.dailymail.co.uk/news/article-449890/The-dirty-truth-Camerons-green-trainers.html

Gilbert, J. (2008) *Anticapitalism and Culture: Radical Theory and Popular Politics* (Oxford: Berg).

Guattari, F. (1989) *The Three Ecologies* (London: Continuum).

Hawkins, G. (2006) *The Ethics of Waste* (Lanham, MD: Rowman and Littlefield).

Institute for Public Policy Rearch and Green Alliance (2006) *A Zero Waste UK* (London: Institute for Public Policy Research).

Littler, J. (2009) *Radical Consumption: Shopping for Change in Contemporary Culture* (Milton Keynes: Open University Press).

Luke, T. W. (1999) 'Environmentality as Green Governmentality', in E. Darier (ed.), *Discourses of the Environment* (Oxford: Blackwell).

Murray, R. (1999) *Creating Wealth From Waste* (London: Demos).

Murray, R. (2002) *Zero Waste* (London: Greenpeace Environmental Trust).

New Economics Foundation (2008) *The Green New Deal* (London: New Economics Foundation).

Terra Plana http://www.terraplana.com/ethical_policy.php

15
Invention and Hard Work

Doreen Massey

Writing now, at the end of the first decade of a new millennium, it is difficult for those of us who lived through it not to think back to another decade when much of what is now crashing to the ground was first established in its dominance. The 1980s, that epochal decade, of Thatcherism and Ronald Reagan, of the establishment of a new dispensation in which individualism and competition, finance and financialisation, privatisation and commercialisation were hammered home as the only possible ways of being in a 'modern' economy and society.

There are many reasons, now, to ponder that earlier moment. A first is to appreciate the profundity and complexity of the changes it involved. This was not just the establishment as dominant of a new way of running an economy ('neo-liberalism', as it has come to be known in short), but the intimate colonising of society by a new common sense. This was, as we can see now, the establishment of a new hegemony and the whole nature of hegemonies is that they come to dominate in such a way that they infiltrate our brains and our imaginations, structure our intuitive understandings of the world, so that we fail to see that there might indeed be 'alternatives'. A second reason, then, to recall the 1980s is that, precisely because of how deep it goes, we can easily forget just how brief and recent has been the dominance of what popular discourse now takes to be natural. This self-evident common sense is only thirty years old. Moreover, and a third reason to remember, the establishment of what now seems natural did not take place without the fiercest of fights (from battles over the governance of cities, to the miners' strike in the UK, from Chile to Nicaragua . . .). So it is a relatively short-lived phenomenon, this neo-liberal hegemony, and it was not set in place without a struggle. All this should give us hope.

Moreover, the 'victory' was never complete. Both within its heartlands, in the USA and the UK, and elsewhere around the globe, there have continued to be resistances to its terms, the imagination of alternatives and concrete demonstrations of other ways of living in a society.

And now, quite suddenly, that settlement is dislocated and on the defensive; economically the whole house of cards is tumbling down. We are now witness to the (potential) implosion, in some senses, of the era which that moment of the 1980s inaugurated. The financial system is facing collapse, the wider economy is facing recession and probably depression and slump. For a host of different proximate reasons (and yet which are connected) people are out on the streets protesting, across Europe and beyond. As I write, there are strikes and mobilisations in Martinique and Guadeloupe. Could it be that this is another epochal moment?

At best, it is only potentially so. One question, one task, maybe one definition, of radical politics today, is how we can help and enable the release of this potential. This is a necessary task. If it is not addressed then the danger is that we shall return to the situation as before; that nothing fundamental will be changed. That there will be no challenge to the credit culture, or to the mechanisms that produce such inequality both within countries and between them, or to the mode of environmentally costly growth, or to the nature of 'growth' itself and the assumption that, whatever form it takes, growth is necessarily a good thing. Worse, the sufferings and discontents inflicted upon different groups and communities, and the protests in which they result, could all too easily degenerate into (and indeed be pushed into degenerating into) a reactionary backlash of parochialism and mutual antagonism, in which the voices saying 'no' end up only in fighting each other.

One thing that can be done, certainly, to avoid such dismal outcomes, is to contribute actively and positively to the 'policy' debate within our own political constituencies and geographical areas. Although it is difficult to learn about them from the usual establishment debates and media outlets, there is in fact a huge plethora of proposals for alternative ways out of this crisis. Just within the UK and European-wide debates there is, for instance, the Green New Deal (New Economics Foundation, 2008), the alternative plan for agriculture coming out through the Soil Association, the arguments against secrecy and (corporate and personal) tax-avoidance, and the proposals for new rules and new geographies of tax, from the Tax Justice Campaign, and the proposals for a different kind of European economy put forward by the EuroMemorandum Group. There are many more. And indeed one thing that is immediately necessary is a conversation between them. They are all carefully thought-through and utterly 'practical'. What they lack is popular currency and political voice.

These attempts to reorientate the political agenda raise other issues. One of these is their tenuous connection with wider social forces. They cannot remain pieces of paper. One of the positive aspects of the Green New Deal is its recognition of this fact. Its aim is to address 'the triple crunch' of the financial crisis, the looming crisis of climate change, and the 'crunch' of the fact that oil will, eventually, run out. By bringing together these three sets of concerns there arises, it argues, 'an exciting possibility of a new political alliance' (New Economics Foundation, 2008: 6).

The question is how such alliances are to be built. The Green New Deal has potential here because its collective of authors is in part drawn from social movements and the proposals themselves are thus already the result of much wider debate. Moreover, because it brings together groups whose main political campaigning has previously been around different issues (tax and finance, the environment, the politics of oil) it has already begun on the most difficult aspect of forming alliances – the recognition of, and address to, the inevitable differences in priorities, and sometimes downright conflicts, that exist between them. Such, often difficult, negotiations in which all of the participants may themselves be changed, is part of the very stuff of politics.

One new potential alliance – Progressive London (www.progressive london.org.uk) – explicitly recognises this. Its first conference took place in January 2009, with a 'starting point' of rejecting 'the Thatcherite dogma . . . that deregulation and the cult of the worst excesses of the financial markets are any kind of way forward for our city'. Aiming to bring together a broad coalition, the opening statement adds: 'unity does not come easily: it requires discussion and debate. Where we agree we will unite. Where we don't we will continue an open discussion. The trade unions, community groups, campaigns and the new media will be important forums where this discussion of progressive policy unfolds.'

Participating in building such alliances is one way of practising radical politics today. And that also emphasises a broader point. And that is the necessity to *engage*. If an alternative way out of this crisis is to be created, one that is radically different from what led to it, then it is necessary to catch people's imaginations. (We desperately need more forums for discussion, more spaces of engagement.) And that in turn means listening, considering seriously why people hold what might seem to be counter-intuitive, even reactionary responses, it means tapping into those trains of thought and feeling that have been developed in the context of the common sense of the last thirty years. The means of doing this can be (must be?) manifold, from serious to fun, from painstaking argument to evocations of the absurd. But to ignore the necessity of doing it would be, quite apart from anything else, undemocratic. (And indeed, the multiplication of forms of democratic engagement must be high on the agenda.)

This kind of politics, however, has to be set within a wider reimagination. The crises that the current system has run into are economic and environmental, the two being intimately linked. What faces us now, on the Left, is the question of how to turn this immense upheaval into one that is also *political*. How to turn it into a moment that also calls into question that cultural common sense on which it has so firmly depended (and which, to make matters more difficult, includes the bizarre notion that the economic is not, itself, a cultural formation)? You'd think this might be our moment, with banks collapsing and being 'nationalised', with protests erupting in a host of places. It is what we have been waiting for; it's what we have predicted. And yet, this implosion of the system is being addressed, largely, within a narrative of the Right. For the most part, 'they' still have hold of the story. And thus, too, of the possible alternatives available for a way out.

It is what has been called a crucial 'conjuncture', just as was that period leading up to and culminating in the hegemonic shift of the 1980s. That last crucial moment was, of course, lost. But one of the things that helped the Left understand it and combat its outcome was attention to a serious analysis of its nature and form.[1] We need, again, to construct an alternative narrative of what is going on. Apart from their recognition of the profundity and complexity of the changes that a hegemonic shift implies, which has already been mentioned, these analyses also stressed two other things which it is vital we pick up again now. First, they combined and moved between the weaving of a broad narrative on the one hand and on the other the intricate excavation of seemingly small and singular events that crystallised the changes under way, that showed how deep they went (and thus helped take the political temperature of society) and that grounded the bigger narrative in lived experiences and incidents that touched base with lives outside the explicitly political. This we must do again, as part of a diagnosis that is at the same time a politics. Second, these analyses brought to light the amount of *work* that had had to be put in to bring about the changes that led to the new settlement and whose terms would come to seem so 'natural'. The preparatory work, in think tanks and institutions, the experimentation – most notoriously in Chile – the suppression of alternatives, all these are well documented. What I want to stress here is the more ordinary, constant, drip drip drip, of their effort to establish their narrative as dominant, and to continue to maintain it as so. Two examples from the UK. First, that story constantly relayed about how the finance sector was so vital to the economy, how without it we would be lost, how any attempt to regulate it would lead all these heroes to flee the City, and so on and so on. This was a fable poured out endlessly from a host of organisations, consultancies and official bodies (Massey, 2007). It took work to establish the obviousness of that story, a story that now seems absurd. Second, as part of the effort to drive down remuneration and pensions to labour, there is a similarly constant stream of voices, pundits and experts, with the sole aim of dividing public-sector workers from private-sector workers. The former have better pensions, it is endlessly argued; this is not fair, they should be reduced. Of course, one could just as well argue the opposite. The point of stressing all this is that it gives us hope. If they have to put so much effort in . . . This work they put in presents opportunities for us to intervene, to counter the arguments, to point to their absurdity, and their real aims.

So, there are some 'small things' going on that deserve our political attention and our own work. Just within the sphere of finance, and within the United Kingdom, there has been over recent months: rising popular anger directed at banks, a big rise in private savings in the Cooperative Bank, and a sharp rise in popularity of the Post Office. Small things, and set within a morass of counter-examples (the privatisation of the public sector continues apace even while privatisation is increasingly discredited). But nonetheless there is a detectable change in mood. An advertisement for a building society, posted in my local tube station, exudes reliability and seriousness, and stresses that it is not a bank but a mutual; it is, in other words, not chasing the fast buck but investing wisely and securely. This little thing both catches at and further disseminates a change in values; it is a tiny reworking of common sense. It picks up on what a contributor said at Progressive London: 'real life is producing changes in understanding'.

However, to make these small things more than ephemeral, to make them *matter*, two things (at least) need to be done. First, they need to be reworked and reinterpreted into a wider narrative. If people have moved their savings to the Coop one reason for this is likely to be an individualistic calculation that they are safer there (i.e. the inherited hegemonic common sense). Yet the *reason* for this greater safety is the nature of the Cooperative and the progressive principles of its investment practice. Can *this* be brought to the surface, as it were, as an element in a new common sense? A new common sense that both reinterprets the state we are in and holds out some vision of what might be possible. Second, there is a need 'to crystallise the disparate and sometimes contradictory elements of dissatisfaction into a new configuration, a new kind of politics' (Hall, 1995: 24). This does not mean dragooning all discontents under one banner. But it does mean digging deeper to find their commonalities, recognising openly their differences, and building multiple lives of open collectivity.

The argument so far has been predominantly within a local or national framing. And yet, at the current moment, few things are more obvious than that we are globally interconnected. How this is to be responded to, if it is to go beyond the romantic and evocatory, and if on the other hand it is not to leave us mired in guilty helplessness, is not so obvious. Yet it is necessary, for reasons primarily of political internationalism. It is necessary too because issues of hegemony play out quite differently when taken at an international level, and because there are real shifts under way – the rise of the BRIC countries, the distinct directions taken by Russia and China, the challenging and progressive alternatives being developed in Latin America. It is necessary because whatever way is taken out of this moment there are likely to be massive changes in the international division of labour and in the world balance of certain forms of power.

The most general thing this implies is a greater 'outward-lookingness' of the political imagination, a greater quotidian awareness of our planetary positioning. The local and the global are not separate spheres; they utterly interpenetrate each other. It is possible to fight through local action for alternative forms of globalisation. This may mean taking responsibility for the activities that make up one's own place, and yet that have international repercussions (what I have called a politics of place beyond place). Now, surely, those of us in the UK should be addressing not only the national but also the global effects of the dominance of financial capitalism, a dominance that was nurtured here. We are told that the current crisis is global and was made in the USA (in other words, don't blame us). It is certainly global in its repercussions and certainly the initial trigger was subprime markets in the USA – though it could easily have been something else. But the preconditions for it, the immense cultural changes it wrought, were, in part, invented and established in the UK, in the City of London, whose unique selling point has been its lack of regulation. This, as well as national concerns, should be integral to the challenge to, and utter reformulation of, finance. This, then, is a politics both of places and of the relations between them.

Second, there is a host of interconnected solidarities and campaigns that already string like necklaces around the world. They may be around particular campaigns (against privatisation, in defence of indigenous peoples), they may be solidarity groups, or experiments with new forms of trade relations. And they may operate through any spatial form, including the national (the new forms of inter-state relations being developed between Latin American countries, and their wider global politics of solidarity). Once again at global level two things are crucial to establish in such struggles. First that they engage with majority populations – in other words that they take seriously the need to establish genuine democratic credentials. And second that they recognise and address the tensions between campaigns, that they take seriously the articulation of differences into something new. A 'common politics' will not just emerge; it will take work.

And finally, especially for those in the First World perhaps, it is necessary to listen and learn. There is a host of experiments, with new forms of economy and society, with new forms of democracy, with new ways of relating between places, already under way, especially in the global South. 'Neo-liberalism' never did have the whole world in its thrall, and that is even more the case now.

Note

1. Much of this kind of work, in the United Kingdom, was initiated by Stuart Hall and the groups, both within and beyond the academy, in which he was active.

References

Hall, S. (1995) 'Parties on the Verge of a Nervous Breakdown', *Soundings: a Journal of Politics and Culture*, 1 (Autumn): 19–33.
Massey, D. (2007) *World City* (Cambridge: Polity).
New Economics Foundation (2008) The Green New Deal (London: New Economics Foundation), http://www.neweconomics.org/gen/uploads/2ajogu45c1id4w55tofmpy552007200 8172656.pdf
Progressive London, www.progressivelondon.org.uk

Part III
Diversity and Difference

16
Progressivism Reinvigorated

Gregor McLennan

Radical politics today has no viable institutional programme. This is partly because those who see themselves as being 'of the Left' do not agree about what is socially and humanly desirable, never mind achievable. There is even significant doubt about whether 'the Left' itself is the right sort of term of reference for radical politics. For example, much today that goes on in the name of multiculturalism, ecology, group rights, anti-globalisation, queer politics, and even the ubiquitous 'social justice' seems at times quite distant from, and even antagonistic to, what used to be the normative capstone of the Left, namely socialism. The key problem has thus been, for many years: can radical politics signal and stand for something over and above the – not always compatible – claims and terminologies of various particularist social movements of a broadly egalitarian nature? This problem has come to a head, because now it is patently clear that without a unifying social imaginary, motivation for constructive egalitarianism quickly flags and effective solidarity fragments. Whilst fully recognising the need for a specific and coherent transformative economic agenda, this contribution nevertheless focuses on the kind of general ethical outlook that also needs re-energising if radical politics is to prosper.

Having experienced a generation of radical thought based on a strongly pluralistic and permissive 'politics of difference', there appears now to be a drift back towards, if not universalism exactly, then at least a search for new common principles. The tide has begun to flow away from disparate multiculturalist takes on social justice. Whilst important, these are perhaps in the end bound to remain pragmatic, volatile, piecemeal currents of ideology and politics. The tide is instead moving towards something more consolidated and general. This mood of restlessness around endless pluralism can be discerned in academic strands of thinking seeking to find a new touchstone for solidaristic change in a neo-liberal world, for example, in the assorted debates concerning cosmopolitanism, planetary humanism, deliberative democracy, and the nature of the global 'multitude'. And multiculturalist spokespersons themselves have started to embrace the previously questioned horizon of a more expansive radical humanism. This all paves the way for a restated vision of social and human progress, bringing into play thoughts and instincts that were not so long ago deemed completely outmoded, or at least kept at arm's length outside the prevailing comfort zone of the politics of difference. But we can see the rediscovered attraction of progressivism in documents like the *Good Society* (Rutherford and Shah, 1996), platform of the British Left-of-centre forum Compass, which until its final version in 2006 lacked any philosophical basis for its hopes of renewing social democratic ideas. Yet what does the new progressivism mean in this context? Actually, it still remains to be properly developed. Indeed, 'progressivism' may not even be the best term for the perspective that we need. But the following elements and emphases must be part of any serious attempt at radical renewal.

Persons

In the multiculturalist style of radical politics, the focus is on groups: group characteristics, group heritages, group experiences, group rights. This is clearly important in various ways, and there is no reason to expect or wish particularistic group politics to cease. But 'groupism' cannot be taken too far, not least because group interests are themselves in part political constructions, and group life, especially when imagined as a series of static and separate cultural practices and values, by no means exhausts the social universe. Also, quite inevitably, the interests and situation of some cultural groups come to conflict with those of others. Elite leadership of groups takes place, strenuous lobbying goes on, and the perception steadily spreads, whether justified or not, that some interests are favoured over others. Claims and counter-claims about justice or injustice, respect and disrespect, fly all over the place. The discourse around group claims, rights and identities becomes moralistic, stultifyingly bound up with expressions of political correctness, such that robust independent thinking on the Left virtually disappears for fear of offending someone's precious sense of self-identity. Then it turns out, naturally enough, that everyone has a precious sense of self-identity that is entitled not only to respect, but to esteem and support as well. Long-term, this kind of multicultural political psychology, full of defensiveness and guilt-tripping, cannot ground any genuinely radical politics.

Karl Marx sought to overcome the negative side of group-ism through the idea of class. Ironically, today, it is routinely assumed even by radicals that what socialists like Marx meant by working class was just another kind of group interest, taking its (important) place alongside others. For Marx it was something much more encompassing. But once you interpret class culturally – let us say with the image of manual workers in factories in mind – it is no longer thought to be sufficient, or even relevant to the way people live now, at least in countries like Britain. But Marx had another way of projecting a kind of universal political project that stretched beyond the confines of group interests, and this was a certain inspiring view of the human, social person: intelligent, active, labouring, thinking, loving, learning, caring, creative, passionate, just. So the task of radical politics might be seen as the creation of a society in which this kind of person comes to prevail, the kind of person that everyone can become, and the kind of person that we subjectively aspire to be. Now feminists have rightly said that there is a dubious masculinist element in this idea of Promethean Man, and apart from that there is always a distinct danger, a dangerous lack of realism, in any picture of our best selves that is so thoroughly wholesome. Many of us will fail to reach the ideal; and there is a side of human life – instinctive, selfish, destructive, creative – that cannot quite be captured by that uplifting moral template. These are important reservations, because they draw our attention to the fact that we cannot be forced or indoctrinated into becoming better people. But on the other hand, radical politics for too long has been complacently contented to lionise and justify people and groups as they currently exist, rather than in terms of what we all can become, and the focus must now shift.

Majorities

Progressivism builds its politics on a sense of what most people share in common rather than what divides them. Its outlook is therefore majoritarian. A radical, socialised, democratic society is one that should be good for all of us, and should be perceived as such by most of us. And however complex deep democracy inevitably must get at times, no political decision-making in democratic style can ultimately function without underwriting in terms of general interests and majority concerns. Yet the radical Left seems at times to have forgotten these basic 'majoritarian' facts about political motivation and the battle of ideas, settling instead for a minoritarian moralism and victimology. One plausible interpretation of Marx's notion of the working class, when freed up from any particular cultural image that immediately dates it in countries like Britain – such as the manual worker in a factory – is all those compelled to engage in paid employment, lacking ownership and control over significant productive resources, and collectively providing the core of those resources. This is a majoritarian conception of the working class, and it can still be applied today, though it is in obvious ways counter-intuitive: we would have to hold that many professionals and middle managers, as well as the cleaners who tidy up their offices, are working class. But the point here is that unless radical politics is majoritarian, it is not radical at all, at least in any progressive sense. We should remember that Thatcher was quite appropriately called a political radical, and that radicalism per se has nothing progressive about it. We could easily decide to drive on the wrong side of the road, set bombs in bus stations, applaud the breakdown of the family, all justified as some kind of radicalism, and even as anarchic or Leftist radicalism. But these acts and thoughts would not (necessarily) be cases of progressive radicalism, which requires a majoritarian horizon.

One of the problems of Left politics, and indeed any kind of democratic politics today, is that the whole majority/minority issue is complex and puzzling. The danger of the tyranny of the majority, especially in multicultural settings, seems more historically acute than ever. The founding democratic fiction that there is one 'people' to whom politicians are accountable turns out to be far from obviously right or desirable, partly because it assumes and encourages the sort of cultural uniformity that is felt to be impossible in pluralistic societies nowadays. Even so, no conception of radical democracy can survive on the basis that the polity is irrevocably split on cultural or any other grounds: there has to be a (majoritarian) principle which specifies the way in which minoritarian expressions or secessions are acceptable to all. Complex though these issues may be, there is simply no way of evading the fact that progressive radicalism, as opposed to sectarian radicalism, must be more positive about the concept of the social majority and must lift its discourse to draw in the concerns of the social majority.

Capacities

Where minoritarian and multiculturalist radicals emphasise the recognition of identities as a condition of social selfhood and democracy, progressivists prioritise the development of our capacities. Identity politics is heavily burdened by the power of the past and by present sectional interests. Capacity politics is more future-oriented, emphasising our ability, individually and together, to go beyond where we have been, and beyond what we are now. Our cultures of education and learning are crucial here, with much thinking on the Right and Left alike seemingly besotted with the notion that our schools and universities must serve and engage with stakeholding communities, whether these be socially classified neighbourhoods, ethnic groups, religious creeds or business enterprises. But instead of this situation of interest-group capture, and despite favoured notions amongst cultural theorists of 'situated knowledge', we need to re-emphasise the inspirational, intrinsic qualities of *dis*interested knowledge, of world- and self-discovery and invention. As the socio-legal theorist Roberto M. Unger insists, the idea is to produce context-breaking, not context-reinforcing minds and energies.

Productivism

Some years ago, the discovery of the fact and the pleasures of consumerism in postmodern capitalism seemed to seal the fate of traditional Marxist benchmarks around economic production and work. Green political arguments had similar effect. But this critique of economism was only partly successful, because only partly valid. Neither the politics of consumption, nor the politics of stewardship, nor even the more profound and legitimate emphasis on the politics of care and concern can ever sufficiently motivate or sustain an alternative societal programme. In fact, the wider meaning of productivism encapsulates far more than an economically functional work ethic – though the continuing need for some such ethic should not be underestimated. Progressive productivism points up the necessity and value of purposeful labour wherever it occurs, and the more cooperative and self-directed the better. It emphasises that we can all be both producers and carers, and that purposeful production encompasses all the rigours and beauty and fantasies of disciplined creativity too. Productive people want to make things happen, they want to innovate, and they want results, whether in the workplace or in their own personal space. The Left cannot allow these indispensable attributes and themes to be colonised by the Right.

It might be thought that, if you put together my emphasis here on creative labour and the previous one on context-breaking intelligence, the kind of image of the desirable social personality reflects essentially middle-class values, or even elitist ones. This perception is correct.

A truly radical progressive politics is not one that says: everything to do with being elitist and middle class is bogus, or is based on unjustifiable privileges that need to be swept away. On the contrary, the point is that the kind of privileged education that middle-class children receive, their general good health and active bearing, the attention given to their creative sides, their lack of a sense of being crushed and brutalised by a life of labour, enforced inactivity, or lack of opportunity – these are precisely the things that should be for everyone. Paradoxically of course, to make this good society come into being, bold and controversial things need arguing through that may seem to hurt the current interests of many middle-class people, not all of them incredibly wealthy or privileged. These could include abolishing independent/sectarian schools, for example, or private medicine alongside guaranteeing that public education and health will be of the highest possible standards, something that no social democratic government has ever seriously attempted.

Secularism

Cultural radicals have, over the past 40 years, become excessively anti-positivist in their attitude to science and scientific ideals. By 'anti-positivist' I mean continually questioning the search for objectivity and truth, and overstating the degree to which scientific knowledge is socially conditioned or socially situated. Of course, we can immediately agree that science *is* socially conditioned and situated. But this does not mean that hard-won knowledge is ever completely reducible to its social context or the social interests surrounding it. We can also immediately agree that we have to be reflexive and critical in relation to scientism – a kind of ideology of science, the naïve belief that science somehow will always show us the best way forward in solving human problems. But at the same time, progressive radicalism must always, as it were, be on the side of science. We should stress the transcultural nature of scientific knowledge (which does not mean that science is anything other than fallible, changing and provisional). We should hail and promote its inspiringly imaginative character; and we should uphold its robust 'rationalism' – that everything is to be subject to public test and unconstrained argumentation.

This firm cultivation of a scientific ethos for social learning, especially amongst the young, is part of what we could call a generally secular approach to social and personal life. But with the revival of religion and spirituality that appears to be going on today, key aspects of the progressivist outlook – secularism, humanism and atheism – have come under increasing questioning and even attack. The idea has taken hold, or at least has not been sufficiently opposed, that society needs to be friendly to religion, and avoid at all costs being 'offensive' to those with cherished beliefs that inscribe who they (think they) are. Progressives need to respond to this challenge by fully accepting the right of religious people (and anyone else) to say what they think in the terms they prefer, and to carry out their faith-work freely, as long as this does not involve aggressive or violent proselytising. People who happen to be religious, like anyone else, are to be respected as people and citizens. And insofar as all the major religions come in versions that are soft on humanism, common cause can often easily and properly be made. But radicals seem to have forgotten that if the Left is to speak effectively to the big issues of our time, it must actually stand for something. So it cannot be infinitely hospitable to all manner of faiths and fancies simply out of common human respect.

With regard to secularism, therefore, progressivists need to argue that in fact we have never been secular; that secularism is anyway not equivalent either to humanism or atheism. Secularism has, if anything, been the saving of religion and religious toleration, not its enemy. As for humanism, progressivists need to emphasise that our understanding of the essential 'this-worldliness' of social problems and solutions differs fundamentally from any outlook in which a (genuine) concern for humanity comes only courtesy of God's will. Atheism, finally, is no more, but also no less, than the considered view that there is no good reason to suppose that supernatural beings and agencies, especially those uncannily resembling human beings and social agencies, either exist, or influence our origins and destiny. None of this means that, in Richard Dawkins' unnecessarily insulting terms, religious people are straightforwardly 'deluded'; nor that religion is anything other than an endlessly fascinating and significant social phenomenon; nor that what we understand by secular society is not badly in need of moral and spiritual uplift. Indeed, we should not forget that in some ways, historically speaking, enlightenment progressivism carries on the 'improving' universalist ethic that the monotheistic religions started. There are many progressive elements in church activities (Make Poverty History) and religious ethical campaigning against the dehumanisation and demoralisation of contemporary consumer capitalist society. But secular progressives must still firmly insist that important moral and political arguments are utterly independent of, and overriding upon, specific religious colorations. And they should urgently oppose theocratic tendencies arising in the public sphere of democratic societies.

The touchstones of identity, pluralism, relativism and multicultural-ism still dominate radical politics today. However, there is a growing turn within the Left which seeks to challenge the trend. While radicals have to be tolerant, they also need to develop a bold and distinctive approach to social and personal life. As a response, in this chapter I have argued for a progressive radical politics, which is majoritarian, capacitarian and broadly secularist.

Reference

Rutherford, J. and H. Shah (2006) *The Good Society: Compass Programme for Renewal* (London: Compass).

17

In Defence of Multicultural Citizenship[1]

Tariq Modood

In this chapter I draw attention to how contemporary radical politics does not embrace ideas of multiculturalism. Indeed, from both the Left and Right, radical politics seems openly hostile to multiculturalism. Going against this grain, I argue that many radicals pay little attention to the possibilities which multiculturalism has to offer today. Multiculturalism, or the politics of difference or identity politics more generally, are all associated with the New Left politics that emerged in the 1960s. Multiculturalism won support for several decades, even while social democracy and Left radicalism were losing ground to more market-oriented approaches to the economy and the provision of welfare. Now that Keyensianism and nationalisation seem to have been rehabilitated, at least temporarily, it is ironic that multiculturalism seems to have lost support amongst radicals and is allowed to be vilified by the Right without a response. For the reasons outlined below, I believe radicals have to review their attitude to multiculturalism.

At the start of the twentieth century, the American social theorist, W. E. B. Du Bois (see Lewis, 1995), predicted that it would be the century of the colour-line. In many ways this was proved to be true but will be transcended in this century, especially in Britain. What should be the appropriate balance between civic attitudes and policies promoting commonality and respecting difference will be one of the major domestic issues. But the focus will not be colour-racism, nor will people divide on it in terms of a racial dualism, whites versus non-whites. The ideological divide will be a form of (post-)liberalism which emphasises the privatisation of religion versus a form of (post-)liberalism based on inclusivity and reaching a modus vivendi in which neither religious nor non-religious people have to 'privatise' their beliefs. It will be a divide in which each side will elaborate a (post-)liberalism with a view to whether ethno-religious groups who refuse assimilation and privatisation, like some Muslims, need to be 'converted' or whether they will be ethical-political partners. I suggest that a civic and dialogical multiculturalism that reworks a sense of national identity can be helpful in this new landscape and should be considered by radicals.

Blaming multiculturalism, blaming Muslims

The relationship between ethnic, religious and social communities in some Western states is mired in a crisis. The term 9/11 is a shorthand reference for it, but the critique of multiculturalism that focuses on Muslims, and is so prevalent today, pre-dates the terrorist attacks of 9/11 and their aftermath. 2001, though, is a pivotal year, at least in Britain. The late spring of that year saw urban disturbances in a number of northern English towns and cities in which young Muslim, mainly Pakistani, working-class and white working-class, men played a central role. The dominant political response was that the riots were due to a one-sided multiculturalism having facilitated, even encouraged, segregated communities which shunned each other. All subsequent events seem to point in the same direction. For example, Gilles Keppel (2005) observed that the 7/7 bombers 'were the children of Britain's own multicultural society' and that the bombings have 'smashed' the implicit social consensus that produced multiculturalism 'to smithereens'.

When reflecting upon the nature and character of radical politics today, we see that multiculturalism has its critics on the Right and the Left. But I continue to be of the view that some reworked version of multiculturalism should be integral to a centre-Left politics of the twenty-first century. So I here restate a conception of multiculturalism, which clearly distinguishes it from relativism and separatism, as well as certain narrow forms of liberalism, and places it squarely within an understanding of democratic citizenship and nation-building.

Multicultural citizenship

Just as social democrats have a notion of positive equality around socio-economic equality, what is called social citizenship, I would like to make a parallel case for positive equality in connection with the symbolic dimensions of public culture. Citizenship is not just a legal status and set of rights, but is amplified by a certain kind of politics. I have nothing specific to say about the former, the basic, foundational levels of citizenship, except that they are necessary – in the way of skeleton to a living body – to all wider meanings of citizenship. T. H. Marshall famously conceptualised a wider citizenship as a series of historical-logical developments, each necessary to later stages, by which legal rights such as habeas corpus were gradually extended to include rights of political participation and then later to social rights, such as the right of citizens to receive health care funded by the citizens as a whole. These developments were a long process of centuries, and involved a history of political struggles, not least in extending the body of citizenry, the rights-holders, from an aristocratic male elite to all adults. With some plausibility it has been argued that through egalitarian movements, such as the politics of difference, the second half of the twentieth century has seen the emergence of a fourth stage in the form of a demand for cultural rights, while simultaneously seeing an erosion of some social rights. Social citizenship has certainly not been accultural. Rather it has been informed by an assumption of cultural homogeneity, such as its support of a male breadwinner model of the nuclear family. The homogeneity has been particularly exposed by social change and change in attitudes, and critiqued by feminists whose work – as with the public–private distinction – others have built upon. I would, however, here like to outline an understanding of this historically developing citizenship – which has not been a simple linear process – in terms of certain overarching characteristics rather than by types of rights.

Like Marshall I believe the citizenship I speak of is particularly informed by British history, though it can be seen at work in many other places too. It is a conception of citizenship that far from being in opposition to multiculturalism, shows how multiculturalism is a progressive development of a dynamic, assertive, empowering and inclusive citizenship. I sketch it below in terms of three features and then explore its relationship to multiculturalism and Muslim identity politics today.

Citizenship is non-transcendent or pluralist

Citizens are individuals and have individual rights. But citizens are not uniform and their citizenship contours itself around specific groups of people with specific cultures and histories. Citizenship is not a monistic identity that is completely apart from or transcends other identities important to citizens; in the way that the theory – though not always the practice – of French republicanism demands. The creation of the UK created new political subjects (for my purpose citizens, though strictly speaking, for most of the history of the UK, subjects of the Crown). But it did not eliminate the constituent nations of the UK. So a common

British citizenship did not mean that one could not be Scottish, English, Irish or Welsh, and so allowed for the idea that there were different ways of being British – an idea that is not confined to constituent nations, but also included other group identities. The plurality, then, is ever present and each part of the plurality has a right to be a part of the whole and to speak up for itself and for its vision of the whole.

Citizenship is multilogical

The plurality speaks to each other and it does not necessarily agree about what it means to be a citizen; there can be a series of agreements and disagreements, with some who agree on X while disagreeing on Y, while some who disagree on X may agree and others disagree on Y and so on. But there is enough agreement, and above all enough interest, in the discussion for dialogues to be sustained. As the parties to these dialogues are many, not just two, the process is more aptly described as multilogical. The multilogues allow for views to qualify each other, overlap, synthesise, modify one's own view in the light of having to coexist with that of others, hybridise, allow new adjustments to be made, new conversations to take place. Such modulations and contestations are part of the internal, evolutionary, work-in-progress dynamic of citizenship. In this way the content of a citizenship can change over time, new groups can be accommodated and new identity formations can emerge within the citizenry.

Citizenship is dispersed

Related to citizenship not being monolithic is that action and power are not monopolistically concentrated and so the state is not the exclusive site for citizenship. We perform our citizenship and relate to each other as fellow citizens, and so get to know what our citizenship is, what it is composed of, not just in relation to law and politics, but also civic debate and action initiated through our voluntary associations, community organisations, trades unions, newspapers and media, churches, temples, mosques etc. Change and reform do not all have to be brought about by state action, laws, regulation, prohibitions etc. but also through public debate, discursive contestations, pressure group mobilisations, and the varied and (semi-) autonomous institutions of civil society also contribute to shaping change. It is not just that the dynamic is bottom-up as well as top-down, but that the sites of action and pressure-points that need to be activated for change to occur are many and of different levels and scale. Moreover, when we say that citizenship is a public not a private identity it is important to clarify what we mean by 'public'. If citizenship involves concern for issues such as poverty or the qualities of prime-ministerial leadership, this can take place in a trade-union meeting or a mosque, or in reading a novel or watching a television documentary in the privacy of one's home. It is the concern for the civic condition that is the issue – not the how and where. So the idea that, for example, religious spaces – mental and physical – are inherently private and non-civic is unnecessarily restrictive and purist.

Even with such a brief sketch of citizenship it should be clear that it is a radical and self-transformative idea and that there is a deep resonance that exists between citizenship and multicultural recognition. Not only do both presuppose complementary notions of unity and plurality, and of equality and difference, but the idea of respect for the group self-identities that citizens value is central to citizenship. Moreover, seeing citizenship as a work in progress and as partly constituted, and certainly extended, by contestatory multilogues and novel demands for due recognition, as circumstances shift, means that citizenship can be understood as conversations and renegotiations, not just about who is to be recognised but about what is recognition, about the terms of citizenship itself. At one point, it is the injuries of class that demand civic attention; at another, there is a plea for dropping a self-deluding 'colour-blindness' and addressing racialised statuses through citizenship. The one thing that civic inclusion does not consist of is an uncritical acceptance of an existing conception of citizenship, of 'the rules of the game' and a one-sided 'fitting-in' of new entrants or the new equals (the ex-subordinates). To be a citizen, no less than to have just become a citizen, is to have a right not just to be recognised, but to debate the terms of recognition.

Muslims and identity

How does this relate to Muslim identity politics, one of the central sources of anxiety and disillusionment about multiculturalism both generally and within contemporary radical politics? British Muslim identity politics was virtually created by the *Satanic Verses* affair of the late 1980s and beyond. Muslims began to make demands for recognition and civic inclusion into a polity which had up to that point misrecognised them (as black or Asian) or had kept them invisible and voiceless; a polity that was struggling to recognise gender, race and ethnicity within the terms of citizenship but was not even aware that any form of civic recognition was due to marginalised religious groups. The conflict that erupted led many to think of themselves for the first time as Muslims in a public way, to think that it was important in their relation to other Muslims and to the rest of British and related societies. This is for example movingly described by the author, Rana Kabbani (1989: ix), whose *Letter to Christendom* begins with a description of herself as 'a woman who had been a sort of underground Muslim before she was forced into the open by the Salman Rushdie affair'. Such shocks to Muslim identity are hardly a thing of the past. The present situation of some Muslims in Britain is nicely captured by Farmida Bi, a New Labour parliamentary candidate in Mole Valley in 2005, who had not particularly made anything of her Muslim background before 7/7 but was moved by the London bombings to claim a Muslim identity and found the organisation, Progressive British Muslims. Speaking of herself and others as 'integrated, liberal British Muslims' who were forced to ask 'am I a Muslim at all?', she writes: '7/7 made most of us embrace our Muslim identity and become determined to prove that it's possible to live happily as a Muslim in the west' (Bi, 2006).

This sense of feeling that one must speak up as a Muslim is of course nothing necessarily to do with religiosity. Like all forms of difference it comes into being as a result of pressures from outside a group, as well as from the inside. In this particular case, both the inside and the outside have a powerful geopolitical dimension. The emergence of British Muslim identity and activism has been propelled by a strong concern for the plight of Muslims elsewhere in the world, especially (but not only) where this plight is seen in terms of anti-imperialist emancipation and where the UK government is perceived to be part of the problem – tolerant of, if not complicit in or actively engaged in the destruction of Muslim hopes and lives, usually civilian. That British, American and Australian (perhaps to some extent most Western) Muslims are having to develop a sense of national citizenship, to integrate into a polity, which has a confrontational posture against many Muslim countries, and is at war, or occupying some of them in what is perceived by all sides to be a long-term project is an extremely daunting task. I suppose one has to say that success cannot be taken for granted. Moreover, domestic terrorism, as well as political opposition, has unfortunately become part of the context. The danger of 'blowback' from overseas military activity is, as events have shown, considerable and capable of destroying the movement towards multicultural citizenship.

The situation is reminiscent of my student days when some Left politics embraced a rhetoric of violent liberation and revolution, iconised armed men such as Trotsky, Che Guevera and Mao and spawned the terrorism of the Baader-Meinhof, the Angry Brigade, the Weathermen, the

Black Panthers and others. Radicalism was able to distance itself from such violence by drawing deeper upon its democratic values. So, similarly must be the case today. One of the reasons why I do not think radical politics should simply give up and pursue a less attractive political goal than multiculturalism is that I am impressed by how many British Muslims have and are responding to the crisis. Namely, with a concern to stand up for their community through civic engagement; with a refusal to give up either on their Muslim identity, or being part of democratic citizenship. Despite a dependency on overseas circumstances outside their control and so where one might anticipate passivity and a self-pitying introspection, many British Muslims exhibit a dynamism and a confidence that they must rise to the challenge of dual loyalties, and not give up on either set of commitments. Ideological and violent extremism is indeed undermining the conditions and hopes for multiculturalism. But, contrary to the multiculturalism blamers I began with, this extremism has nothing to do with the promotion of multiculturalism, but is instead coming into the domestic arena from the international.

National identity and being British

Multiculturalism has been broadly right and does not deserve the desertion of support from the centre-Left, let alone the blame for the present crisis by many 'radicals'. It offers a better basis for integration than its two current rivals, namely, 'social cohesion' and 'multiculture'. For while the latter is appreciative of a diversity of interacting lifestyles and the emergence of new, hybrid cultures in an atmosphere of 'conviviality', it is at a loss as to how to deal sympathetically with the claims of newly settled ethno-religious groups, especially Muslims, who are too readily stereotyped as 'fundamentalists'. Some advocacy of multiculturalism has, however, perhaps overlooked, or at least under-emphasised, the other side of the coin. This is not just equally necessary but is integral to multiculturalism. For one can't just talk about difference. Difference has to be related to things we have in common. The commonality that most multiculturalists emphasise is citizenship. I have argued that this citizenship has to be seen in a plural, dispersed and dialogical way and not reduced to legal rights, passports and the franchise (important though these are). I would now like to go further in suggesting that a good basis for or accompaniment to a multicultural citizenship is a national identity.

Many radicals, focusing upon abstract idealism, have overlooked a practical reality. Where multiculturalism has been accepted and worked as a state project or as a national project – Canada, Australia and

Malayasia for example – it has not just been coincidental with, but integral to, a nation-building project; to creating Canadians, Aussies and Malayasians etc. Even in the USA, where the federal state has had a much lesser role in the multicultural project, the incorporation of ethno-religious diversity and hyphenated Americans has been about country-making, civic inclusion and making a claim upon the national identity. This is important because some multiculturalists, or at least advocates of pluralism and multiculture (the vocabulary of multiculturalism is not always used) – even where they have other fundamental disagreements with each other – argue as if the logic of the national and the multicultural are incompatible. Partly as a result many Europeans think of multiculturalism as antithetical to, rather than as a reformer of, national identity.

Moreover, it does not make sense to encourage strong multicultural or minority identities and weak common or national identities. Strong multicultural identities are a good thing – they are not intrinsically divisive, reactionary or fifth columns. But they need a framework of vibrant, dynamic, national narratives and the ceremonies and rituals which give expression to a national identity. It is clear that minority identities are capable of having an emotional pull for the individuals for whom they are important. Multicultural citizenship requires, therefore, if it is to be equally attractive to the same individuals, a comparable counter-balancing emotional pull. Many Britons, for example, say they are worried about disaffection amongst some Muslim young men and more generally a lack of identification with Britain amongst many Muslims in Britain. As a matter of fact, surveys over many years have shown Muslims have been reaching out for an identification with Britain. For example, in a Channel 4 survey carried out in spring 2006, 82 per cent of a national sample of Muslims said they very strongly (45 per cent) or fairly strongly (37 per cent) felt they belonged to Britain (Channel 4, 2006). Of course there is a lot of anger and fear around these issues, especially in relation to the aggressive USA–UK foreign policies and terrorism. While I do not feel that we are at all close to undoing the mess we have got into with these policies, to not build on the clear support there is for a sense of national belonging is to fail to offer an obvious counterweight to the ideological calls for a jihad against fellow Britons.

So, I cannot conclude on a clear note of optimism. But we do need some optimism and self-belief if we are to even limit the damage that is currently being done to our multicultural politics and prospects for the future. The twenty-first century is going to be one of unprecedented ethnic and religious mix in the West. In the past multicultural societies have tended to only flourish under imperial rule. If we are to keep alive the prospect of a dynamic, internally differentiated multiculturalism within the context of democratic citizenship, then, going against the grain of radical politics, we must at least see that multiculturalism is not the cause of the present crisis, but part of the solution. Civic multiculturalism is not a full-blown political philosophy or ideology. It is not a substitute for or in competition with political programmes based on, say, human rights or economic redistribution – both of which are crucially important to ethnic equality. It is an elaboration of civic equality in the context of contemporary ethno-religious and other forms of difference. A radical politics that does not accommodate it by engaging with it is dangerously incomplete.

Note

1. I am grateful to Jonathan Pugh for his editorial support. The full argument is presented in my *Multiculturalism: a Civic Idea* (Cambridge: Polity Press, 2007).

References

Bi, F. (2006) ' "Alienation", the London bombs, one year on', *OpenDemocracy*, 3 July, http://www.opendemocracy.net/conflict-terrorism/july7_3706.jsp#six

Channel 4 (2006), http://www.channel4.com/news/microsites/D/dispatches2006/muslim_survey/index.html

Kabbani, R. (1989) *A Letter to Christendom* (London: Virago Press).

Keppel, G. (2005) 'Europe's Answer to Londonistan', *OpenDemocracy*, 23 August, available at http://www.opendemocracy.net/conflict-terrorism/londonistan_2775.jsp

Lewis, D. L. (ed.) (1995) *W. E. B. Du Bois: a Reader* (Canada: Fitzhenry, Whiteside Ltd.).

18
New Left and Old Far Right: Tolerating the Intolerable[1]

Nick Cohen

This chapter criticises what passes for contemporary Left-wing radical-ism. My main concern is as follows. While it is obvious that a radical, psychopathic movement of the far Right is sweeping the world, it is far from obvious that Left-minded and liberal-minded people are prepared to oppose it. A characteristic of the Left, I would argue a defining charac-teristic, is that Left-wingers excuse, turn their eyes from, or on occasion, openly support movements which are against everything they profess to believe in. Before going on to briefly explore why this situation has come about, I'll give you a few examples to illustrate my point.

When Martin Amis returned to Britain from two years living over-seas, he found a liberal-Left wallowing in self-delusion. Asked by the *Independent* what had shocked him most since he got home he replied:

> The most depressing thing was the sight of middle-class white demon-strators waddling around under placards saying, 'We Are All Hezbollah Now'. Well, make the most of being Hezbollah while you can. As its leader famously advised the West: 'We don't want anything from you. We just want to eliminate you.' (Amis, 2007)

Critics could say that Leftists boasting of their conversion to Islamism were a fringe phenomenon, but Amis made it clear that he was talking about the mainstream, not the fringe, when he went on BBC's *Question Time*, the most popular political discussion programme of the day.

> A woman in the audience, her voice quavering with self-righteousness, presented the following argument. Since it was America that supported Osama bin Laden when he was fighting the Russians, the US armed forces, in response to September 11, 'should

be dropping bombs on themselves!' And the audience applauded. It is quite an achievement. People of liberal sympathies, stupefied by relativism, have become the apologists for a credal wave that is racist, misogynist, homophobic, imperialist and genocidal. To put it another way, they are up the arse of those that want them dead. (Amis, 2007)

About the same time that Amis was speaking to the *Independent*, Ken Livingstone, the ex-Mayor of London, invited me to a 'Clash of Civilizations' conference. I refused to go, as I knew the form for this type of Left-wing meeting. The token liberal speaker's sole function is to be ritually denounced by a packed platform and packed audience. However, friends of mine went, and shocked accounts of what they saw are all over the internet. However, it took a French feminist from the secular republican tradition to speak plainly. Agnès Poirier (2007) pulled out because although there were no special facilities for Christians, Hindus and Jews, Livingstone had provided separate prayer rooms for Muslim men and Muslim women. 'Is Ken Livingstone's idea of multiculturalism, one that acknowledges and condones segregation?' she wanted to know (Poirier, 2007).

The conference was indeed packed but in my opinion in an original way. The white Left was in alliance with the Islamist far Right. The attacks on the London Underground were, speakers agreed, 'reprisal events'. To oppose radical Islam was to oppose all Muslims and hence mark oneself as an 'Islamophobe'. This wasn't a one-off but a long-term strategy. For several years now I believe, Livingstone, Left-wing journalists and the leaders of the Stop the War coalition have been pumping up the Muslim Brotherhood and its south Asian sister organisation Jamaat-e-Islami.

Sheikh Yusuf al Qaradawi, the Brotherhood's chief theologian seems to excuse female circumcision, as well as wife beating, so long as the husband does it lightly with his hands, avoiding her face and other sensitive areas (Gay and Lesbian Humanist Association, February 2005). When it comes to gays, he says that

> Muslim jurists hold different opinions concerning the punishment for this abominable practice. Should it be the same as the punishment for fornication, or should both the active and passive participants be put to death? While such punishments may seem cruel, they have been suggested to maintain the purity of the Islamic society and to keep it clean of perverted elements. (Outrage Dossier, no date)

Across the Arab world, liberals have risked their lives by challenging these ideas. Iraqi, Jordanian and Tunisian writers organised a petition to the United Nations by 2,500 Arab intellectuals which condemned 'individuals in the Muslim world who pose as clerics and issue death sentences against those they disagree with. These individuals give Islam a bad name and foster hatred among civilizations' (Hashim et al., 2004; Lakhdar et al., 2005).

If I were to ask you to name the most prominent Left-wing politician in Britain, you would probably name Ken Livingstone. Yet he has welcomed those who oppose feminism and democracy in the Arab world. The Stop the War coalition was no better. One of the largest demonstrations in British history, it was led by Trotskyites who proclaimed themselves to be Left wing, and then formed an alliance with ultra-Right-wing Islamist groups rather than Muslims of liberal background. The protest's chief figure was George Galloway, who during a visit to Iraq in 1994 was reported to have commended the 'courage' of Saddam Hussein (BBC News, 22 April 2003). The Left did not mind that it was being led by a man who had apparently praised a genocidal dictator. Indeed Galloway was elected to Parliament at the last election as the first allegedly far Left-wing MP in 50 years.

The point I want to emphasise, indeed the point I can't emphasise to you strongly enough, is how bizarre and unprecedented our present situation is. If readers of this chapter come from the old Left, they will remember that in the twentieth century we used to have a hierarchy, or at least we pretended we did. At the top was some form of socialism which we argued about continuously and like the kingdom of God never came. Next was what we had here in Britain: namely, liberal democracy with its freedoms and a mixed economy and a welfare state. At the bottom were fascist and ultra-Right wing movements that spouted ethnic or religious totalitarianism usually with large dollops of Adolf Hitler's raging conspiracy theories thrown in.

Not just in Britain, but overwhelmingly and everywhere, liberals and Leftists are far more likely than conservatives to excuse fascistic governments and movements. Not their native far-Right parties. As long as local racists are white, they have no difficulty in opposing them in a manner that would have been recognisable to the traditional Left. But give them a foreign far-Right movement that is anti-Western and they treat it as at best a distraction and at worst an ally. The reverse side of the debased coinage of modern Leftish thinking is a poignant spectacle. Democrats, feminists and socialists in the poor world, who are suffering at the hands of the extreme Right, turn for support to the home of democracy, feminism and socialism in the West, only to find that the democrats, socialists and feminists of the rich world won't help them or acknowledge their existence.

If you think the phenomena I am describing are simply the result of the disastrous Bush administration, I would agree with you up to a point. But they were developing long before Bush came to power and show every sign of continuing after he has gone. In any case, a Left that still had life in it and a European liberal tradition that meant what it said would have had no difficulty in dealing with Bush in an honourable manner. It would have opposed the second Iraq war, deplored the errors and brutalities of the occupation while supporting those Iraqis who fought Al-Qaeda and insisted that they wanted something after 35 years of the genocidal Baathist regime. Support was forthcoming from parts of the old and declining labour movements, but the dominant voices on the liberal-Left in the media, universities and political parties stayed silent as Al-Qaeda slaughtered Iraqis without compunction. 'Internationalism', 'solidarity' and 'fraternity' now feel like dead words from a lost age.

Even the one foreign cause that does inspire the European Left, the Israeli confrontation with the Palestinians, is far less altruistic than it seems. Very few on the Left are prepared to support Fatah, which for all its faults is a recognisable national liberation movement that may build a Palestine worth living in, while deploring Hamas, which wants to impose intolerable burdens on Palestinian women, gays, trade unionists, secularists and Christians. The inability to discriminate between democrat and theocrat is a sign of vacuity. Today's Left cannot tell its friends from its enemies because it has no programme for a better world. Blaming its decadence on Bush is as foolish as holding America responsible for every conflict in the world. Deeper historical trends explain the crisis of our times, which as promised in the introduction to this chapter, I will now explore.

The rise of consumer politics

In the 1960s, those who longed for a radical transformation of the status quo, as many people do at some time in their lives, could draw comfort from revolutionary Leftish movements that were sweeping the world from Cambodia to Chile, as well as the strength of the student radicals in their own countries. History was on their side. Millions were moved by their slogans. Since the fall of socialism, revolutionary Leftism has died everywhere except in Latin America, and even there it is sickly and shallow. The main threat to the status quo comes from radical Islam and the corrupt nationalisms of China and Russia. Far Leftists are open in their support for jihadis. The apologias from some liberals are so comprehensive that they must also support radical Islam in their hearts. At some level, these people understand that they have nowhere else to go now that the revolutionary guerrillas and communist regimes of the twentieth century are history. A love of violence and hatred of their own societies – well merited or otherwise – leads them to conclude that any killer of Americans is better than none.

Noam Chomsky in his political writings, the cultural theorising of Michel Foucault and the postmodernists anticipated the twenty-first century Left ideology. Read them and you find a Leftism without a practical political programme has taken the place of socialism and anti-fascism. All they have is a criticism of the existing order. In this mental universe, no movement that challenges the existing order can be unambiguously condemned. Say what you like about them, but a communist or social democrat in the 1940s had clear ideas about how to transform society. Today, there is no radical alternative that serious people believe they can use, just practical ways of adapting to changes in the economy and environment.

A paradoxical consequence of the death of the socialist idea is that Leftism now suits the consumer society very well. Because there is no coherent Left-wing political programme, anyone can affect a Leftish posture, just as anyone can walk into a shop. For example, if I were a socialist, you might agree with a proposal I was making on a cause you endorsed. Maybe I would say that we should do more to improve the treatment of animals on factory farms or increase our aid budget. But because I believed in socialism I would have to add that I also wanted the nationalisation of the commanding heights of the economy, penal taxation, and workers' control. If not you, then other readers might back away saying that after hearing my programme they could not possibly define themselves as Left wing. Modern Leftists do not have to risk alienating potential sympathisers with proposals that might make them uncomfortable. They rarely have proposals for a new ordering of society. They are merely against the West in general or America in particular, both of which, God knows, provide reasons aplenty for opposition. If someone points out that as Leftists they have a duty to fight crimes committed by ultra-reactionary movements, the new Left ideology instructs them to say that it is 'hypocritical' for Westerners to criticise when they carry so much guilt. The correct course is to do and say nothing.

The collapse of socialism also explains the general inability of Leftists in Europe and North America to work on behalf of feminists, democrats and Leftists in the poor world. If you do not have a positive programme yourself, how can you see strangers as comrades who have the right to your support? These perfidies may be scandalous but they chime with the psychology of modern consumerism. Shoppers don't like altruistic commitments. They have no appetite for boring meetings to raise public consciousness and the lobbying of politicians to change policy.

When I go into the homes of the richest people I know, I see Naomi Klein and Michael Moore on their shelves and think, 'Why am I surprised? The Left is no threat to the wealthy any longer. Being a Leftist is a lifestyle choice. It carries no costs and no obligations.'

Liberal disillusion

So far I have been talking about the consequences of defeat. But the second half of the twentieth century also saw enormous triumphs. European Left-wing movements gave the masses better housing, full-time education, employment rights and comprehensive health cover. But the triumph had the unexpected consequence of turning the liberal intelligentsia against the white working class. The workers let down the intellectuals. They did not lead the charge towards a socialist society as the intelligentsia told them to. On occasion, they voted in large numbers for politicians the middle-class Left despised – Reagan, Thatcher, Bush and Sarkozy. And all too clearly in the cities of Europe and North America, the utopian plans of the twentieth-century social reformers did not always create a better society but welfare dependency, family breakdown and crime.

You can see the disappointment of the middle class in the attempts to prevent democratic votes and deny freedom of speech. The centralisation of decision-making in the undemocratic bodies of the European Union, the fondness for asking unelected judges to take political decisions and politically correct speech codes all flow from a belief that the working class cannot be trusted to think as the middle classes would like it to think.

Beyond a fear that they cannot win majorities in open elections, the liberal middle class across the developed world feels a deeper unease. History no longer seems to be going its way. Market economies undermine the status and comparative wealth of the public sector managers who dominated modern states at the high tide of social democracy in the mid-twentieth century. Financiers and industrialists have acquired fantastic wealth and political status, while the liberal middle classes lingered in jobs their rulers despised for their failure to be market-orientated. Modern democracy is a system that no longer pleases them. They are less likely than they once would have been to oppose clerical fascist movements and stand up for the best values of their societies.

Multiculturalism and its discontents

Our Left-wing radical of the past would be as astonished by the triumph of human rights as by the growth of the welfare state. Women, homosexuals and blacks – groups which had been discriminated against for millennia – have won full legal equality. A measure of the transformation is that it is now impossible for a conservative politician who is against equal rights for homosexuals to become the leader of a mainstream European centre-Right party, let alone go on to win an election.

Again, there is an ambiguity, however. Although the extraordinary success of campaigns against sexism, racism and homophobia vastly improved the lives of millions of individuals, postmodern liberals did not see them as individuals but as categories. They developed an identity politics based on group definitions that was anti-individualist in its assumptions. They treated women, members of ethnic minorities, gays and others as blocs with communal interests. Their simplifications weren't always pernicious – a campaign to tighten the law on domestic violence, for example, is a campaign for women, not this or that woman. But postmodern multiculturalists have taken the liberal idea of tolerance and pushed it into an extreme relativism which holds that it is wrong for liberals to attack previously disadvantaged groups – 'the other' – even when 'the other' espoused ideas which were anti-liberal.

In short, it has become racist to oppose sexists, homophobes and fascists from other cultures. Such attitudes are a disaster for progressive forces in the poor world, most notably in the Arab world and Europe's immigrant communities. We are now in the extraordinary position where liberals consider it 'Left wing' to argue that the emancipation of women is good for white-skinned women in London but not for brown-skinned women in Tehran. Postmodern multiculturalists have picked up the reactionary anti-universalist philosophies of the counter-Enlightenment and dressed them in modern clothes.

Fear

From the 9/11 atrocities on, the stupidest citizens of the Western democracies could be in no doubt that forces were swirling around the globe that would murder them on a vast scale. This is a short and simple point to make, but we are frightened and think it is better to say nothing about the treatment of women, the attacks on freedom of speech, the psychopathic ideologies, medieval hatreds and raging conspiracy theories in case we provoke the killers. Fear is the most powerful of human motives.

Add in the despairing and reactionary turn modern Leftish thinking took after the collapse of socialism, the tolerance of the intolerable inculcated by postmodernism and the doubts about democracy in the liberal mainstream, and I hope you can see why so many can't oppose totalitarian movements of the far Right or even call them by their real names.

However understandable the denial, it remains as pitiful a response to Islamism as climate change denial is to global warming. Both sets of deniers believe that we can carry on as before living our safe, consumerist lives as if nothing has changed.

We cannot in either case, and must face the threats of our time. Reasonable men and women can disagree about how we face them, but we will not be able to see them plainly until we have cleared away the mountains of junk that block our view. The twenty-first century will not have a Left that is worth having until we do.

Note

1. This chapter is an edited version of my 2007 Isaiah Berlin Memorial Lecture.

References

Amis, M. (2007) *The Independent*, 15 January, http://www.independent.co.uk/news/people/martin-amis-you-ask-the-questions-432146.html

BBC News (22 April 2003) 'Profile of George Galloway', http://news.bbc.co.uk/1/hi/uk_politics/2966199.stm (accessed 27 July 2009).

Gay and Lesbian Humanist Association (February 2005) 'Response to the Mayor of London's Dossier concerning Sheikh Yusuf Al-Qaradawi', http://www.galha.org/briefing/qaradawi.html (accessed 28 July 2009).

Hashim, J., S. Al-Nabulsi and L. Lakhder (no date) 'Open Letter from liberal Arabs and Muslims: request to the United National Security Council and the United Nations Secretary General for the Establishment of an International Tribunal for the Prosecution of Terrorists', http://iraqthemodel.blogspot.com/liberal%5B1%5D%5B1%5D.arabs03.edited.pdf

Lakhdar, L., S. Al-Nabulsi and J. Hashim (2005) 'Arab Liberals: Prosecute Clerics who Promote Murder', *The Middle East Quarterly*, 12(1) (Winter), http://www.meforum.org/700/arab-liberals-prosecute-clerics-who-promote-murder#_ftn3 (accessed 28 July 2009).

Outrage Dossier: Livingstone exposed over Al-Qaradawi, http://www.indymedia.org.uk/en/regions/world/2005/02/305315.html

Poirier, A. (2007) 'A Clash of Hidden Agendas', *The Guardian*, 24 January, http://www.guardian.co.uk/commentisfree/2007/jan/24/post968

19
Clashing the Civilisations

Amir Saeed and David Bates

This chapter will examine how British Muslims have responded to being subjected to suspicion and scrutiny as part of an ideological offensive which must be seen in the context of the broader politics of globalisation, and in particular the government's 'war on terror'. The question of British Muslims being 'radicalised' is one which has preoccupied politicians and commentators all the more since '9/11' and '7/7'. But we will argue here that while many British Muslims have indeed decided to embrace radical politics, the vast majority of these Muslims, contrary to popular belief, reject the use of indiscriminate violence to achieve political ends. Nevertheless we argue that to be seen as 'Muslim' in Britain in 2007 is to be seen as 'radical' and also therefore to be seen as 'violent', 'fundamentalist' and 'anti-Western'.

Diversity, race, ethnicity and culture

In the most recent census of the British population, the number of Muslims living in Britain was found to have grown from 21,000 in 1951 to 1.6 million in 2001 (Peach, 2006). In an analysis of the census results, Ceri Peach commented that the enquiry into people's religion on the 2001 census form seemed to have been driven by the question: 'How many Muslims?' The focus, Peach observed, was on religion as cultural background more than actual religiosity, and this in itself as a reflection of the times, with religion playing an increasing role in how 'ethnic minorities' were perceived by the majority. According to Peach (2006: 631): 'The events of 11 September, 2001 in the United States, the Iraq war of 2003, the Madrid bombs of 11 March 2004, the London bombings of 7 July 2005, the riots in the banlieus of Paris in January 2006 and the continuing Middle East crises, magnified an already focused attention on the Muslim population of Britain' (also see Saeed, 2004).

Contemporary racism is manifested in many ways. Its agency is premised on a number of false assumptions about 'race', and on grouping people into simple homogeneous groupings. Even now racism can still resemble the biological arguments employed to justify slavery and imperialism.

> All Muslims, like all dogs, share certain characteristics. A dog is not the same animal as a cat just because both species are comprised of different breeds. An extreme Christian believes that the Garden of Eden really existed; an extreme Muslim flies planes into buildings – there's a big difference. (Cummins, 2004)

Simultaneously, cultural racism is evident with politicians questioning the success of a multicultural society. The moral panic surrounding the events of 9/11 and 7/7 have led to a Right-wing led debate under the guise of community cohesion that has suggested a return to 'core national values/culture' (note that the debates suggest the lack of precise meanings for these terms, 'national' and 'culture') alongside stricter immigration and policing controls. Recently a new dominant neo-Right-wing discourse has been formulated that questions the whole concept of multiculturalism. In summary it seems that Right-wing commentators fear the concept of multiculturalism because it implies an erosion of core, national values in favour of diverse cultures, whilst more liberal commentators appear to suggest that the concept actually creates divisions in society by emphasising difference rather than stress the common ground. What makes this different from previous Right-wing criticism of multiculturalism is that much of this criticism is coming from previously centre-Left commentators. Much of this language has taken even the more sinister view of questioning the need of immigration, questioning minority communities and questioning the actual benefits of a multicultural society.

These reactionary and conservative arguments fail to adequately examine social, political and even cultural reasons for contemporary events. Thus deep ideological and institutional factors such as British/Western foreign policy, poverty, 'white flight' or anti-Muslim racism are marginalised or glossed over. Furthermore, a lot of the 'blame' for the failure of multiculturalism has been attached to Islam's incompatibility with living within the 'democratic' principles of the West.

Islam and the war on terror: a clash of civilisations?

In the aftermath of the terrorist attacks in the USA on 11 September 2001, a long-standing preoccupation with the problem of Islam resurfaced in much Western culture. Drawing upon Samuel Huntington's (1993) theory of a 'clash of civilisations' was the idea that Islam posed a threat to the enlightened Western way of life, its culture and its values. In the days, weeks, months and years after 9/11 this anti-Islamic discourse acquired new efficacy particularly among politicians, journalists and commentators in the USA and the UK.

Huntington's thesis, which first appeared in 1993 under the title *Clash of Civilizations?*, became an instant bestseller post-9/11 (albeit in full-length book form and minus the question mark). It could be argued that the mainstream media in the West have adopted Huntington's argument into the classical Orientalist framework of 'Us and Them'. In the conclusion to Huntington's (1993: 49) original article the author stressed the importance of identifying 'elements of commonality between Western and other civilizations' and made clear his view that 'for the relevant future there will be no universal civilization, but instead a world of different civilizations, each of which will have to learn to coexist with others'. Nevertheless the danger inherent in Huntington's tendency to divide the world into 'the West and the rest' was perhaps more evident in the foreboding conclusion to his book *The Clash of Civilizations and the Remaking of World Order* (Huntington, 1996):

> The underlying problem for the West is not Islamic fundamentalism. It is Islam, a different civilization whose people are convinced of the superiority of their culture and are obsessed with the inferiority of their power. (Huntington, 1996, cited in Sardar and Davies, 2002: 49)

The 'clash of civilisations' discourse was to become a key ideological component of the explanatory framework established to justify the war on terrorism launched by the Bush administration in September 2001. For example, sixty prominent academics, led by Huntington, Theda Skocpol, Michael Walzer, Francis Fukuyama and Amitai Etzioni, have signed a ten-page petition endorsing the war on terrorism on the grounds that it defended 'American values', 'our way of life', and the 'achievements of civilization'.

Likewise in the UK the then prime minister Tony Blair (reported in *The Guardian*, 2006) implored British Muslims to take collective responsibility and accept British values.

When it comes to our essential values – belief in democracy, the rule of law, tolerance, equal treatment for all, respect for this country and its shared heritage – then that is where we come together, it is what we hold in common. It is what gives us the right to call ourselves British.

In 2006 Blair told a House of Commons committee that it was the responsibility of Muslims to 'root out' extremism in their communities, and in doing so criticised those who held that British and American foreign policy was a factor in generating terrorism.

If we want to defeat the extremism, we have got to defeat its ideas and we have got to address the completely false sense of grievance against the West . . . We can only defeat it if we have people in the community who are going to stand up and not merely say 'you are wrong to kill people through terrorism . . . you're wrong in your view of the West', the whole sense of grievance, the ideology is wrong, is profoundly wrong. (British Broadcasting Corporation News, 2006a)

Earlier that year, Home Secretary John Reid (British Broadcasting Corporation, 2006b) used a speech in the East End of London to make an appeal to Muslim parents to look out for tell-tale signs of radicalisation and extremism in their children. Likewise, in January 2008, Conservative Party leader David Cameron (2008) commented that for him that year's World Economic Forum at Davos had been mostly about 'the issue of how we in the west stop and reverse the process of the radicalisation of Muslim youth'.

Furthermore a recent number of Right-wing think tanks associated with the Conservative Party have produced reports that suggest Muslim civil liberties must be restricted in order to combat terrorism. What is more worrying is that these reports also question mainstream Muslim organisations such as the Muslim Association of Britain who have attempted to express Muslim concerns. This questioning seems to associate even moderate Muslims with extremist views.

It is in this context of the war on terror – which saw the USA and the UK invade and occupy Afghanistan and then Iraq, continually support Israel, and detain (often without trial) Muslims suspected of terrorism-related offences either at home or in Guantanamo Bay – that has come to be seen by some Muslims as a war on Islam. Clearly such policies had a disproportionate effect on Islamic people across the world and were accompanied by an upsurge in anti-Muslim rhetoric in Britain and elsewhere.

'The enemy within'

In an echo of Huntington's 'clash of civilisations' discourse which dominated in the USA, Pakistani and Bangladeshi communities in the UK – often lumped together and described simply as 'Muslim' – have been represented as separatist, insular and unwilling to integrate into mainstream society, with whom they are said to be at odds due to a clash of cultures. Muslims have been singled out as the culturally distinct minority whose difference is constructed as a threat to national cohesion and security. Muslims have effectively been told not only that they must make a special effort to integrate, but also that they must assume collective responsibility for the terrorist actions carried out in the UK and elsewhere in the name of the Islamic faith.

However much they seek to identify themselves as British, young Muslims regularly find that others assume them to be first and foremost Muslim. In Britain today, especially after the events of 9/11 and the beginning of the 'war on terror', it is now Muslims who have been identified as a group of potentially 'false nationals' and systematically constructed as the other. A discourse has been produced that directly links British Muslims with support for terrorism, fundamentalism, illegal immigration and an Oriental stereotype of the East. British Muslims are repeatedly implored by voices in the media and by politicians of all sides to make more strenuous efforts to integrate into British society, and reassert their loyalty to the British state in a manner that no non-Muslim anti-war group would ever be instructed. In short, demands for integration seem to be associated with 'be quiet and behave'. However, it could be argued that as well as this 'racist' discrimination, the history of Muslims also bears witness to class oppression. As a whole, Muslims are one of the poorest sections of British society. One in seven job-seeking Muslims is unemployed, compared with one in twenty for the wider population. The two biggest Muslim communities in Britain, those originating in Pakistan and Bangladesh, are particularly impoverished.

British Muslims and radical politics

There exists in Britain a long and proud history of radical working-class struggle by Muslims and other non-white minorities. Much of this struggle has reflected wider political issues. For example, in the 1970s and 1980s Muslim identity was subsumed within the wider 'Black' struggle against racism and fascism. In short, religious identity was second to 'racial' identity. This 'racial' identity was then accompanied within a broader 'Black and White Unite and Fight' class-consciousness. The 1990s and the emergence of identity politics alongside the development of 'cultural racism', increasingly saw Muslim communities asserting their religious distinctiveness. This distinctiveness has been further highlighted with the 'war on terror'.

Despite the negative connotations attributed to Muslims' 'radicalism', a survey of British Muslims undertaken by the 1990 Trust (a UK national Black organisation set up to articulate the interests and influence policy-making on the behalf of Britain's Black communities) in 2006, found that whilst 82 per cent of its respondents thought that Muslims were becoming more radicalised, a majority (65.2 per cent) crucially did not associate radicalism with violence. Instead radicalism was primarily associated more with activities such as letter writing, demonstrations, becoming involved in organisations or disengaging with mainstream politics (1990 Trust, 2006). Ironically, when Muslims do try to participate within society they have been treated with suspicion both by the Left and 'liberal' elements of society.

In the aftermath of the anti-war demonstrations in 2003, sections of the Marxist Left in Britain (led by the Socialist Workers Party) launched 'RESPECT – The Unity Coalition', an electoral front supported by the Muslim Association of Britain. Although this prompted criticism from many on the radical Left, who saw the coalition as opportunistic, 'communalist' and overly influenced by conservative community leaders, it nevertheless succeeded in attracting a layer of Muslims into Left-wing community activism.

RESPECT's recent modest electoral success has been met with the criticism that it is a 'Muslim' party. Yet in the areas where RESPECT gained seats (East London), the demographics would suggest that even if every Muslim in these wards voted for RESPECT, they would not win. In short, non-Muslims were attracted to the Left-wing manifesto that offered an alternative to Labour. However, for many, including Muslim members of the Labour Party, the class element was diluted from the politics. Indeed some elements on the Left even argued that RESPECT was a Muslim party that did not address the needs of the other sections of the working class. Likewise, the mainstream media assumed RESPECT was a Muslim party and represented it as such. In short, Muslim willingness to participate in democratic politics was viewed with suspicion and debate rather than just simply being welcomed.

In spite of the political and cultural onslaught, more and more Muslims are attempting to engage with radical politics. British Muslims have affirmed their political vibrancy and diversity in a number of other ways. Thousands of British Muslims took part in the million-strong multicultural demonstration against the Iraq War in London in February 2003. As anti-war campaigner Shahed Saleem (2004) comments: 'It is one more step to expand this common protest against a neo-imperial war to a common ideological understanding of the mechanisms of global capitalism and its associated war machine, but it may be possible.' This point was reaffirmed by Adam Riaz Kha (2007), writing in *The Chartist*: 'If a Muslim and a Marxist can agree that we must get rid of a system which breeds the divisions of racism, nationalism, patriarchy and exploitation, then the anti-war and indeed the anti-capitalist struggle is clearly one struggle.' Birmingham councillor Salma Yaqoob (2007) recently wrote of British Muslims' appetite for:

> The ideas of universal healthcare; a living wage; participatory democracy; public services that are accountable to the people who use them; food, medicine and shelter as a human right; these are not particularly radical ideas. They are common sense ideas enshrined in the UN Charter. Add to that list a foreign policy that places a premium on diplomacy, and international cooperation, plus more decisive action on climate change, and there is the basis of a manifesto a sizeable slice of the British public would sign up to. Why are these ideas so radical today? At one stage most would have been regarded as the bread and butter of social democracy. They appear radical now only because of the way neo-liberalism has shifted political discourse to the right over the last 20 years. All the while the gap between what the politicians do, and what people want, has widened.

Conclusion: the similarities between Muslims and the traditional Left

Radical British Muslim politics today does not have to mean a politics dominated by religion but may use Islamic faith as a basis to challenge all inequality. From a personal perspective one of the authors of this article has previously noted

> Rather than seeing Islam just as a religion, a closer examination of the Koran showed me that it also offered a political ideology that could provide a framework for understanding contemporary capitalist society. For me capitalism, in simple terms, puts 'profit before people'. Whilst mainstream popular culture and public opinion seem

to decry the inhumane nature of Islam following 9/11, the following passage from the Koran seemed highly relevant: 'Whoever slays a soul . . . it is as though he slew all mankind, and whoever keeps it alive is as though he kept alive all mankind' (Al Quran 5:35). In Islam it is clear that life is to be respected and the right to life is to be accorded to all beings. Unfortunately those who appear to be strongest critics of Islam seem to have the weakest knowledge of it. (Saeed, 2004: 58)

Muslims need to realise the West's foreign policy is linked to domestic policy on issues such as housing, education and welfare. Muslims need to recognise that oppression does not begin with imperialist foreign policy but with domestic welfare cuts that target the most vulnerable in society, Muslim or non-Muslim. In short, Islamic fundamentalism that divides the working classes is not the greatest threat but market fundamentalism that promotes racism both abroad and at home. The challenge here is to engage with Muslims and non-Muslims and offer an alternative to free market capitalism. This is where the heart of true integration and participatory democracy lies. One of the authors of this chapter is a secular Marxist, whilst the other is a Muslim. In writing it, both have a common dialogue based on mutual respect and willingness to confront the inequality in the New World Order.

References

British Broadcasting Corporation News Online (2006a) 'Muslims Must Root Out Extremism', http://news.bbc.co.uk/1/hi/uk_politics/5144438.stm

British Broadcasting Corporation News Online (2006b) 'Reid Heckled during Muslim Speech', http://news.bbc.co.uk/1/hi/uk/5362052.stm

Cameron, D. (2008) 'Davos 08: Tackling Radical Islam is My Priority', http://www.guardian.co.uk/commentisfree/2008/jan/25/theworldeconomicforumat

Cummins, W. (2004) 'Muslims are a Threat to Our Way of Life', http://www.telegraph.co.uk/opinion/main.jhtml?xml=/opinion/2004/07/25/do2504.xml

The Guardian (2006) 'Radical Muslims Must Integrate, Says Blair', http://www.guardian.co.uk/uk/2006/dec/09/religion.immigrationandpublicservices

Huntington, S. P. (1993) 'The Clash of Civilizations?', *Foreign Affairs*, 72(3): 22–49.

Huntington, S. P. (1996) *The Clash of Civilizations and the Remaking of World Order* (New York: Simon & Schuster).

1990 Trust (2006) Faith-related documents, http://police.homeoffice.gov.uk/publications/equality-diversity/faith/?view=Standard&pubID=581918

Peach, C. (2006) 'Muslims in the 2001 Census of England and Wales: Gender and Economic Disadvantage', *Ethnic and Racial Studies*, 29(4): 629–55.

Riaz Kha, A. (2007) 'Atheists, Anarchists and Muslims Unite', http://www.chartist.org.uk/articles/britpol/may03riazkahn.htm

Saeed, A. (2004) '9/11 and the Consequences for British-Muslims', in J. Carter and D. Morland (eds), *Anti-Capitalist Britain* (London: New Clarion Press).

Saleem, S. (2004) 'Capitalism, Socialism and Islam Meeting', http://www.workersliberty.org/node/2004

Sardar, Z. and M. W. Davies (2002) *Why Do People Hate America?* (Oxford: Icon Books).

Yaqoob, S. (2007) 'Practising What We Preach', *Red Pepper*, http://www.redpepper.org.uk/article1051.html

20
Radicalism is Nostalgia

Alastair Bonnett

> Survivors of the twentieth century, we are all nostalgic for a time
> when we were not nostalgic. But there seems to be no way back.
>
> (Boym, 2001: 355)

We used to hate nostalgia. The sentimentalism, the conservatism, the
sheer vulgarity of it were beneath contempt. In 1962 Eric Hobsbawm
brusquely observed that ideologies that offer 'resistance to progress
hardly deserve the name of systems of thought' (Hobsbawm, 1962: 290).
But something has changed. Nostalgia is getting noisy. Today's socialist
movement is shot through with fond yearning for a time when Left-wing
varieties of radicalism were a real force in Western politics. The taboo on a
sense of loss, on wistful recollection, remains powerful but is crumbling.
To call someone nostalgic remains a wounding insult. Yet the radical Left
is, in so many ways, the politics of the past. To be on the Left is to inhabit
a political landscape where all the familiar faces and all the significant
events are of yesteryear.

So, goodbye radicalism? Perhaps not. My argument is not that radicalism is finished but that it's time to rethink the relationship between
radicalism and nostalgia. Confronting and engaging nostalgia is a useful
corrective for radicals who have forgotten something rather important.
It is simply this: that radicalism needs nostalgia. In an era of massive and enforced social change resistance becomes wedded to memory.
When landscapes and communities are blasted, over and again, into
ever smaller units of disconnected consumer atoms, then a sense of
loss becomes an inevitable and necessary resource. Early radicalism in
England was based on this understanding. Unfortunately, by the dawn
of the last century it had been forgotten. The ideological modernism

179

of twentieth-century socialism and communism turned the past into an arena of shame and guilt. But the grip on radicalism of the last century's muscular red heroes is now palsied. The secret that all those forward-facing, flint-featured comrades worked so hard to repress is now out and open: radicalism is a response to loss. This is a hard fact to acknowledge. Nowhere harder than in the politics of multiculturalism; a politics which some on the Left have used to recast and refetishise anti-nostalgic modernism. The unconvincing nature of this latest attempt to repress loss forms the focus of the latter half of my essay.

Nostalgia's revenge

Today the identification of the past with political conservatism is not as easy as it once was. Nevertheless, there are still plenty of voices on the Left who seem to see their project as akin to a rocket blasting into the future or as an act of violence inflicted on the dead. The durability of these dramatic poses is remarkable, not least in the wake of the widespread incredulity that they now inspire. In his wide-ranging attack of the Left's festishisation of the idea of progress, *The True and Only Heaven*, Christopher Lasch (1991) identified the psychological cost of maintaining a revulsion towards attachments to the past for those whose continued existence is cast by the wider world as an anachronism. It is the 'belief in progress', Lasch (1991: 36) tells us, that explains 'the Left's curious mixture of complacency and paranoia':

> Their confidence in being on the winning side of history made progressive people unbearably smug and superior, but they felt isolated and beleaguered in their own country, since it was so much less progressive than they were.

The 'pretence of standing out against the prevailing intellectual fashion of sentimental regret' is, for Lasch (1991: 57), a Left 'trademark', marked by a 'tone of bluff and jocular dismissal'. Lasch takes a cruel delight in vivisecting Leftist hopes to be the party of the future. But his eye for the postures that accompany this claim is savagely accurate.

Nostalgia is gaining its revenge on those who would let the dead bury the dead. Within orthodox communist factions, a Marxist nostalgia both of itself and for itself has become prominent. This perception also arises from the fact that even those activists who are still very much with us are today often cast as representatives of lost worlds of political militancy. As socialism has turned into an act of remembrance it has become easier to see the strains that have accompanied the repression of nostalgia in earlier decades. David Lowenthal's (1989) cheeky intervention in the History Workshop conference in 1985 was an early sign of the changing mood. In his counter-orthodox chapter in *The Imagined Past*, the edited volume which emerged out of these sessions, Lowenthal (1989: 20) offers a lurid portrait of the mood of gleeful nostalgia bashing: 'Diatribe upon diatribe denounced [nostalgia] as reactionary, regressive, ridiculous.' Lowenthal cannot resist turning the tables on these assumptions. If the Left wants to find a culture of nostalgia, he implies, it should look in the mirror. Indeed, he points out that the idea of a 'History Workshop' is itself laden with nostalgia: an attempt at 'validating our endeavour by linking it with olden horney-handed toil' (Lowenthal, 1989: 28).

Another provocation came with *The Revolt Against Change: Towards a Conserving Radicalism* by Blackwell and Seabrook (1993: 3–4). They drew on their long experience with the new Left, to develop a manifesto for a different kind of relationship between radicalism and the past:

> we were becoming uneasy about the recurring theme that 'people must change' . . . The experience of industrialisation had been of driven and relentless change, and continues to be so . . . So why should we expect exhortations to change will be welcomed by those who have known little else for at least two centuries? In this context, the desire to conserve, to protect, to safeguard, to rescue, to resist becomes the heart of a radical project.

Perhaps the most strikingly novel aspect of the new wave of writing about nostalgia lies in the attempt to depict the role of nostalgia amongst communities who have long remained marginal to radical representations of those who are to give voice to the poetry of the future. The Native American story-tellers discussed by the anthropologist Jenifer Ladino (2005) articulate a sense of loss and remembrance that reflects their experience of modernity as a racialised condition which has shown little interest in *their future*.

However, the insistence that nostalgia is to be taken seriously only when it can be presented as a useful political tool, a disposable weapon of resistance, fails to fully meet the challenge posed by this chronic response to the modern condition. The instrumental deployment of oppositional pasts demands that these pasts be reduced to mere cogs in the engine of progress. The currently fashionable notions of counter-nostalgia and counter-memory, although important in provoking new attention to the topic, do not necessarily represent a clean break with automatic suspicion of attachments to the past. And why do we need to break from such suspicion? Because nostalgia is not a choice; not something we can opt in and out of. It is an inescapable part of the radical project. To flee it is to run towards it.

No hiding from loss: the melancholia of multiculturalism

We are familiar with the heroics of cosmopolitanism. Intellectuals have long cast themselves as citizens of the world city. The post-national political claim that follows is also familiar. Thomas Paine framed it thus: 'my country is the world, my religion is to do good to mankind' (cited in Lasch, 1991: 123).

Over the past forty years or so these beneficent aspirations have been democratised into a radical vision of ordinary multiculturalism; of the cosmopolitan, multiracial city as an arena of resistance and creativity. The diverse metropolis has become a political talisman and, in a post-communist era, a landscape of solace for the Left.

The turn towards inclusivity is certainly welcome. Less so the perpetuation of a hostility towards issues of loss and nostalgia. For in this new metrocentric multiverse, nostalgia is routinely reduced to a racist grunt, an ugly noise made by place-bound primitives. But it has also become an awkward and disruptive presence, a discordant sigh of regret; an embarrassing lapse in the up-beat sound track for a tirelessly celebratory urban radicalism. We can look at this process in more detail with the help of an example: Paul Gilroy's (2004) resolutely anti-nostalgic *After Empire: Melancholia or Convivial Culture?* With reference to this book we can show how, even amongst those who profess to despise it, nostalgia creeps in and makes its presence known.

In *After Empire* Paul Gilroy diagnoses British culture as afflicted with yearning. In Gilroy's Britain loss has metastasised and requires urgent treatment. His remedy is convivial culture; a 'radical openness'; a way of being that 'makes a nonsense of closed, fixed, and reified identity' (Gilroy, 2004: xi). The conviviality Gilroy offers in opposition to melancholia is defined as 'the processes of cohabitation and interaction that have made multiculture an ordinary feature of social life in Britain's urban areas' (Gilroy, 2004: xi). Gilroy sets convivial culture against the 'anxious, fearful, or violent' culture of a Britain awash with 'multiple anxieties' (Gilroy, 2004: 13). The former is cast as insurgent and full of a youthful, rascally charm. The latter is understood to be dominant but aged, decrepit, contemptible. It generates the 'guilt-ridden loathing and depression that have come to characterise Britain's xenophobic responses to the strangers who have intruded upon it' (Gilroy, 2004: 98).

How could anyone object to conviviality? Yet it is the *ingratiating* nature of the concept that first provoked my unease with *After Empire*. Gilroy ties it to another equally unobjectionable project he calls planetary humanism. The very agreeability of these ideas seems designed to construct nostalgia as misanthropic and monstrous.

Gilroy's critical focus is on emotional attachments to empire and memories of World War Two. The following passage is also illustrative of the tone of jocular dismissal he favours:

> For about three decades, the brash motto of true-Brit sporting nationalism was supplied by the curious boast: 'Two world wars and one World Cup, doo dah, doo dah'. Future historians will doubtless puzzle over this odd phrase, which, as it echoed around many British sports venues, became an ugly chant. (Gilroy, 2004: 117)

Gilroy's (2004: 131) future historians will no doubt contrast this sorry scene with the 'convivial metropolitan cultures of the country's young people'. They might, however, have a hard time finding much evidence. For Gilroy's emergent Britain is represented by a creaking line-up of popular youth and media culture. It is through the comedy character Ali G, the BBC television comedy *The Office* and the pop band The Streets that we learn about conviviality. What Gilroy is looking for in this kind of material are intimations of a street level and anti-authoritarian scrabbling of fixed images of racial and national identity.

White or black young men are Gilroy's vehicle of change and the site of nearly all his depictions of conviviality. One of the striking ironies of the book arises from Gilroy's minimal concession to the fracturing of notions of blackness, or the rise of religion as an axis of conflict. A one-sentence depiction of those 'young black Europeans' who are 'willing to hitch their hopes for a just world to the absurd engine of an Islamic revolution' (Gilroy, 2004: 144) suffices to despatch the ambitions of Islamism. Gilroy shows even less interest in Britons of Asian, Chinese, Arab, Scottish, Welsh, Irish or of continental European origin. Whilst Gilroy's (2004: 23) vision of the 'warring totalities of blackness and whiteness' secures blackness as a location of struggle, it undermines the reach and generosity of his own convivial disposition. His attempt to rescue a radical subject clashes with his claims of radical openness, leaving readers with the queasy feeling that Gilroy's political vision is anything but inclusive.

The clichés of youthful resistance, the anachronistic insistence on warring totalities, combine with Gilroy's melodramatic vignettes of the sins of melancholia, to create a pressing sense of nostalgia's unacknowledged presence. The past that looms largest in *After Empire* is not that of the British Empire but of socialism. 'Multiculture' is made to do the work of popular solidarity and resistance; it is fashioned into a vehicle of resistance which both challenges and somehow renews the socialist lineage. In this way cultural mixture is stripped of its diverse political content and history and cast as reflecting, perhaps even fulfilling, all that was ever best in socialism.

The political struggle Gilroy applauds takes place in a world where multiculturalism is politicised. At the same time the deployment of politicised internationalism and cultural syncretism that may be found time and again in the history of state socialism (in Leninism but also in Maoism and Stalinism) is forgotten. Yet whilst the ghosts of world socialism are not acknowledged, readers can feel their presence on every page. This presence sometimes takes the form of a rather tired stereotype of gleeful young transgressors, struggling against a reactionary old order. More explicitly, this presence can also be found in those passages of *After Empire* where Gilroy registers a bleak sense of being overtaken by history. Gilroy repeatedly suggests that his political vision is out of kilter with its time; a lonely fight against an oncoming tide. '[T]his book', he tells us, 'offers an unorthodox defence of [the] twentieth-century utopia of tolerance, peace, and mutual regard' (Gilroy, 2004: 2).

There is a certain pathos in Gilroy's harking back to a simpler time when mutual regard was valued. This Golden Age is painted with the broadest strokes, creating a shimmering but vague spectacle of a time before the 'flight from socialistic principles' (Gilroy, 2004: 135). In those days: 'Neither women nor workers were committed to a country. They turned away from the patriotism of national states because they had found larger loyalties' (Gilroy, 2004: 5).

This hazy Eden is conjured by transforming socialist history into an untarnished quest for transnational fellowship. We are assured that within this twentieth-century utopia 'Socialism and Feminism . . . came into conflict with a merely national focus because they understood political solidarity to require translocal connection' (Gilroy, 2004: 5).

One might hope that socialists at the start of the twenty-first century could admit that the relationship between internationalism and social-ism has been difficult, often tragic. But Gilroy is not concerned with this compromised political landscape. His portrait is a nostalgic one: it uses myths of the past and of a departed fellowship of radicals to critique the present. And who would not feel melancholic for this lost world when confronted with the ghastly orthodoxies of the present?

> The fundamental point is that today, cosmopolitan estrangement and democracy-enriching dissent are not prized as civic assets. They are just routine signs of subversion and degeneration. (Gilroy, 2004: 27)

In today's 'beleaguered multiculture' Gilroy (2004: xi) offers himself as a lost prophet of larger loyalties. Nostalgia is not a minor theme in *After Empire*. The book strains to identify itself with the new and emergent and, by so doing, allows a hostility to nostalgia to shape its political and intellectual structure. At the same time, *After Empire* is tortured by a sense of loss. The past is deployed as a place of certainty, of community and of morality, and used to critique the present. The presence of loss in *After Empire* may be tied to the specific contemporary context in which the book was written, a time when socialists of many different stripes are turning to the past for compensation and inspiration. However, Gilroy's unreflexive antagonism to nostalgia is indicative of the fact that a sense of loss remains a site of anxiety and denial.

Conclusion

For many years William Morris' (1915: 57) exhortation to 'cling to the love of the past and the love of the day to be', has curled many a radical toe. It was an embarrassing relic of the incoherent and immature naïvety of the early movement. Today that judgement appears too hasty: the shame of nostalgia is fading.

It is perhaps fitting that it is radicals at the iconoclastic edges of cul-tural life who are beginning to grapple with the fact that the poetry of the future is no longer enough. In *London Orbital*, Iain Sinclair's (2003) account of his ramble around the M25's noisy margins, we find a jour-ney in and against the contemporary landscape: an act of retrieval of radical histories now by-passed. *London Orbital* is one of the central examples of the nostalgic (and place-obsessed) turn that can be iden-tified in British literary culture from the early 1990s. The ambition is to explore and reimagine the forgotten nooks and crannies of ordinary landscapes: to re-enchant and remythologise prosaic geographies. The resultant effect is disorientating; funny yet melancholic; utterly of our time but ill at ease with modern Britain. Released from the censorious gaze of socialist progressivism, the hesitant openness to the past exhibited by earlier avant-garde engagements is being taken further and into new territory.

In a post-communist era the pursuit of radicalism takes place in a curious atmosphere of freedom and doubt. It is a moment of adventure but also of bewilderment. Both paeans for a lost age and anti-essentialist celebrations of the disintegration of organic community seem equally ill judged. Where else to begin? The nostalgic turn in contemporary culture provides us with clues because of its vulnerability, its urgent search for both home and uncertainty. It encourages us to finally admit that we look to the past with mixed feelings, with yearning as well as disgust. Admitting to a sense of loss provides little comfort but offers a necessary understanding that we are all both in and against our age.

It seems that nostalgia is gaining its revenge on the Left, at least upon those who continue to deny it. The attempt to transform multiculturalism into a new radical dawn creates many an awkward moment. The attempt to politicise 'conviviality' generates new forms of partisanship and exclusion. Transferring its own anxieties outward, Left multiculturalism (at least as presented to us by Gilroy) claims to be battling against a conservative and gloomy politics of loss. Some acts of transference pass unnoticed but not this one. The first years of the twenty-first century saw neo-liberal capitalism at its most triumphal and cosmopolitan. The narcissistic and self-congratulatory global consumer was almost fit to burst with its own sense of success. It was not a great moment to pass off the venerable canard that the dominant society is culturally backward and that the radical Left is all things fresh, funky and forward-looking. Even after the neo-liberal bubble burst the Left still looks anachronistic, a voice from the past. So, can we finally admit it? Radicalism has always been about loss and yearning. Today this close and uncomfortable relationship can no longer be repressed. In order to come to terms with the new century, we must come to terms with our relationship with the past.

References

Blackwell, T. and J. Seabrook (1993) *The Revolt Against Change: Towards a Conserving Radicalism* (London: Vintage).

Boym, S. (2001) *The Future of Nostalgia* (New York: Basic Books).

Gilroy, P. (2004) *After Empire: Melancholia or Convivial Culture?* (London: Routledge).

Hobsbawm, E. (1962) *The Age of Revolution, 1789–1848* (New York: New American Library).

Ladino, J. (2005) 'Rediscovering Nostalgia: the Significance of Counter-nostalgia in American Literature', paper presented to the Nostalgia and Cultural Memory English Graduate Conference, University of Victoria, 4–5 March.

Lasch, C. (1991) *The True and Only Heaven: Progress and its Critics* (New York: W. W. Norton).

Lowenthal, D. (1989) 'Nostalgia Tells it Like it Wasn't', in C. Shaw and M. Chase (eds), *The Imagined Past: History and Nostalgia* (Manchester: Manchester University Press).

Morris, W. (1915) *The Pilgrims of Hope and Chants for Socialists* (London: Longman, Green and Company).

Sinclair, I. (2003) *London Orbital* (London: Penguin).

21
Universal Conditions: Modern Childhood

Ken Worpole

Radical politics has become dominated by the politics of difference, rather than what makes us all the same. Universal conditions – such as childhood – have taken second place to identity politics in recent years. While the struggles of discriminated groups were once predicated on the need to build the good society for all, in many cases such campaigns mutated into claims for separate and unique status. In this politics of competing identities and *ressentiments*, the common good was overlooked. Politicians played one group against the other, and indeed many identity groups came to believe that the marketplace held out the best arena for the fulfilment of their wishes.

As a consequence, radical politics has ignored the lives and interests of children for at least a generation now. This is most certainly so in the UK and wherever else neo-liberal economics holds sway. As economics has prioritised low-tax, market-led solutions to what were once collective forms of social provision, the needs of those without spending power – notably the young, the vulnerable and the elderly – have been marginalised or left to be dealt with by state provision as a last resort.

The credit crunch and the collapse of the banking system have dealt a blow to those dreams. Furthermore, the large demographic changes lying ahead, in which a minority of those of working age will need to support a large non-working population, now means that universal state provision is coming back with a vengeance, though it may take more flexible forms. When the Tory party talks of the need to mend a broken society, then issues of shared values, common provision (the NHS is still lit by a seemingly inextinguishable idealistic political flame), and inter-generational equity and respect, return to the political table. Nowhere does this shift back from economic and cultural relativism to universalism in public provision seem more urgent than in the way we provide and care for children.

Consider this. Britain came bottom of the league table for child well-being across twenty-one industrialised countries, according to a UNICEF report published in 2007 (UNICEF, 2007). One of the report's authors stated in a BBC interview that under-investment in children's facilities and a 'dog-eat-dog' society were to blame for the UK's poor performance (BBC, 2007).

More children between the ages of 10 and 14 are currently being locked up in England and Wales than in any other Western European country. The cost of keeping a young person in a secure children's home was estimated to be £185,000 per annum in 2008, six times the cost of sending a child to Eton. This is the politics of retribution and the economics of despair.

According to a YouGov national survey of 2,000 adults in 2008 commissioned by Barnardo's (2008) 'half of the adult population in Britain is fundamentally prejudiced against the current generation of children and critical of their "animal" behaviour'. Not only are they antagonistic towards children, but they believe children's problems are nobody else's concern but their own. Half of the Barnardo's sample disagreed with the statement that 'children who get into trouble are often misunderstood and in need of professional help'. We appear to be returning to a world of original sin. A separate survey (The Guardian, 2008) found that 43 per cent of UK adults think that 14 is the earliest age for children to be allowed out unsupervised. Furthermore, children in Britain complain more about lack of play facilities than in most other European countries, and the percentage of them who walk or cycle to school is lower than in other parts of Europe, suggesting they may be less healthy too.

That is the glass half empty scenario. The glass half full view is that most children and young people in Britain today are healthier, better educated and have better life opportunities than ever before – and there are plenty of statistics to underpin that perspective equally. Nevertheless, for a significant number of children and young people life is still a dangerous and occasionally even fatal lottery, and the troubled terrain of childhood is one that progressive politics seems to have abandoned. This was not always so.

Until recently most political movements or currents of thought committed to social change, put the life opportunities of children at the head of their political agenda, conjuring up a vision of joyful young people at school and at play as symbols of a better world to come.

That imagery then went missing, as PR and marketing agencies engaged by political parties targeted day-to-day adult concerns – mortgage rates, tax cuts, low inflation, crime reduction – rather than raise longer-term concerns over larger environmental or social issues. Election posters are usually the same wherever you go in the world: photographs of well-fed, grey-haired men promising economic stability and security. Children and young people are rarely seen or heard today in the political imaginary.

As a result we are in danger of losing a generation of young people conscious of belonging to civil society, however loosely or tightly this is defined. Any programme of political reform needs to look at the opportunities provided for children and young people to develop an attachment – no matter how critical or qualified – to an agreed range of public values and institutions, which ultimately provide the overall structure, security and safety-nets to their lives. This is as true of the home as it is of the school or the public realm. The American philosopher and progressive educationalist, John Dewey (1916), once described education as 'the constant reweaving of the social fabric'. There is no reason why such a principle should not coexist with an equal commitment to individual liberty and the nonconformist conscience – in fact one hardly works without the other.

While the market is adept at creating all kinds of goods and services in the name of personal fulfilment or flourishing, it shows less interest in supporting a range of public goods without which a participatory or educated democracy cannot flourish, such as safe streets, parks, playgrounds and public libraries. There are now places in contemporary Britain where a significant number of young people have given up hope of educational or social fulfilment by the age of 10, and are now intent – by omission or commission – on bringing down the neighbourhood around them. Bea Campbell's (1993) exploration of some of Britain's poorest and most socially and geographically isolated neighbourhoods and estates in her book *Goliath* may be over-alarmist, but her descriptions of what has gone wrong are rooted in direct observation and enquiry.

This is not an issue that is marginal to radical politics, even though it may be so socially complex that reformers find it easier to formulate problems elsewhere in the web of public life and culture. There should always be proper concerns about the state intervening too directly into domestic and local social milieu, especially around issues of public morality. Even so, where poverty, crime, personal violence or group intimidation are abroad in the public domain, then there are adequate grounds for revisiting this lost tradition of child-centred public policy.

Historically, images of children as bearers or symbols of a better world to come have occurred at significant moments of social upheaval and demographic change. They can be seen in the *kinderspelen* paintings of the early Dutch school, where children were often portrayed as playing street games against the backdrop of the town hall, suggesting a transition from one world of rule-making (games) into another (civic democracy). Such symbolic proxies were central to the Romantic movement in the work of Wordsworth and Blake, and emerged again in the Victorian campaigns against child labour and in twentieth-century public health campaigns to combat tuberculosis and rickets in Britain's airless slums. The health and well-being of the child – but particularly the child of the slums or of rural penury – was seen as a litmus test for the state of the nation.

In the aftermath of World War Two a belief in the regenerative powers of free play sprang up everywhere across Europe: architect Aldo van Eyck famously created 700 new playgrounds in Amsterdam alone. Adventure playgrounds proliferated in Scandinavia, and in Britain play provision was put at the centre of planning for the new towns. On the bomb-sites, and in the streets and school-playgrounds, anthropologists, writers and photographers found a resonant symbol of the post-war social settlement. Think also of how film-makers used such symbols. In Akira Kurosawa's great film, *Ikiru* (Living, 1952), the life of an ageing bureaucrat is finally given meaning when he devotes himself to bringing about a children's playground in a slum district. By contrast, Luis Bunuel's *Los Olvidados* (The Forgotten Ones, 1950), tragically portrays the hopeless and brutalised life of the slum children in Mexico City, whose only way out of poverty is a violent death.

In recent times films such as *Made in Britain* (UK, 1982), *Boyz in the Hood* (USA, 1991), *La Haine* (France, 1995), *City of God* (Brazil, 2002) and *This is England* (UK, 2007), emphasise how unforgiving life is in the slums, projects and housing estates of cities as different as Paris, Birmingham, Los Angeles, Rio de Janeiro, and elsewhere in the world. While progressive politics is not simply about capturing popular emotions in the endless battle of symbolic signs and meanings, nevertheless the social imaginary is shaped by symbols and metaphors, particularly if and when they have their roots in the achievements of public policy, which they clearly have in the social democracies of northern Europe. The Netherlands, Sweden, Denmark and Finland not surprisingly take the top four places in UNICEF's child well-being survey.

These sympathies for the proper nurturing of childhood have a philosophical basis. Central to the Enlightenment and to the later Romantic movement, in which the ideas of Jean-Jacques Rousseau were dominant, was the notion that each and every child was born with the propensities to achieve happiness and greatness, given the right environmental circumstances and guiding education. This assumption informed the theories of philosophical and educational innovators such as David Hume, John Locke, Froebel, Montessori and John Dewey, as well as poets and novelists such as Coleridge, Goethe, Wordsworth and others. At the beginning of the twentieth century, radicals such as the Macmillan sisters, Bertrand and Dora Russell, Homer Lane, A. S. Neill and Caldwell Cook, charted a course for what came to be known as child-centred education, admired and emulated throughout the world.

Progressive educational thought in Britain – which gave fresh impetus to this new sympathetic attitude towards children – first found organisational form with the setting up of the Fellowship of the New Life in 1883 by the Scottish philosopher Thomas Davidson. Early members included the poet Edward Carpenter, sexologist Havelock Ellis and future Fabian secretary, Edward R. Pease. Although tiny in membership its influence irradiated much early twentieth-century thought, particularly in ideas about education. The New Education Fellowship, founded in 1921, continued the ideals of the earlier movement, and comprised people such as Homer Lane, and many others already mentioned. Its journal, *The New Era in Home and School*, had been the bedside companion of the older women lecturers at the college where I trained to be a teacher in the 1960s. Rarely a sentence passed their lips which did not refer to the work of Caldwell Cook, a teacher at the Perse School in Cambridge, whose book *The Play Way*, published in 1917, became the most influential work of classroom pedagogy for generations.

Central to this child-centred pedagogy was the belief that the child was a sovereign being with innate capacities to grow and develop socially and intellectually, given time, sympathetic educational stimulation and respect. The Hadow Report on primary education in 1931 could not be more graphic in its support for the view that education was about respecting the individuality of the child in every detail. Of the education process it asserted that:

> It will best serve the future by a single-minded devotion to their needs in the present, and the question which most concerns it is not what children should be – a point on which unanimity has hardly, yet, been reached – but what, in actual fact, children are. Its primary aim must be to aid children, while they are children, to be healthy and, so far as is possible, happy children, vigorous in body and lively in mind. (Cited in Darling, 1994: 38)

No mention of SAT tests there. This appreciation of the innocence and inner vitality of the child was not solely a rural concern, as it sometimes seemed in its Wordsworthian idiom. In the 1950s, photographers such as Nigel Henderson in London's East End, Roger Mayne in Notting Hill, Jimmy Forsythe in Newcastle and Bert Hardy and Edith Tudor Hart working for *Picture Post* across Britain, all went to great lengths to capture city children at play – on bombsites, in back alleys and in the empty streets. In 1959 Iona and Peter Opie finally published their peerless anthology of children's street songs, *The Lore and Language of Schoolchildren*, with a cover photograph by Roger Mayne. The Opies had been collecting rhymes and games for more than a decade across the length and breadth of Britain. They observed that whereas city children played more games (perhaps because they didn't have to work when away from school), the rural children knew more proverbs and sustained a wider repertoire of folk beliefs. In Edinburgh, J. T. R. Ritchie published his anthology of Scottish children's games, *The Singing Street*, in 1964. For so long invisible to the world of politics and public policy, the image of children at play suddenly became a symbol of something better, even of national vitality.

Furthermore, this was a realm of public performance and social presence in which young girls played an equal, and at times dominant, role. Dan Jones, the artist and human rights activist who has been collecting children's rhymes for more than forty years now, recently told me that the enthusiasm with which young girls of all races and cultural backgrounds still chant and sing rhymes and play traditional games in school playgrounds remains unabated, even if many of their verses have been given a contemporary pop music or television celebrity twist.

If there is to be a progressive future, then it is surely this tradition which has to be rediscovered and renewed. There are many things which can be done, and since New Labour came to power in 1997, some things have begun. The Sure Start programme which provides additional resources to children and families in deprived areas seems to be making genuine if modest improvements in a significant number of children's lives. The number of children's centres built since New Labour came to power is now around 2,500 (of the 3,500 promised by 2010), and these most certainly add a valued public asset to the otherwise declining repertoire of public buildings in many neighbourhoods. Thus by 2010 every community will have its own Sure Start Children's Centre, and brings back into public policy at least one small element of universal provision.

Participation in organised physical activity in school is once again on the rise after nearly disappearing in some places, with nine out of ten school-children now taking part in at least two hours of physical activity each week, and a welcome rise in inter-school sports events and games. The government is committed to the support of free swimming for everybody under 16 in school and municipal pools across the country, though these are not evenly distributed. There is finally a coherent National Play Strategy which is paying for a new generation of playgrounds across the country which will not simply be metal 'sheep-pens' of the old deadly municipal design, but will emphasise exploration and risk. The government's £235m Fair Play initiative launched in April 2008 aims to improve or build 3,500 play areas by 2011, create 30 new adventure playgrounds and train 4,000 play-workers to agreed levels. This is on top of the £155m Big Lottery Fund Children's Play Initiative, which was launched in 2006. These figures are for England only. There will also be a new national indicator to measure children's satisfaction with local play opportunities.

Such have been government fears around the issue of child-obesity, resulting from a lack of physical activity as well as parental fears of letting children play outdoors unsupervised, that schools are now under pressure to organise walk or cycle to school regimes and out of school activities in addition to their preoccupation with tests and exam results. Britain still lacks, however, the summer camp tradition found in other parts of the world, where children could learn something about living with others away from the family home, and learning to explore the natural world through hiking, climbing and outdoor pursuit activities. A class analysis of who is to be found walking the hills and dales of Britain today, or engaged in other kinds of outdoor pursuits or activity sports, would probably make dismal reading. Yet there was a time when walking and climbing were perceived to be radical activities, and a part of progressive working-class life and culture – another element of that lost tradition of popular self-education and an appreciation of the natural world through outdoor recreation.

In abandoning a historic concern for the condition of childhood, radical politics has abandoned its claim on universality. There may be a radical politics based on holding the ring in a competing world of interest groups – and on deliberating between claims and counter-claims to resources and power – and there is no reason why such a politics may not deliver important forms of social change. But childhood belongs to everybody, affects everybody and, in the end, prioritising the needs of children in public policy may be the true litmus test of a good society, whatever else happens later on.

References

Barnardo's (2008) 'The Shame of Britain's Intolerance of Children', 17 November, www.barnardos.org.uk

British Broadcasting Corporation News (2007), http://news. bbc.co.uk/1/hi/uk/6359363.stm

Campbell, B. (1993) *Goliath: Britain's Dangerous Places* (London: Methuen).

Caldwell Cook, H. (1917) *The Play* Way (London: Heinemann).

Darling, J. (1994) *Child Centred Education and its Critics* (London: Paul Chapman Ltd.).

Dewey, J. (1916) *Democracy and Education*, http://en.wikisource.org/wiki/Democracy_and_Education

The Guardian (2008) 'Britain in Danger of Demonising its Children, claims Barnardo's', *The Guardian*, London, 17 November, p. 15.

Hadow Report (1931) *The Primary School*, http://www.dg.dial.pipex.com/documents/hadow/31.shtml

Lowe, R. (2007) *The Death of Progressive Education* (London: Routledge).

Opie, P. and I. Opie (1959) *The Lore and Language of Schoolchildren* (United States: New York Review of Books).

Ritchie, J. T. R. (1964) *The Singing Street* (Edinburgh: Oliver & Boyd).

Worpole, K. (2000) *Here Comes the Sun: Architecture and Public Space in 20th Century European Culture* (London: Reaktion Books).

United Nations Children's Fund (UNICEF) (2007) *Child Poverty in Perspective: an Overview of Child Well-being in Rich Countries*, http://news.bbc.co.uk/nol/shared/bsp/hi/pdfs/13_02_07_nn_unicef.pdf

22
A New Politics of Innovation

Sheila Jasanoff

Radical politics defines itself in opposition to a settled order of things, a condition or set of conditions that most people so take for granted that it requires extreme action, and a rebellious imagination, to bring about systemic change. That imagination is easiest to set free when tyranny rules and the governing visions of a few make intolerable the lives of the many. It is harder in a time like ours, when democratically elected political leaders take public welfare and equality for granted, and see their task as merely that of expanding the pie of resources so that everyone gets a slice that keeps them happy. Where to focus radical action becomes a puzzle in this era of pervasive and complacent benevolence, troubled only by spectres of global catastrophe. To restore security and order in such a world, it is the proclaimed rationality of ruling imaginations that needs to be challenged, and for that it is necessary to restore the political to much that has been silently depoliticised. In this chapter, I question the growing tendency throughout the world to equate human development with technological advancement. That seemingly rational strategy makes no sense, I argue, without an accompanying politics that probes the social foundations, presuppositions and purposes of innovation.

Looking backward helps bring the problem of today's radicalism into sharper relief. In the short twentieth century, from World War One to the collapse of the Iron Curtain, it hardly seemed necessary to ask what radical politics should be about. Inequality and domination inscribed their fault lines on the world; dreams of emancipation drove a politics of liberation. Bloody or non-violent, nationalist or cosmopolitan, the themes of radical politics were astonishingly similar: from Russia's October Revolution in 1917 to China's Cultural Revolution in 1966; from Gandhi's Salt March to India's west coast in 1930, to Nelson Mandela's release from prison near Cape Town in 1990; from the trampling to death of the suffragette Emily Davidson at the Epsom Derby in 1913 to Martin Luther King's 'I have a dream' speech just fifty years later; and from America's counter-cultural revolution of the 1960s to Europe's student revolutions of 1968. All were propelled by a hunger for self-determination, and many who took part in the great liberation movements wrote movingly about the links between their actions and their aspirations.

George Orwell was one of these. In his *Homage to Catalonia*, Orwell repeatedly praised the self-organising egalitarianism of the Spanish militias he lived and served with:

> In theory it was perfect equality, and even in practice it was not far from it. There is a sense in which it would be true to say that one was experiencing a foretaste of Socialism, by which I mean that the prevailing mental atmosphere was that of Socialism. Many of the normal motives of civilized life – snobbishness, money-grubbing, fear of the boss, etc. – had simply ceased to exist. The ordinary class-division of society had disappeared to an extent that is almost unthinkable in the money-tainted air of England. (Orwell 1952: 104)

It is not so much Orwell's celebration of a specifically socialist ideal that resonates with contemporary audiences. Rather, it is the youthful energy that led Orwell and countless other twentieth-century insurgents to risk (and often give) their lives fighting against the divisions of money, class, sex and race that suffocate initiative and create insuperable hierarchies among men and women. Revolution was about creating a space of collective action where anyone committed to equality could breathe free, or die fighting.

Today, that revolutionary energy seems naïve and misguided, though admirable in spirit. The ideal of equality achieved through forcible erasure of economic and social disparities looks like a dangerous pipe dream. Orwell's Catalonian moment, after all, yielded to Orwell's own bleak foreshadowing of 1984. The classless society vanished as an unattainable, perverse and, at its extremes, inhuman vision. The ideology of equality that took its place, and that still reigns supreme, is the equality of the marketplace, in which access matters more than endpoint, and where everyone is free in principle to pursue any legitimate desire and, with luck and energy, to gratify it. The goal of politics is not mainly, in Barack Obama's controversial campaigning words, to 'spread the wealth' – at least not through mandatory redistribution. It is to spread opportunity, so that anyone who is inclined to do so can rise up the ladder of success and plenty. At his inauguration as 44th President of the USA, this is precisely the goal Obama articulated: 'The time has come to reaffirm our enduring spirit; to choose our better history; to carry forward that precious gift, that noble idea, passed on from generation to generation: the God-given promise that all are equal, all are free and all deserve a chance to pursue their full measure of happiness.'

In politics, sonorous words often elide difficult questions. How should opportunity be spread, and whose 'full measure of happiness' is the standard the world should live by? Despite all the gains brought about by science, technology, markets and democracy throughout the twentieth century, the 'bottom billion', so named by the economist Paul Collier (2007), remains mired in disease and poverty. Meanwhile, an overheated climate, recklessly mismanaged finances, and novel risks to food and health threaten our common future. What kind of politics is needed to pull the world's poorest of the poor up to something like the minimum standards of living that the rest of us see as essential perks of humanity? And in a period when global economic expectations and global environmental threats are both rising, what can ensure that the opportunities enjoyed by the most privileged billion will not only be spread more equally, but will be regulated so that the planet itself can be passed on more or less intact to the next generation and the next?

Imagining sustainable ways forward for global humanity has become, in my view, a parochial affair in the minds of today's best and brightest. Borrowing Thomas Kuhn's use of the label 'normal' for paradigmatic science, we can say that the idea of human progress is governed today by a kind of 'normal politics', spearheaded largely by the wealthy nations of the G7 (or G8) and the OECD, with their favoured international institutions, such as the World Bank, the International Monetary Fund and the World Trade Organization, exercising disproportionate influence. In their policy imaginations, the best that the world's backward populations can hope for is to catch up to their more fortunate earthly neighbours, perhaps 'leapfrogging' some historical stages as a result of ingenious technological improvements. To get outside that box, to set free more diverse and creative visions of humanity's prospects, we need to re-examine the rationalities that underlie the previous half-century's failed prescriptions for development. The radical politics of today has to liberate new imaginations that challenge the very ideas of growth and opportunity defined by today's political, economic, and technological elites.

Here, the politics of science and technology must figure centrally. If any single dream guides present visions of global progress, it is that salvation lies in the pursuit of knowledge – most often equated with scientific knowledge – closely partnered with technological innovation. Governments and their expert advisers have invested heavily in that vision, creating a whole new discourse of knowledge politics in the process. So today we live in knowledge societies, elect governments that promise to expand our knowledge economies, create public–private knowledge partnerships, and watch the rise of new knowledge classes. States compete with one another over the percentage of the GDP to be invested in research, count patents as measures of innovation, ask for sophisticated audits of research productivity, and offer prizes, grants and excellence awards to build more incentives for scientific and technological advancement. The European Union's Lisbon Agenda of 2000, promising to make the EU 'the most dynamic and competitive knowledge-based economy in the world', unambiguously endorsed such commitments. Even the administration of President George W. Bush, anti-science in its policies towards such acknowledged global hazards as climate change and AIDS, initiated a new government funding programme, to support a catchily designated 'science of science and innovation policy' in the USA.

Yet, stubbornly, knowledge gains and technological advances remain distributed along lines that replicate the ancient divisions of geography, class and race that aroused violent resistance in the past century. Today's knowledge plutocracies look surprisingly similar to yesterday's political elites, with just enough ethnic and cultural diversity at the top to keep alive the reassuring myth of progress. This should not surprise us. The knowledge that drives prosperity needs not only a steep staircase but also a high plateau to climb from, a plateau constructed in equal parts of material, intellectual and social resources.

Redistributive policies in the West have been targeted towards building better access roads to such plateaus, but those roads exist mainly for the benefit of the less advantaged of each nation's citizens. The richest private universities in the USA, for example, have adopted 'need-blind' admissions policies because, in today's highly competitive knowledge societies, those who win entry tickets to the best education gain priceless competitive advantages. It is not accidental that a Harvard College dropout named Bill Gates founded Microsoft and became one of the richest men in the world; nor that Mark Zuckerberg, another Harvard dropout, founded Facebook, a wealth-generating social networking tool that lets more than 100 million people create their own public personas and connect to friends and acquaintances around the world. These men drew on connections, social practices and imaginations forged at, or on the way to, Harvard. The technologies they helped invent carry within them particular, localised and (as it happens) saleable understandings of how the world works. But what resources and imaginative alternatives exist for those who will never come within ten thousand miles of Harvard and whose aspirations are rooted in radically different desires, needs and resources?

Two shibboleths need to be challenged: first, that technological innovation is the most reliable driver of human advancement; and, second, that transfers of technological capability from North to South, or West to East, is the highest imperative for global public policy. Both normative ideals carry enormous weight with contemporary governments and international donor agencies; indeed the consensus on these propositions amounts almost to a global constitutional agreement among states of all political persuasions. Technological innovation – for environment, energy, transportation, food, health, communication – is one of the key instruments by which the Obama administration hopes to implement the president's promise of change. Yet both norms ignore the fact that technology is ultimately a form of social organisation, a human–material hybrid whose transfer entails tacit extensions of social arrangements, including relationships of dominance, that are built into technological systems themselves. Unlike environmental sustainability, successful inventors often think locally and act globally, but the capacity for global action remains very unequally distributed.

Complex technologies work much like legal constitutions. They enable and constrain human capabilities in fundamental ways; they alter settled forms of life, making some obsolete and others exceedingly desirable. Yet – unlike constitutions – technology usually achieves its restructuring impacts without transparency, without open debate, and often without opportunity for organised resistance.

Opening up dominant technological imaginations to reformist inputs from below, or from sideways, will not be easy. For one thing, technological fixes seem appealingly simple and demand no hard-to-enforce behavioural changes, let alone a radical rethinking of the mantra of growth. Given a chance, who would not prefer to find a source of cheap energy that ends all our worries about consumption, conservation and waste disposal? Second, through centuries of habit, technology has come to be identified only with its good outcomes: better health, food, longevity, ease of movement, domestic comforts. The adverse consequences are seen as 'unintended', which leaves undisturbed the master narrative of progress even when a technologically supersaturated world is hurtling towards war or other disaster. Third, there have been serious wrong turns in opposing technology from which a radical politics of innovation will have to distance itself. What I have in mind is not the nationalist impetus that led Thabo Mbeki to deny anti-retroviral treatment to South African people with AIDS; nor the politically expedient alliance with Christian fundamentalists that prompted George W. Bush to withhold federal support for stem cell research. Rather, the aim of political action should be to uncover and challenge the lock-ins of the imagination that drive innovation in particular directions, heedless of history, culture or social context, and sometimes with tragic consequences.

There are two ways to pry open the black box of present-day innovation policies, one modest and the other radical. The modest route does not challenge the technological status quo or the dominant narrative of progress. Instead, it tries to make technology's demonstrated benefits for the wealthy more readily accessible to the less privileged. In the process, technical barriers may be broken and new potentialities liberated. Thus, the drive to create the $100 laptop at MIT's Media Lab, in order to meet the worldwide goal of 'One Laptop Per Child', led to breakthroughs in the use of electricity to suit the low to no electricity environments of developing countries. However, as Nicholas Negroponte, the project's charismatic chief architect likes to proclaim, an early consequence of disseminating the laptop was to introduce Cambodian and Rwandan children to Google and Skype. The lesson: content, and the myriad economic and social implications of conceiving and providing it, remain firmly lodged in the places where the laptop's hardware was invented. How long it will take to reverse such persistent imbalances in the means of innovation remains an open question.

Modest imaginations can grow anywhere, of course, and may decentralise the opportunities for wealth creation. In the case of Tata's recently introduced 'Nano', the cheapest car in the world, inventiveness similar to that of Negroponte's $100 laptop had its roots in the Indian automotive industry. If the car reaches even a fraction of its intended market, it will revolutionise transport for the Indian urban middle class; it may make India a net exporter of low-cost electric and hybrid vehicles, thereby reducing the projected per capita carbon emissions from motor vehicles as developing country citizens take to the road in larger and larger numbers.

Similarly, India's generic drug industry, one of the largest in the world, developed its own business model, taking advantage of significantly lower production costs in India to provide cheaper alternatives to expensive but life-saving pharmaceutical products invented in the West. In an economically and socially layered world, this kind of innovation made good use of comparative advantages in the social side of technology's social–material complex. At their best, such developments may redress some of the inequalities associated with ruling technological imaginations, but they do not take issue with the deeper visions of public benefit that feed and water them. At worst, as in the case of generic drugs, these sorts of efforts to remedy gross economic stratification in the world may be undercut by more powerful forces. Ambiguities in the WTO Agreement on Trade-Related Aspects of Intellectual Property Rights (TRIPS Agreement) offer one example. In a recent case, generic drugs that Indian manufacturers claimed were lawfully in transit to countries with inadequate manufacturing capacity, and hence with demonstrated need for the drugs, were seized in transit through the European Union on grounds that their shipment violated TRIPS.

A more radical approach has to begin with the proposition that the process of innovation is deeply and intrinsically political. Instead of fighting rearguard actions against specific inequities built into the production of specific goods and services, what is needed is a more comprehensive political imagination granting publics who might be affected by technological innovation a *constitutional* right to be consulted. In the emerging global order, built around allegedly shared norms of reason and progress, and around technological systems that increasingly seek world markets, recognition of such a principle seems a minimum condition of democratic accountability.

Incremental movements throughout the world suggest that there is growing awareness of the constitutive aspects of innovation. It is present when a group of international activists allies with unlikely partners such as the Rockefeller Foundation to keep Monsanto from investing in sterile seed technology (the 'Terminator gene') that would force farmers to buy new seed in each planting season. It is there when massive consumer rejection forces the UK government to conduct an unprecedented nationwide consultation on public attitudes towards genetically modified crops. It helps explain the worldwide disenchantment with nuclear power and the consequent moratorium on nuclear expansion in many countries, though expert risk assessors keep insisting that far fewer people have died from nuclear plant accidents than from coal mining or oil drilling. This objection misses the point that it is not the nuclear threat but its non-governance on the global stage that arouses anxiety and mobilises opposition.

A comprehensive political theory of innovation would give coherence and meaning to these scattered bursts of activity. It would provide reasons why technological trajectories must bear reasonable relationships to the lives people want to live, as opposed to those that inventors have made possible. Piecemeal acknowledgement of the need for wider public involvement can be found in academic writings and in policies or practices clustering under such headings as 'ethics', 'upstream public engagement' and 'real-time technology assessment.' All these moves recognise that technology has social and moral as well as intellectual and material dimensions, and that the former need to be deliberated when design choices are still fluid and malleable, long before finished products, with built-in social costs and presumptions, hit the market.

Like the sleek shafts of windmills springing up around the coast lines of the Northern world, technological innovation offers at first blush few handholds for the political imagination. These things arrive, and once with us they seem preordained. And yet those material miracles grew from mundane beginnings that are profoundly and unavoidably social. A Swiss inventor goes for a walk in the woods and finds in clinging burdock seeds the idea for a fabric fastener called velcro. But it takes twenty years and the resources of the US National Aeronautics and Space Administration, in its mission to win the Cold War's bipolar technological race, to capitalise on the product's uses in gravity-free environments, and so to popularise Velcro for ordinary consumer markets.

Telling such stories, and multiplying them thousands of times over, will begin to rewrite the taken-for-granted narratives of technological progress in ways that account for shortfalls as well as successes, tragedies as well as triumphs, and most of all power as well as plenty. In turn, more critically aware civic understandings of what is at stake in innovation will help lay the groundwork for a global charter of rights and responsibilities, giving voice to those who will be most affected by innovation's advances. Through strategic analysis and selective resistance, an enlightened radical politics of innovation may build a world in which the race is not only to the swiftest, but also to imaginations that are thoughtful, just and humane.

References

Collier, P. (2007) *The Bottom Billion* (Oxford: Oxford University Press).
European Union (2000) Lisbon Agenda, http://www.europarl.europa.eu/summits/lis1_en.htm
Orwell, G. (1952) *Homage to Catalonia* (New York: Harcourt Brace).

23
Universities are Radical

Nigel Thrift

One of Joseph Wright of Derby's most famous pictures is called 'A Philosopher giving that Lecture on the Orrery, in which a Lamp is put in place of the Sun'. I want to argue that Wright's picture, by a man who never went to a university, can stand foursquare for the ambition of the university. Though putting a lamp in place of the sun may seem a modest ambition, as Wright's picture shows, it can produce a surpassing beauty, one which is well worth hanging on to.

This brief introductory paragraph straightaway signals that I am going to make an argument about what counts as radical politics that will not only sound weedy to the full-blooded, testosterone-fuelled radical but probably even reactionary. So be it. My argument is that universities are not only important and need preserving, but that they are vital civilisational forces without which we would all be worse off. In other words, they need to be defended.

This is not to argue, I hasten to add, that I think universities are perfect or exemplary institutions. That would be patently absurd. But it is to argue that they are worth fighting for, even more so in these difficult times. And the times are very difficult. The planet is being held captive by a version of humanity that seems all too willing to demonstrate the venal side of its nature. The environment is being ravaged. Warfare is a permanent state of affairs. The distribution of income in many parts of the world is grotesque. States frequently trample on their citizens' human rights and traduce the existence of all manner of species. And so on. In such circumstances, the future of universities may seem a small thing, of little consequence. But I think not. In other words, I am going to argue in this chapter for what I still consider to be an important site of radical politics if 'radical' is understood as pushing and prompting new ways of thinking about the world.

'Civilisational' conjures up all kinds of difficult resonances, of course. Nowadays it can sound as though it is a part of some colonial enterprise. Equally, it can sound rabidly Platonic, interested in the eternal pursuit of truth as though that were a fixed pole of being. Or it can sound heroic in an inflated and self-important kind of way. But I still want to use it because I think there is a sense in which the civilisational role of universities is important, precisely at a time which is so difficult. Put another way, I want to argue that a certain kind of conservatism, understood as a respect for a past which is then made amends for in the future, is actually a radical move in our present circumstances.

Certainly, I think that the time may be right to restate this case. In the West at least, the last few decades have undoubtedly been an era of private achievement. But these decades of affluence (and I am well aware that not everyone has shared in their fruits) have also been a time in which opportunities for repair and maintenance of the social and environmental fabric have often been squandered and the public sphere has fallen into disrepair. In the more temperate times that now face us, times of fiscal squeeze and struggles over scarce resources in which 'the children are left to grapple with the burdens of their elders' (Brooks, 2008), it may be that universities can once again come into their majority as genuine citizens of the world.

Of course, for the researcher whose contract is coming to an end with no other contract in sight, for the cleaner who is on the minimum wage and has become a prisoner of overtime, and for the adjunct faculty who have to string together multiple part-time jobs, all this highfaluting talk about the role of universities will no doubt ring hollow. But I am not trying to construct a high-minded smokescreen. Rather, I am trying to remind people what universities are and must be there for.

Threats to the idea of the university

No one would want to deny that what we pass on to future generations is important and deserves debate. But a debate also needs to be had about how we do that too, since so many values need to be shown, not just told. And that's what universities do: they are both a store of knowledge that has been passed on and a means of passing that knowledge on so that it promotes real and long-lasting engagement and so generates new knowledge. Richard Sennett (2008) has made precisely this point in his recent book, *The Craftsman*. Universities are, first and foremost, about good work for its own sake. Its members are (or, at least, ought to be) continually acquiring skill, at first through working with those who have demonstrated they have those skills and then by interacting in a community in which that skill is valued and which they are able to become an active contributor to. Indeed, in time, they may be able to play a part in changing what that skill consists of.

But, upholding the values of the university as a shuttle between the generations is a more complicated move than it once was. To begin with, the soubriquet 'university' covers a host of quite different kinds of institution. In the United Kingdom, for example, it takes in Oxford and Cambridge and Staffordshire or Greenwich Universities. Most commentators would find it hard to argue that these institutions are doing quite the same things. In the USA, as one other example, it can take in private and endowed-up-to-the-hilt Ivy League universities, the full range of state universities and all kinds of other private universities and community colleges. Then, universities are being painted as the solution to all manner of troubles. Think of just a few of the extra strings that have been added to their bow in recent years. So universities are now meant to be in the vanguard of the economy. They are there to pass on the values of innovation and entrepreneurship in the pursuit of wealth and to act as regional economic magnets and magnifiers. Again, universities are painted as social engineers, there to widen participation and promote fair access. Finally, they are seen as guardians of social stability, there to make sure that students think generally pacific thoughts and act nicely.

The charge sheet

So let me begin by putting the case against universities. I will make three main charges for the prosecution. The first is that universities are simply slaves of the usual vested interests of class, state and business. The prognosis varies from country to country. For example, in France Pierre Bourdieu once argued that universities were primarily agents of the state nobility and indeed that much of the intellectual work they carried out consciously or unconsciously mirrored that function. Meanwhile, commentators in the USA argue that they have produced unfair hierarchies of labour by institutionalising cheap teaching by underpaid and overworked graduate assistants (Bousquet, 2008).

Now universities undoubtedly reproduce all manner of malign influences. It is right for people to be sceptical of them, for their sometimes overt elitism, for their offputting air of superiority, for their too cosy relationship to establishment interests. But, all that said, universities are no longer quite the conveyance of a gilded elite that they used to be. For example, in the United Kingdom, though the overall number of institutions that might style themselves as having higher education ambitions of one form or another has shown only a modest increase, there has been a substantial increase in the average size of institutions which has produced a considerable change in the character of higher education (Scott, 2008). In fact, in the United Kingdom, much of the controversy seems to be as much about the size of pathways into the few elite universities as much as anything else, thereby unconsciously reproducing the sins of earlier generations but in a quite different situation.

The second charge is that universities have moved away from the vocation that Max Weber understood as their defining characteristic and have yet to find a new one. Insofar as they are no longer refuges from the market, there to allow a few good men and women the opportunity to think great thoughts unsullied by worldly imperatives, their calling has been compromised. Universities have become addicted to sources of income that can only compromise that Weberian vocation, and indulge in activities which some see as distasteful or even morally repugnant. There are a number of variants on this argument about vocation. To begin with, there is the issue of being shackled by the dictates of the commercial imperative. Secure in his Harvard eyrie, Derek Bok (2003) has written of the rampant commercialisation of some North American universities, leading to the notion of a 'corporate university', which has become increasingly inseparable from business. But, rather like Steven Shapin (2008), I would not want to sign up to a Manichean vision in which university and industry are simply opposing poles of reciprocal condescension and condemnation. After all, nowadays, science is not just a calling. It's a job that employs many millions of people around the world and it no longer seems automatically reprehensible that, as Shapin (2008: 149) puts it, 'entrepreneurial science . . . may appeal to scientists who want to make something, to see ideas embodied in products, and, perhaps, in products contributing to the social good' – which is not, of course, to say that there is no balance to be struck. Then, there is the fact that many universities are involved in what are seen by some as malign activities, particularly military and defence-related work and animal experimentation. Again arguments rage about what balance to strike between worldliness and unworldliness. Then again, a number of commentators, on both the Left (as proponents) and the Right (as critics), want to see universities as hotbeds of dissent, leading the charge against capitalism, imperialism and just about every other 'ism' too. Should university faculty save the world on their own time, as Stanley Fish (2008) would have it, or should they become actively involved in changing the world, as some would see it, by declaring their political and other allegiances in class and journal?

It is right for people to be critical, of course. But it is not easy to see instant and practical ways out of some of these dilemmas, partly because they are dilemmas and partly because so many people now rely on universities for employment and succour that it is no simple thing to backtrack to a period when vocation could be equated with an almost Edenic purity of mission and motive.

The third charge is that universities have sacrificed quality to quantity, particularly in teaching but maybe also in research. I think it is undeniable that most universities (except for the very richest ones) have changed their character as institutions over the last few decades as they have grown in size and function. As they have expanded and diversified, so the experience of teaching has changed, and not necessarily for the better.

But a price had to be paid for expansion and it is difficult to argue that we should go back to a time of tutors serving sherry to the gilded elite in front of a gas fire. What we need is a way to keep the best of the craft of teaching whilst understanding that the nature of the student body has changed. The problem is that the solution to this problem has generally been associated with the practices of audit whose ways of being bear most similarity to modern enterprise management systems and certainly not to anything resembling craft.

The case for the defence

So, given this charge sheet, what are the values that universities can demonstrate to the world? I will fix on six. The first value that universities can attest to is, quite straightforwardly, solutions to global problems. Universities will never be very good at certain kinds of innovation, especially the kind of tinkering that goes on day to day on the shopfloor or in the office or, indeed, in someone's backyard shed. But they excel in producing innovations which switch an accepted tramline of thought onto new rails. Those solutions can be of several kinds. One is framing problems that were hard to see but turn out to be vital. I am thinking here of the example of climate change which was spotted by university scientists and, in part, framed as a problem that needed to be addressed by them. Other problems may be less tangible but just as important for people's lives. The point is that these problems can only be solved by new imaginative framings, and universities are constantly producing these framings, twisting and wrenching and yawing the world into new configurations that yield new questions. Some of these reframings will turn out to be trivial or even batty, but enough of them stick to produce genuine changes in perception and practice.

Another value that typifies universities is cosmopolitanism. Universities have become mixing-grounds for peoples from all kinds of cultures. As a result, universities have increasingly become locations that promote knowledge and understanding of – which is not the same as agreement with – others' viewpoints. And they are places where people can agree to disagree without incurring instant penalties. That is no easy function. It requires the bolstering of the slow realisation that people from other cultures are not easily comprehended stereotypes but really do think differently. It requires refereeing what can often be righteous anger but is sometimes self-involved posturing. It requires the management of a certain kind of structured exasperation, if you like. But, very often in day-to-day interaction in universities people not only learn to rub along – they have to do that in most of the great cities of the world, after all – but begin to negotiate difference and produce what Jean-François Bayart (2007) calls a 'dense transnationalism' which has its own ethical demands. What I particularly like about this kind of cosmopolitanism is that it produces uncertainty – which is not the same quality as scepticism. Building up this courage to be uncertain is and must be a key feature of the university.

A third value that universities can demonstrate is conscience. Truth to tell, much of what we might regard as the modern conscience has been invented or at least codified in universities. That might seem a strong statement to make but think of the ways in which universities have been crucial nodes in the generation of women's rights, the rights of children, animal rights, and so on. The record is certainly not perfect. Sometimes it has resulted in the arid point-scoring occasioned by political correctness. Sometimes it has produced an obsessive interest in differences that, when all is said and done, mean very little at all. Sometimes it has produced mere stridency. But enough creditable work has emerged that it can be argued that universities have acted and continue to act as resources for founding the kind of social and cultural questioning that is a key characteristic of the active citizenship that must typify any healthy society.

A fourth value universities must hold dear is the constant work of making memory. Often, the arts and humanities are seen as the preserve of people who sit isolated in rooms producing work of vaulting abstraction which will only ever be read by like-minded people. But I want to see them as, in large part, enacting the paying back of a debt to those who made our history by constantly reinterpreting the lives and works of people who once lived, sometimes well, sometimes badly, but always fiercely. This cultural quilting is central in all manner of ways. It puts a brake on the kind of self-serving half-truths that we are all susceptible to. It reminds us that the past is not just a mirror of our present concerns. It binds us to a common culture of remembrance which is more than just the sum of manifold fragments each recollecting their own selective suffering or a Cook's tour through the moral lessons of history. Tony Judt (2008) has written about the 'sin of forgetting' and, given that contemporary societies usually produce either a casual insouciance or instant victimhood when they consider the past, we too often commit that sin. Universities are about passing on different lessons which, in turn, can produce a more open and creative future.

A fifth value universities must cleave to is seriousness. We live in a time when cultures have been affected by all manner of viruses that undermine the ability to think seriously over concentrated periods of time – the pleasures of celebrity culture, the constant stream of screened information, the formation of fast communities on the internet and the consequent propensity for emotional firestorms, the casual cruelties of media reporting and internet comment . . . For those who have studied history, there is an inevitable element of déjà vu about these complaints. 'Twas always thus, one might say. Sages through the ages have rancorously decried the supposed intellectual shallowness of their particular societies. And yet there do seem to me to be peculiarly distressing characteristics about the current situation. The sheer profusion of agents vying for our attention seems to be producing less capacity for analytical thought and more likelihood of whizzing through tasks and simply cutting and pasting information. If this analysis is correct, universities become even more important, especially for their ability to tend abstract things that cannot be easily valued – or even valued at all. What might be called 'slow thinking' has its own importance in this world of fleeting interest.

Finally, there is one other value that universities can and must demonstrate. That is wonder. After all, thinking is a passion. Richard Holmes' (2008) latest book describes the 'age of wonder' that was the lot of science at the end of the eighteenth century but, if we have the wit to see it, that age of the apprehension of simultaneous beauty and terror has never really faded. Science is producing discoveries that continue to amaze all but the most hidebound, and most of those discoveries come from or are associated with universities. Just in the last year, for example, the following moments have brought me up short: The volcanic landscape of Mercury revealed by Mercury Messenger. The plume of dark matter created by two galaxies colliding. Exoplanets around the star Fomalhaut. Playing with aerogels. The possibility that glial cells are more than just the brain's cement. Some of the extraordinary discoveries associated with animal cultures. A car made from vegetable matter. I can extend this sense of wonder into the humanities and social sciences. I think, for example, of work I have read over the last year in anthropology on the markedly varied spatial cognition of different peoples in the world, or the extraordinary meetings that were produced by the circulations of trade in prehistory, or the different apprehensions of the world being unleashed by new modes of digital performance. And that is before I get to the wonders unleashed by new interpretations of novels, poems, artworks and film, and all manner of historical events that I thought I knew well. In the end, it is probably this core of wonder I am most concerned to protect and the way it immunises us against what Whitehead (1944) called minds in a groove, for minds in a groove cannot come up with the new solutions that we so desperately need. Whitehead was writing about the professions and the inadequate comprehension of human life that they derived from particular kinds of abstraction, but the point is a more general one which has a lasting importance.

Conclusions

Universities are concerned with ideas and ideas are fragile. We should be careful not to snuff out the potential that universities have to generate new ideas – by loudly proclaiming universities' irrelevance, by ceaselessly attacking every one of universities' bona fides as though they must inevitably be self-serving, by auditing universities out of existence. All of these tactics are possible. Very often, they have been carried through into cynical policies that have caused needless damage to institutions that cannot afford the luxury of cynicism.

In the end, being radical is not just about knowing what needs to be replaced and doing something about it. It is also about knowing what needs to be kept and doing something about that too. Universities are certainly not suns. But they can be lamps. And lamps, however imperfectly, do light the way. We need to keep them.

References

Bayart, J.-F. (2007) *Global Subjects: a Political Critique of Globalization* (Cambridge: Polity Press).

Bok, D. (2003) *Universities in the Marketplace: the Commercialization of Higher Education* (Princeton: Princeton University Press).

Bousquet, M. (2008) *How the University Works: Higher Education and the Low-Wage Nation* (New York: New York University Press).

Brooks, D. (2008) 'A Date with Scarcity', *New York Times*, 5 November.

Fish, S. (2008) *Save the World on Your Own Time* (Oxford: Oxford University Press).

Holmes, R. (2008) *The Age of Wonder: How the Romantic Generation Discovered the Beauty and Terror of Science* (London: Harper Press).

Judt, T. (2008) 'What Have We Learned, If Anything?' *New York Review of Books*, 1 May, pp. 16–20.

Scott, P. (2008) 'Beyond the Market: Higher Education in 2020', Association of University Administrators, Eleventh annual lecture, 21 October, The Rembrandt, 11 Thurloe Place, London SW7 2RS.

Sennett, R. (2008) *The Craftsman* (London: Allen Lane).

Shapin, S. (2008) *The Scientific Life: a Moral History of a Late Modern Generation* (Chicago: Chicago University Press).

Whitehead, A. N. (1944) *Science and the Modern World* (New York: Macmillan).

24
Radical Politics After the Crisis[1]

Will Hutton

To begin with, it is important to draw attention to three components that are needed for radical politics. First of all you have got to have a cause. You have got to have a grievance. You have got to have a belief that you can make tomorrow better than today. This has its roots in a belief in utopianism; or that there is a utopian constructible 'thing' that is prosecutable, that will make tomorrow better than today. That is usually informed by, if it is going to be a radical politics that works, an overarching worldview to bring together sufficient people to deliver. You cannot do radical politics by yourself. You do it (and that is the second point) as a movement. You do it in groups, and if you are going to bring disparate people together, there has to be an overarching story. Generally speaking, in Western democracies, that is a political economy story – that's a political economy of the Left, that's a political economy of the Right. You have got to have such a theory. If you are on the Left you need a theory of capitalism. This should address what is generating the inequalities, monopolies, instabilities and grievances that you want to do something about, to create a better tomorrow. And if you are on the Right you similarly have a political economy of capitalism. You are taking the view that capitalism is an order that really works and you look to what will make it work more.

Of course there has been a radical politics over the last 30 years. It is called American neo-conservatism. The network that Jon Pugh directs[2] does not have any neo-Conservatives in it. But neo-Conservatives have been the radicals of our generation and how successful they have been. How successful they have been!

I think that we underestimate in Britain the degree to which our own thinking is coloured by what takes place in America. It is the hegemonic power. It is the place where there is a lot of money spent on intellectual generation. It takes time and effort to write and produce ideas. I was lucky, I was at *The Guardian* at a particular time in my life and the publishing industry was rich enough to pay advances to allow me to take sabbatical terms and to write my books. The kind of economics that supported an individual public intellectual that existed ten years ago has eviscerated, even in our country. Now in the USA they spend a lot of money on ideas. They spend a lot of money on ideas in universities, they spend a lot of money on ideas in the great think tanks, particularly on the Right. Those neo-conservative think tanks generating those radical ideas have a huge impact on our society: the arrival of free market fundamentalism; the deregulation of financial markets; the lack of resilience in the energy system; the beating back of regulation in the car industry; the line that was taken on climate change; the line that we all learnt that the government was bad, that public action was always going to fail. All this came out of America over the last 25 years. It has been hugely radical. There is a radicalised Republican Party, and of course the twenty-first-century American movement around Bush who launched the war in Iraq could hardly have been more radical. They had a project about a utopian tomorrow. There was a group of them that did it.

Here is the third thing. You cannot have radical politics unless you have got some kind of institutional structure in which you can feasibly prosecute your radicalism. Radical politics in the nineteenth century (and in the first half of the twentieth century) did require a nation state. It required a viable nation state within whose territorial jurisdiction you could gain control of the National Assembly (if you were on the Left) and you could do things that would move that society tangibly and realistically towards that utopia that you had in mind. One of the difficulties of radical politics since the mid-1970s has been the rise of (what Philip Bobbitt calls) 'the Market State'. This perception can be more important than the reality. I mean states *are* slightly more constrained than they were but to those who say that globalisation really constrains states, I say well look at the bail-out of the last six or eight weeks. Look at the way in which when push came to shove, it was nation states that had to write taxpayers' money to support Western banks, and suddenly we were all reminded that these nation states that allegedly had little or no power were, when the system broke, the only thing that you had.

There has been a perception, at least for the last 25 years, that states cannot do much. You wouldn't want to put up corporate taxation or marginal rates of taxation, would you? You wouldn't want to tax non-domicile residents in the United Kingdom, would you? You wouldn't want to attack the engines of wealth generation, would you? The wind of radicalism has been blowing from the Right.

I want to now briefly return to the idea of utopianism, in order to make an important point. I think utopianism comes from the better side of human nature, a belief that to live a life well requires not doing it wholly individualistically, associating one's own preferences, tastes and feelings. It is about acting collectively. As some examples, to live a life well means being in love with somebody or loved by somebody. It means being in a group of friends in a family, in a kinship network, in a community of interests, of people. We human beings are profoundly social. And my point is this – utopianism springs from social aggregation.

You have got to have some sense of utopianism for radical politics, and if it is going to be a rational utopianism, it is built on something that will bind people's different interests. Some people may have a grievance about the climate, others may have a grievance about gender or ethnicity, others about disability, poverty or class. Bring those disparate interests together. You can only do it if you can build a political alliance, and that political alliance requires a common thread for everyone to relate to. This is why a political economy that underpins Left thinking or Right thinking is so important. It is the only way that you can get to the next stage of bringing people together. Then hopefully you need a third stage of credibility. It is all only credible if there are instruments that you can gain control of that would allow you to change stuff radically.

All of that has been weak in Britain in the last 30 years, and it has been weak in Britain because there has been a genuine rise in individualism. People have not looked to live lives socially or collectively, even acknowledging reciprocity of obligation in a marriage, in a family or in a community. It has been a 'me first' assertion of my individualistic appetite. I am going to move up a hierarchy of needs, and I am going to satiate my individual taste and preferences and needs. That story has really undermined radical politics because what these people are radical about is how they can live better themselves, as individuals. They are not radical about how they collectively might make the world a better place.

There has been an undermining of a Left political economy. Sometimes, when I get bleak moments, I wonder why I bothered writing *The State We're In* (Hutton, 1995). The best-selling economics book in the twentieth century was John Maynard Keynes' *The Economic Consequences of the Peace* written in 1919, and the second best-selling book in the twentieth century was unbelievably *The State We're In*. But actually it made absolutely no difference at all. New Labour did what they did as if it had not been written, although Gordon Brown sometimes says that he went for the independence of the Bank of England because it's recommended in *The State We're In*. In response, I have said, 'Yes Gordon, but actually the whole point of that was to be the centrepiece of a new regulatory order for finance. The point was to make it independent while you increase regulation in the City of London, split investment banking from commercial banking, have a new system of company law to get a less transactional financial system to generate more long-termism. That was the point of the exercise. It wasn't for you to cherry pick and to give them independence and set an inflation target and then give all those speeches cheer-leading deregulation, which has ended in, as any Keynesian could have foretold, the disaster through which we're currently living.'

Although I seem to be mostly critical of New Labour, I also understand the times. In 1997 when they came to power, as Peter Mandelson often talks about, they were in the politics of reassurance. The wind was blowing ferociously from the Right, intellectually and commercially and in the real world. It seemed for a long time that Keynesian ideas or radical Keynesianism, of the type that I championed, was a fools' errand; it was a fools' mission. No one would believe in nonsense like that anymore. Keynes said there was an existential problem in the relationship between the financial markets and the real economy because of the speed of adjustment in the financial markets (their time horizons) which the rate of interest could not possibly mediate. He wrote a book, *The General Theory of Employment, Interest and Money* to prove it. Well I believed it all my life. I spent the first six years of my career working in the City. I know it to be true. But in 2007 I could not have convinced a cat that that's where the burden of evidence seemed to be.

A lot of us are now very critical. I am sure you are all very critical. But everybody – I should suspect a large part of this lecture room – colluded in what took place. I am sure you wag your fingers at the regulator and say 'How could they bear to allow Northern Rock to do what it did?', and how disarming it is for Newcastle that Northern Rock is where it is. The FSA, the worst people in a job, I am sure you said that in the pubs and clubs round here. I am sure you've also wagged your fingers (those of you who are Labour Party members) at how Gordon Brown could possibly have allowed it all to take place. Of course you are right. But you are also partly wrong because all of you simultaneously will have been, between 2000 and 2007, very much enjoying conversations about how much your house price was rising in value. Did you deter your children from putting down extravagant deposits on a house because we all knew that house prices would go up next year compared with this year? We as a national community all colluded in this credit boom and enjoyed this asset price bubble, all of us – government regulators, populists, commentators (except for one or two – I put my hand up – I did try). Who wanted to believe it would end in tears, or even if you did think it would really end in tears, who really wished for a different kind of economic and social organisation in that period?

Although I do not like the fact that *The State We're In* was completely ignored, I understand why it was. It is a pity I hadn't written the book now, rather than eleven or twelve years ago, and indeed I'm about to try a revisited version.

So when you come to now, how optimistic can one be about radical politics? Well I think the great thing about the financial crisis is that there is now almost nobody left who believes in a proposition (the intellectual position of the 1980s, 1990s and the naughties as they are called) of the efficient market hypothesis: that because financial markets are pluralist, with many runners and riders, that information is widely shared and instantaneously, that there are very few barriers to trade entry into the industry, that prices are sending instantaneous information to lots and lots of actors simultaneously, and that this is the precondition for an efficient market. So this market above any other will be efficient. Nobody now believes that, not even the high priests of financial theory. Of course, Alan Greenspan said that in testimony to Congress. It has been absolutely, for him, a life-changing event. He always thought that shareholders would make sure that the managers of the enterprise they owned did rational things and that markets behaved rationally. This is an honest admission, from a great man actually. But when Alan Greenspan runs up the white flag, you know that there is a clear opportunity for us to try something new.

I wrote an article a while ago called 'Will the Real Keynes Stand Up' and to my surprise not only was I asked to go and talk about it to Alistair Darling in the Treasury, but I also got a phone call from David Cameron who wanted to explore this particular conception of Keynesian economics and to what extent, as a conservative, you would now have to rethink through the Tory philosophy, meant in Keynesian terms. For us, and I'm a man of the liberal Left, I think it is game on.

Unlike Tony Giddens, I do not believe in the radical Centre. I just don't think that is a smart way of thinking about politics or values. I do not think there are such things as 'Centralist' values. I think there's a portfolio of values, a prism of looking at the world, which is broadly liberal Left. It's a belief in pluralism, it's a belief in equity, it's a belief in fairness, it's a belief in dissent, it's a belief that human beings shape the world and need to shape the world. It is a recognition that human beings need reciprocity to express their altruism. There is another cluster of views on the Right which broadly take the view that human beings are fallen, they are imperfect, that you cannot design, that you have to be very careful about giving too much power to any political institution in particular, because fallen human beings are dangerous and make mistakes and are power hungry, and they will use that power over you, and they will make mistakes. This leads to coercion and the infringement of freedoms. The best society is one which permits individuals to express their choices and their freedoms unconstrained. The Left and Right are two bodies of values and they sit in tension. And here's the point: society needs them both. All of us carry these values, we are yin and yang, we are man and woman in our head, we are also Left and Right in our head. We all of us carry a value system in our heads and we need political parties who champion these things, because at various moments in time one set of values is more appropriate to the objective situation than another.

The Centre is a normal bunch of people who have been moved by the Right to join them or by the liberal Left to join them. In themselves there is no radicalism in Centralist values. But what I think is emerging at the moment is both optimistic and dangerous. And I will finish on this. For someone like me, and what makes me optimistic, is that a lot of people are recognising that a life lived well is not about just having a more valuable house next year, better clothes next year, designer clothes next year, trying to be a celebrity. A life lived well does require some capacity to express oneself in concert with others.

Secondly, I think what has happened in finance and the financial crunch has opened up once again a Keynesian politics, a Leftist politics that allows the Left to put together an overarching political economy which allows it to start building much more inclusive coalitions than it was able to do hitherto.

Thirdly, I think there is a new recognition that states, government and the public really matter. Because without them we certainly would not have a banking industry. If we are going to reshape the car industry, as another example, it is clearly going to have to happen in concert with public and government. Reshape the business mould of the car industry and radically rethink the deployment of cars.

That is a source of optimism I think for radical politics, but the pessimistic side is this. Where the Right will go, I am afraid, is nationalism and religion. Blood, the colour of your skin, the religion you adhere to and the national community to which you belong will become dangerous sources of radicalism.

The next decade is going to be an interesting one. But I think we will look back on the last ten years (despite its lack of radical politics) with some kindness. We have had some very good times.

Notes

1. This chapter is an edited transcript of a public talk given by Will Hutton, at Newcastle University, on 5 December 2008. This was entitled 'What *is* Radical Politics Today?', and moderated by Jonathan Pugh. For a full video of the event, which also included Anthony Giddens, please see http://www.spaceofdemocracy.org
2. The *Spaces of* Democracy and the *Democracy of* Space network (see http://www.spaceofdemocracy.org).

References

Hutton, W. (1995) *The State We're In: Why Britain is in Crisis and How to Overcome It* (London: Jonathan Cape).

Part IV
The Role of the State

25
Anarchism

Saul Newman

We've heard a lot of talk recently about 'change', the 'need for change'. Was this not the catch-cry of the Obama presidential campaign in 2008? The precise changes proposed were never really spelled out – they merely signified the idea of a break with the past, a new direction for the future of the USA. Of course, it remains to be seen what kinds of changes a new administration in Washington will actually implement. There will probably be a few reforms here and there – reforms that are no doubt important, such as closing Guantanamo Bay and withdrawing troops from Iraq. But if we are expecting major social and economic transformations, the chances are we will be disappointed.

Radical politics is certainly about change, but unlike the vague and empty slogans of political parties, radical politics contends that real change cannot come about through the formal system of power and representation – it must come from outside it. I realise that this position puts me at odds with many people, even those on the progressive side of politics. Some (Left-liberals and social democrats) would say that the representative political system is by no means perfect – that indeed its imperfections are many and run deep – but that it can nevertheless be used to implement much-needed reforms: egalitarian and redistributive measures, for instance, or better regulation of financial markets. Others (Marxists, Leninists – and there's not many of them around these days) would say that real social and economic change can only come through a revolutionary form of politics; but this nevertheless involves a vanguard party seizing political power and using the structures and mechanisms of the state to carry out an economic transformation of society (after this, the state was supposed to wither away, although historical experience proved precisely the opposite was true). Both these positions – different

223

as they are – work within the paradigm of the state; the state is seen as the instrument for implementing social change.

By contrast, the position that I take is one that is closer to anarchism. Anarchism has always been viewed as a heretical doctrine, even (and especially) by the Left. Historically, anarchism has been marginalised both as a philosophy and a revolutionary practice: the expulsion of the anarchist Mikhail Bakunin from the First International in 1872 – an expulsion instigated by Marx at the end of a long and bitter dispute over revolutionary tactics – found its ultimate conclusion in the massacre by Trotsky of the rebellious libertarian sailors of Kronstadt in 1921.

What was so threatening about anarchism? What was the challenge that the anarchists posed for radical politics? What lessons does anarchism have for us today? To answer these questions, we must take a closer look at the situation of radical politics today. My contention here is that – contrary to what many have argued – this is not a time for despair and faux-radical hand-wringing. Rather, that we are witnessing a disengagement of many people from traditional modes of political activity, and an invention or reinvention of alternative and more autonomous political practices. The political practices are not centred around participation in formal political structures – indeed they express a clear suspicion and, indeed, rejection of these arrangements and institutions. Radical politics today, I would argue, is increasingly anarchistic and embodies a desire for greater autonomy from political power.

Why are many people increasingly suspicious of power? It seems that there is a growing sense that governments – even democratically elected ones – no longer represent the desires of the people, and are no longer accountable to the people. There is a real crisis of legitimacy of our political institutions. Was not this absolute chasm between the people and power revealed in the startling symbolism of millions of people around the world protesting in 2003 against the decision of their governments to go to war against Iraq, only to be met with the indifference and utter contempt of their political elites? In the United Kingdom, the government actually used these demonstrations as an excuse to ban political protests within a 1 km radius of the Houses of Parliament in Westminster. The sight of noisy and unruly protesters was too much, it would seem, for the delicate nerves (or guilty consciences?) of our hard-working parliamentarians, those tireless servants of the common good! Do the Houses of Parliament in Westminster – that great seat of democracy – not increasingly resemble a besieged citadel, with its armed police guards, surveillance cameras, concrete fortifications; does it not symbolise both the contempt and fear of the people, the attempt to shut the people out from power?

This is perhaps not surprising. As the elite theorists always told us, democracies were simply a mechanism by which elites perpetuated their rule. This has been referred to as the 'iron law of oligarchy', a term coined by a German syndicalist (a libertarian trade unionist) and sociologist Robert Michels (1962), to describe the workings of socialist parties in Europe in the early twentieth century. Even then there was a sense of despair felt by many radicals about the activities of the formal Left, by their betrayal of working-class movements, their authoritarianism and hierarchical organisational structures.

Imagine what someone like Michels (1962) would make of the social democratic parties today – imagine what he would make of a perverse and monstrous creation like New Labour, with its utter complicity with global neo-liberalism and the American Empire, and with its relentless and obsessive drive for more security, surveillance and social control. Neither the Labour Party in the UK – nor social democratic parties anywhere else for that matter – have anything to offer us except more authoritarianism. Having abandoned even the most modest attempts to ameliorate the capitalist system, the only sphere in which such parties can intervene – the only area in which they can be seen to be doing *something* (and notice how central the term 'reform' became to New Labour discourse) – is in the intensification of state control and surveillance. Whether under the guise of the social wars it wages against crime, deviancy, 'anti-social' behaviour, political dissent, welfare fraud or terrorism, governments have used every available opportunity to increase the power of the state to spy on us, stop and search us, detain us without charge, monitor our electronic communications, pry into and regulate just about every aspect of our lives – from the way we bring up our children, to the way in which we put our wheelie bins out for collection, to the exercise of what we once thought were our fundamental political rights and freedoms. Every morning on my way to work, I go through my local borough, Lewisham (a suburb in south-east London) – and I pass by numerous posters put up by some government agency saying something like 'We Are Closing In', with a picture of a stereotypical 'welfare cheat' – depicted as an unprepossessing, badly dressed, overweight woman, or a very shifty looking man, upon which has been superimposed the image of a target. Is this sort of crack-down propaganda – of which I see many examples in London on a daily basis, not to mention the ubiquitous surveillance cameras and other signs of social control – not virtually identical to the propaganda one might find in totalitarian regimes? Once again, we as a society are invited to close in around various 'class enemies' – no longer the bourgeoisie, but what Marx would call the lumpenproletariat. The aim of such propaganda is to construct an image of social unity – a stable social identity – through the exclusion and targeting of various social enemies, whether the teenage thug, the welfare cheat, the illegal immigrant, the sexual deviant, the Muslim terrorist. Its aim is also to take the attention away from the failings of government, its inability to prevent the social dislocation wrought by capitalist markets.

State authoritarianism and police power have of course been ramped up since the declaration of the 'war on terror'. Under the ubiquitous term 'security' what were previously thought unthinkable in a liberal democracy – detention without trial, the use of 'harsh interrogation' techniques – have now become commonplace practices. We should not assume that security is a politically neutral or benign idea – something that simply protects us from external attack: security is an ideology, it is a fundamentalism to which every other concern is subordinated; its logic is inexorable and without limit – we can never have too much security. And have we not seen these security measures being used not only against terrorist suspects, but against everyone else, from protesters, people sending their children to school outside their catchment area, and even against Icelandic banks?

The only thing that governments today have to offer is more security and, what is just as bad, more paternalism. Governments today – and once again the so-called social democratic ones are often the worst here – busy themselves with 'tackling' (a word they simply love!) 'teenage binge-drinking' and 'obesity epidemics'. The body itself has become the site for the deployment of excessive state power, a phenomenon mirrored and fetishised in those ghastly reality TV shows about 'Embarrassing Medical Conditions'. The French philosopher Alexis de Tocqueville (1994: 667), in his exploration of American democracy in the nineteenth century, spoke of new despotism there, 'an immense and protective power' that stands above the race of men and keeps them in perpetual childhood, covering 'the whole of social life with a network of petty, complicated rules that are both minute and uniform'. Today we can find this 'protective' power operating in societies like ours, where state surveillance and paternalism combine to hold us in perpetual thraldom and dependency – a permanent infantile state. We have all heard the expression the 'nanny state' – the idea that the state has taken over the role of parenting, treating us like children who need guidance and firm discipline. It is time to rescue this very apt term from Right-wing tabloid newspapers and mobilise it instead on the radical Left. We should no longer see the state as part of the solution, but as part of the problem – and

I think this realisation is dawning on many people today. Of course, as Tocqueville alluded to, we also develop a dependency on power: state domination is not only overt and top-down, it is also micro-political in the sense that it weaves itself into the social fabric at the infinitesimal level, generating a psychological dependency on power, even a desire for one's own repression. This is one of the major obstacles that radical politics has to deal with – and this is something I shall return to later.

The signs, however, are hopeful. The argument I have made thus far is that radical politics should have no truck with the state and with representative democracy – representative democracy is simply the ritual that symbolically legitimises state domination and confirms the iron law of oligarchy. This dissatisfaction with representative democracy is being borne out by an overall decline in levels of voter turnout in many societies – something that we should not necessarily interpret as a giving up on politics, but as a giving up on a certain very limited form of politics. In its place, people are doing politics differently, experimenting with different modes of political activity – including mass protests and social movements, but also more innovative forms of politics such as social forums; direct action (against, for instance, weapons installations, refugee detention camps, biomedical labs, GM farms); satirical spectacles and *detournement* (a form of cultural subversion involving techniques such as 'ad-busting' as a way of undermining dominant capitalist messages and drawing attention to contemporary society through the staging of alternative spectacles); 'Temporary Autonomous Zones' (TAZs) (practices, spectacles in which the current order is temporarily suspended and where new forms of freedom can be experimented with); the building of permanent autonomous communities; internet blogging and alternative media centres; through to computer hacking and various forms of sabotage (here I can only feel moved by a strange sense of awe and sympathy with that young man in the UK who was convicted in 2007 of engaging in a letter bombing campaign against what he saw as the 'surveillance society'; who has the right to laugh at or condemn as naïve his impotent, lonely and violent rage against a society that increasingly resembles a giant, hi-tech prison?).

Some of these practices have been on display in the massive mobilisations that we have seen in recent years against the G8 and WTO summits; others are less obvious and more everyday and imperceptible, but nevertheless just as important. I do not want to suggest that these new modes of politics are in themselves changing the world – although I think in small ways they are, or at least might do in the future – or that they are unproblematic. But they nevertheless represent a new way of practising politics, and they provide us with a new political language. That they are threatening to the current order can be evidenced by the massive police presence and security measures that are now deployed at these summits – our global political and economic masters are obviously worried about something.

What interests me about these new forms of politics is that they are essentially anarchistic – indeed, this anarchist quality has been commented on by many others (see for instance Graeber, 2002; Gordon, 2008). This can be seen in a number of ways. Firstly, as I have argued, it is a form of politics which refuses the state and works outside representative political structures: activists are not interested in running in elections or in seizing state power. This does not prevent them from making demands on the state – demands which at the same time call into question the very sovereignty of the state. For instance, the demand for an end to the draconian policing of borders and the detention of refugees and asylum seekers, at the same time calls into question the state's sovereignty over its own national territory, as well as drawing attention to the central contradiction of global capitalism: that it encourages the free flow of goods and capital across borders, while at the same time leading to greater restrictions on the movement of people. Secondly, in the actual practices and organisational structures of many of these radical movements there is an emphasis on direct action and decentralised, grassroots decision-making. This is a form of politics without a vanguard party, without anyone in the leadership role. Sometimes this can prove problematic and inconvenient, especially when coordinated action is called for – but on the whole, I see this refusal of hierarchy, leadership and authority as a good thing. It invokes the anarchist idea that any sort of revolution against political power must be libertarian in form as well as aim; that a project which seeks to overthrow power through authoritarian means – as in the idea of a centralised Leninist party vanguard – already falls into the trap of power and will only end perpetuating it. Thirdly, this new radical politics goes beyond both the Marxist politics of class struggle, as well as the identity politics that was predominant throughout the 1980s and 1990s. It is not a class-based politics in the traditional sense, because it incorporates a greater range of issues than strictly economic ones (even though these are often related to global capitalism) – such as the environment, state power, autonomy, indigenous rights, the status of 'illegal' migrants and so on. On the other hand, it is not a politics that is based on the assertion of an identity – cultural, ethnic, religious, sexual: there is a recognition that a differential identity does not, in itself, threaten the system of power (state capitalism is a system that is able to accommodate identity difference up to a certain point – in fact, it even actively endorses it, promoting sexual, ethnic and religious diversity, provided it does not transgress a certain limit, and provided it remains depoliticised). Indeed, I would argue that the radical politics of the future is more likely to be a politics of *dis-identification*, by which I mean not simply a questioning of established identities, but a kind of withdrawal from the system of power. To clarify this, I would like to invoke the nineteenth-century German existentialist philosopher Max Stirner's (1995: 280) notion of 'the insurrection' and the sense in which it is different from revolution:

> The Revolution aimed at new arrangements; insurrection leads us no longer to let ourselves be arranged, but to arrange ourselves, and sets no glittering hopes on 'institutions'. It is not a fight against the established, since, if it prospers, the established collapses of itself; it is only a working forth of me out of the established.

What Stirner is getting at here is that our relationship with power is much more complex than we imagine, that we have a psychological investment in power and even a desire for domination that we have to dislodge before we can liberate ourselves. So not only does the insurrection *not* seek to go through institutions – as the revolution does – but it can also be seen as a kind of personal insurrection, an attempt to work ourselves out of the bind of power. The insurrection can take a number of forms – indeed there are multiple insurrections at the level of everyday life. One of the most important, however, is the experimentation with alternative political practices and ways of life that are not regulated by the state: in other words, to show that lives can be lived and communities organised without the involvement of the state, is already a liberation from its power. This is not an escape from politics – precisely the opposite: it is an *active withdrawal* that fundamentally calls into question the symbolic authority of the state. The state's power over us depends on our recognition of this power, and, as Stirner (1995: 280) says, if we no longer recognise this power, then 'the established collapses of itself'.

References

Gordon, U. (2008) *Anarchy Alive! Anti-Authoritarian Politics: From Practice to Theory* (London: Pluto).

Graeber, D. (2002) 'The New Anarchists', *New Left Review*, 13 (Jan/Feb): 61–73.

Michels, R. (1962) *Political Parties: a Sociological Study of the Oligarchical Tendencies of Modern Democracy* (New York: Free Press).

Stirner, M. (1995) *The Ego and Its Own*, ed. D. Leopold (Cambridge: Cambridge University Press).

Tocqueville, A. de (1994) *Democracy in America*, trans. G. Lawrence (London: Fontana Press).

26
The Importance of Engaging the State

Chantal Mouffe

The way we envisage social criticism has very important consequences for radical politics. Radical politics today is often characterised in terms of desertion, exodus and refusal to engage with existing institutions. Whereas I believe that radical politics should instead be concerned with building political engagement, through developing competing, antagonistic political claims. My aim here is to highlight the main differences between these two characterisations. The first could roughly be described as 'critique as withdrawal'; the second as 'critique as engagement'. I will argue that, ultimately, the problem with the form of radical politics advocated by 'critique as withdrawal' is that it has a flawed understanding of the very nature of 'the political' itself.

Critique as withdrawal

The model of social criticism and radical politics put forward by Michel Hardt and Antonio Negri in their books *Empire* (2000) and *Multitude* (2004) is a good illustration of 'critique as withdrawal'. *Empire* is often referred to as the Communist manifesto for the twenty-first century in academic and activist conferences. In this book, the authors call for a total break with modernity and the elaboration of a postmodern approach. In their view such a break is required because of the crucial transformations of globalisation and the subsequent workers' struggle experienced by our society during the last decades of the twentieth century. According to Hardt and Negri, these transformations can be broadly summarised in the following way:

1. Sovereignty has taken a new form: there is a new global sovereignty, which Hardt and Negri call 'Empire'. They argue that this Empire is a

new imperialism that replaces the attempt by nation states to extend their own sovereignty beyond their borders. In contrast to old-style imperialism, the current Empire has no territorial centre of power and no fixed boundaries; it is decentred and deterritorialised, progressively incorporating the entire global realm with open, expanding frontiers.

2. This transformation corresponds, they say, to the transformation of the capitalist mode of production. The role of industrial factory labour has been reduced. Priority is instead given to communicative, cooperative and affective labour. In the postmodernisation of the global economy, the creation of wealth tends towards regulating and mediating life itself. It permeates every aspect of our life. The scope of the rule of Empire is social life in its entirety. All aspects of our life are controlled – from the way we work and exchange ideas across international borders, through to how we think about our body image.

3. We are witnessing the passage from a 'disciplinary society' to a 'society of control' characterised by a new paradigm of power. In the disciplinary society, which corresponds to the first phase of capitalist accumulation, command is constructed through diffuse networks of apparatus. These produce and regulate customs, habits and productive practices with the help of disciplinary institutions like prisons, factories, asylums, hospitals, schools and others. The society of control, in contrast, is a society in which mechanisms of command are less obvious. The society of control is dominated by the many mechanisms of the globalised, postmodern capitalist society, which seek to directly organise the brain and body (from the internet, through to complex global systems of trade). What is directly at stake is the regulation of life itself. This is what they call 'biopower'.

4. Hardt and Negri produce new terms to help explain this situation. These are 'mass intellectuality', 'immaterial labor' and 'general intellect'. The central role previously occupied by the labour-power of mass factory workers in the production of surplus-value is today said to be increasingly filled by intellectual, immaterial and communicative labour-power. For Hardt and Negri, the figure of immaterial labour involved in communication, cooperation and the reproduction of affects occupies an increasingly central position in the schema of capitalist production.

5. A new term is needed to refer to this collective worker that Hardt and Negri call the 'Multitude'. They believe that the transition to Empire – where territorial state sovereignty is less important – has opened up

new possibilities for the liberation of this Multitude. The Multitude have shaped a new form of globalisation, which means that previous systems and structures of exploitation and control, such as the state, are no longer needed. This is why their book *Empire* is so often referred to as the Communist manifesto of the twenty-first century. According to this manifesto, the creative forces of the Multitude are capable of constructing a counter-empire, of overthrowing the state apparatus of control. The present systems of control are no longer necessary. An alternative political organisation of the global flows of exchange now dominates in this era of globalisation. We can, therefore, get rid of territorial sovereignty because it only serves to oppress our creativity. Hardt and Negri therefore clearly illustrate what I previously called, in my introduction to this chapter, 'critique as withdrawal': a refusal to engage with existing institutions.

At this point it is worth introducing the work of Paolo Virno to complement the picture. Virno's analyses in his book *Grammar of the Multitude* (2004) dovetail in many respects with those of Hardt and Negri. But there are also some significant differences. For instance, he is much less sanguine about the future. While Hardt and Negri have a messianic vision of the role of the Multitude, which will necessarily bring down Empire and establish an 'Absolute Democracy', Virno does not. For Virno, the present conditions are not right for a communist future. It is unlikely that the sort of 'Absolute Democracy' that Hardt and Negri envisage will actually take place. Instead of seeing the generalisation of immaterial labour as a type of 'spontaneous communism' like Hardt and Negri, Virno tends to see post-Fordism as a manifestation of the 'communism of capital'. Under post-Fordism, consumers pursue different goals, with services responding accordingly. This means that today, for Virno, capitalistic initiatives orchestrate material and cultural conditions for their own benefit. And the role of political action should be to create a sphere of common affairs – which he calls the 'Republic of the Multitude' – to challenge this situation. Virno proposes two key terms to describe the type of political action which he thinks is necessary. These are 'exodus' and 'civil disobedience'. And for me, they again illustrate what I call 'critique as withdrawal': something which is an important and influential trend in radical politics today because exodus advocates mass defection from the state. This requires the development of a non-state public sphere and a radically new type of democracy. It involves experimenting in new forms of non-representative and extra-parliamentary democracy, organised around leagues, councils and soviets. The Multitude never aspire to transform themselves into a majority. They develop a power that refuses to become government. This is why, according to Virno, civil disobedience needs to be emancipated from the liberal tradition. He does not just want to ignore specific laws if they do not conform to the principles of a given territorial constitution or state. For Virno, like Hardt and Negri, radical disobedience goes much further – it puts the existence of the state itself in question.

In both Hardt and Negri, and Virno, there is therefore emphasis upon 'critique as withdrawal'. They all call for the development of a non-state public sphere. They call for self-organisation, experimentation, non-representative and extra-parliamentary politics. They see forms of traditional representative politics as inherently oppressive. So they do not seek to engage with them, in order to challenge them. They seek to get rid of them altogether. This disengagement is, for such influential personalities in radical politics today, the key to every political position in the world. The Multitude must recognise imperial sovereignty itself as the enemy and discover adequate means of subverting its power. Whereas in the disciplinary era I spoke about earlier, sabotage was the fundamental form of political resistance, these authors claim that, today, it should be desertion. It is indeed through desertion, through the evacuation of the places of power, that they think that battles against Empire might be won. Desertion and exodus are, for these important thinkers, a powerful form of class struggle against imperial postmodernity.

According to Hardt and Negri, and Virno, radical politics in the past was dominated by the notion of 'the people'. This was, according to them, a unity, acting with one will. And this unity is linked to the existence of the state. The Multitude, on the contrary, shuns political unity. It is not representable because it is an active self-organising agent that can never achieve the status of a juridical personage. It can never converge in a general will, because the present globalisation of capital and workers' struggles will not permit this. It is anti-state and anti-popular. Hardt and Negri claim that the Multitude cannot be conceived any more in terms of a sovereign authority that is representative of the people. They therefore argue that new forms of politics, which are non-representative, are needed. They advocate a withdrawal from existing institutions. This is something which characterises much of radical politics today. The emphasis is not upon challenging the state. Radical politics today is often characterised by a mood, a sense and a feeling, that the state itself is inherently the problem.

Critique as engagement

I will now turn to presenting the way I envisage the form of social criticism best suited to radical politics today. I agree with Hardt and Negri that it is important to understand the transition from Fordism to post-Fordism. But I consider that the dynamics of this transition is better apprehended within the framework of the approach outlined in the book *Hegemony and Socialist Strategy: Towards a Radical Democratic Politics* (Laclau and Mouffe, 2001). What I want to stress is that many factors have contributed to this transition from Fordism to post-Fordism, and that it is necessary to recognise its complex nature. My problem with Hardt and Negri's view is that, by putting so much emphasis on the workers' struggles, they tend to see this transition as if it was driven by one single logic: the workers' resistance to the forces of capitalism in the post-Fordist era. They put too much emphasis upon immaterial labour. In their view, capitalism can only be reactive and they refuse to accept the creative role played both by capital and by labour. To put it another way, they deny the positive role of political struggle.

In *Hegemony and Socialist Strategy: Towards a Radical Democratic Politics* we use the word 'hegemony' to describe the way in which meaning is given to institutions or practices: for example, the way in which a given institution or practice is defined as 'oppressive to women', 'racist' or 'environmentally destructive'. We also point out that every hegemonic order is therefore susceptible to being challenged by counter-hegemonic practices – feminist, anti-racist, environmentalist, for example. This is illustrated by the plethora of new social movements which presently exist in radical politics today (Christian, anti-war, counter-globalisation, Muslim, and so on). Clearly not all of these are workers' struggles. In their various ways they have nevertheless attempted to influence and have influenced a new hegemonic order. This means that when we talk about 'the political', we do not lose sight of the ever present possibility of heterogeneity and antagonism within society. There are many different ways of being antagonistic to a dominant order in a heterogeneous society – it need not only refer to the workers' struggles. I submit that it is necessary to introduce this hegemonic dimension when one envisages the transition from Fordism to post-Fordism. This means abandoning the view that a single logic (workers' struggles) is at work in the evolution of the work process; as well as acknowledging the pro-active role played by capital.

In order to do this we can find interesting insights in the work of Luc Boltanski and Eve Chiapello who, in their book *The New Spirit of*

Capitalism (2005), bring to light the way in which capitalists manage to use the demands for autonomy of the new movements that developed in the 1960s, harnessing them in the development of the post-Fordist networked economy and transforming them into new forms of control. They use the term 'artistic critique' to refer to how the strategies of the counter-culture (the search for authenticity, the ideal of self-management and the anti-hierarchical exigency) were used to promote the conditions required by the new mode of capitalist regulation, replacing the disciplinary framework characteristic of the Fordist period. From my point of view, what is interesting in this approach is that it shows how an important dimension of the transition from Fordism to post-Fordism involves rearticulating existing discourses and practices in new ways. It allows us to visualise the transition from Fordism to post-Fordism in terms of a hegemonic intervention. To be sure, Boltanski and Chiapello never use this vocabulary, but their analysis is a clear example of what Gramsci called 'hegemony through neutralisation' or 'passive revolution'. This refers to a situation where demands which challenge the hegemonic order are recuperated by the existing system, which is achieved by satisfying them in a way that neutralises their subversive potential. When we apprehend the transition from Fordism to post-Fordism within such a framework, we can understand it as a hegemonic move by capital to re-establish its leading role and restore its challenged legitimacy. We did not witness a revolution, in Marx's sense of the term. Rather, there have been many different interventions, challenging dominant hegemonic practices.

It is clear that, once we envisage social reality in terms of 'hegemonic' and 'counter-hegemonic' practices, radical politics is not about withdrawing completely from existing institutions. Rather, we have no other choice but to engage with hegemonic practices, in order to challenge them. This is crucial; otherwise we will be faced with a chaotic situation. Moreover, if we do not engage with and challenge the existing order, if we instead choose to simply escape the state completely, we leave the door open for others to take control of systems of authority and regulation. Indeed there are many historical (and not so historical) examples of this. When the Left shows little interest, Right-wing and authoritarian groups are only too happy to take over the state.

The strategy of exodus could be seen as the reformulation of the idea of communism, as it was found in Marx. There are many points in common between the two perspectives. To be sure, for Hardt and Negri it is no longer the proletariat, but the Multitude which is the privileged political subject. But in both cases the state is seen as a monolithic apparatus of domination that cannot be transformed. It has to 'wither away' in order to leave room for a reconciled society beyond law, power and sovereignty. In reality, as I've already noted, others are often perfectly willing to take control.

If my approach – supporting new social movements and counter-hegemonic practices – has been called 'post-Marxist' by many, it is precisely because I have challenged the very possibility of such a reconciled society. To acknowledge the ever present possibility of antagonism to the existing order implies recognising that heterogeneity cannot be eliminated. As far as politics is concerned, this means the need to envisage it in terms of a hegemonic struggle between conflicting hegemonic projects attempting to incarnate the universal and to define the symbolic parameters of social life. A successful hegemony fixes the meaning of institutions and social practices and defines the 'common sense' through which a given conception of reality is established. However, such a result is always contingent, precarious and susceptible to being challenged by counter-hegemonic interventions. Politics always takes place in a field criss-crossed by antagonisms. A properly political intervention is always one that engages with a certain aspect of the existing hegemony. It can never be merely oppositional or conceived as desertion, because it aims to challenge the existing order, so that it may reidentify and feel more comfortable with that order.

Another important aspect of a hegemonic politics lies in establishing linkages between various demands (such as environmentalists, feminists, anti-racist groups), so as to transform them into claims that will challenge the existing structure of power relations. This is a further reason why critique involves engagement, rather than disengagement. It is clear that the different demands that exist in our societies are often in conflict with each other. This is why they need to be articulated politically, which obviously involves the creation of a collective will, a 'we'. This, in turn, requires the determination of a 'them'. This obvious and simple point is missed by the various advocates of the Multitude. For they seem to believe that the Multitude possesses a natural unity which does not need political articulation. Hardt and Negri see 'the People' as homogeneous and expressed in a unitary general will, rather than divided by different political conflicts. Counter-hegemonic practices, by contrast, do not eliminate differences. Rather, they are what could be called an 'ensemble of differences', all coming together, only at a given moment, against a common adversary. Such as when different groups from many backgrounds come together to protest against a war perpetuated by a state, or when environmentalists, feminists, anti-racists and others come together to challenge dominant models of development and progress. In these cases, the adversary cannot be defined in broad general terms like 'Empire', or for that matter 'Capitalism'. It is instead contingent upon the particular circumstances in question – the specific states, international institutions or governmental practices that are to be challenged. Put another way, the construction of political demands is dependent upon the specific relations of power that need to be targeted and transformed, in order to create the conditions for a new hegemony. This is clearly not an exodus from politics. It is not 'critique as withdrawal', but 'critique as engagement'. It is a 'war of position' that needs to be launched, often across a range of sites, involving the coming together of a range of interests. This can only be done by establishing links between social movements, political parties and trade unions, for example. The aim is to create a common bond and collective will, engaging with a wide range of sites, and often institutions, with the aim of transforming them. This, in my view, is how we should conceive the nature of radical politics.

References

Boltanski, L. and E. Chiapello (2005) *The New Spirit of Capitalism*, trans. G. Elliott (London: Verso).

Hardt, M. and A. Negri (2000) *Empire* (New York: Harvard University Press).

Hardt, M. and A. Negri (2004) *Multitude: War and Democracy in the Age of Empire* (London: Penguin).

Laclau, E. and C. Mouffe (2001) *Hegemony and Socialist Strategy: Towards a Radical Democratic Politics*, 2nd edn (London: Verso).

Virno, P. (2004) *A Grammar of the Multitude: For an Analysis of Contemporary Forms of Life*, trans. I. Bertoletti and J. Cascaito (Semiotext(e)) (New York and Los Angeles: Casson. Distributed by MIT Press, Cambridge, MA and London, England).

27
Common-sense Beyond the Neo-liberal State

David Featherstone

In July, 2007 going home one night after a day spent working in Glasgow's Mitchell Library, I ended up chatting with a porter. He was working late providing cover for an event happening after the library had closed and was not particularly happy about this. I empathised with his complaints about having to work late. What I found interesting, though, was that his chief bone of contention was that the event he was providing cover for was private. He argued that such an event was not a correct use of the library's facilities and was outside the proper function of the library as a public space.

Much has been written about the success of the neo-liberal project in making many of its central claims about politics and the economy part of the common-sense of our times. The terms of our conversation, though, were firmly at odds with such a position. There was a shared understanding about the importance of public sites like libraries and the 'proper' distance they should have from the market. The conversation reminded me of the importance of seeing common-sense as contested and in process rather than accepting that the neo-liberals had successfully remade common-sense in their own image. As Gramsci (1985: 421) argued, 'common-sense' is not a stable end point or consensus, but is characterised by instability and is a terrain of contestation.

This chapter seeks to engage with the significance of the contestation of neo-liberalism for radical politics today. Through doing so it engages with the changes and transformations that shape radical politics today. The first part of the chapter discusses debates about the emergence of a 'radical centre' or Third Way politics which has sought to accommodate social democratic goals with neo-liberal globalisation (Giddens, 1998). I engage with claims by Chantal Mouffe and Slavoj Žižek that this has produced a contemporary epoch that is post-political. I argue that their critiques of the radical centre, while important, tend to ignore the ways in which the neo-liberal structuring of globalisation has been brought into contestation by transnational resistances. I refer to these movements as 'counter-globalisation movements' rather than 'anti-globalisation' to signal the way their political project is as much about generating alternative forms of globalisation as contesting globalisation per se. The second section engages with the alternatives to neo-liberal globalisation that such movements have articulated. It draws out four key elements of these alternatives that are of particular significance in relation to the current crisis and which might contribute to a common-sense beyond neo-liberalism.

Space, neo-liberalism and contestation

A central claim of theorists and politicians associated with the radical centre and the Third Way has been that 'old' styles of politics ordered around political antagonisms, most significantly between Left and Right, are no longer relevant. Anthony Giddens (1998), for example, has claimed that politics is a domain that can now be characterised by harmonious negotiation rather than the definition of adversaries or enemies. Giddens' consensual construction of politics isolates citizens' engagements with the unequal power relations that shape processes like globalisation. He argues that 'the overall aim of Third Way politics should be to help citizens pilot their way through the major revolutions of our time' (Giddens, 1998: 64). He removes conflict from the political through setting up 'globalisation, changes in family structure and the transformations of our relationship to nature' as 'transformations that citizens should be "piloted through"' (Giddens, 1998: 64). This language is instructive. Giddens' work develops a passive construction of citizenship. This denies citizens any role or agency in negotiating, shaping or engaging with such transformations. Such a passive construction of citizenship, and the role of politics more generally, has been central to the project of Third Way political parties such as New Labour.

The consensual politics associated with the Third Way has been critiqued by a number of authors who have characterised the current 'era' as being 'post-political'. The political theorist Chantal Mouffe (who also contributes to this volume) has persistently argued for a reassertion of the significance of antagonism for contemporary politics (see Mouffe, 2005). Her central contention is that the move away from a notion of the political centred on conflict and contestation has had devastating consequences for both understandings and practices of politics. For Mouffe the radical centre denies the role of conflict in the political, and is based on an inadequate understanding of the constitution, and persistence, of collective political identities. She argues that the key challenge facing contemporary politics is not to move beyond conflict, but to find ways of dealing with conflict in democratic terms. If conflict isn't negotiated as part of democratic politics she contends that grievances can be articulated in ways which threaten democratic norms and values, for example by Right-wing populists like Jorg Haider. Žižek (1999), in similar vein, argues that conflict re-emerges, in post-political times, in the guise of fundamentalisms.

The reassertion of the importance of conflict and unequal power relations to the political by theorists such as Mouffe and Žižek is significant. There are tensions, however, in their identification of the contemporary moment as 'post-political'. Their account of contemporary political life as defined by a move beyond conflict and antagonism depends on a limited notion of what constitutes the political and of the geographies through which politics is conducted (Featherstone, 2008). They construct the national as the key site where political antagonisms are to be constructed and negotiated primarily through parliamentary politics. This has consequences. It makes it difficult to engage with some of the key movements that have brought the unequal geographies of neo-liberal globalisation into contestation. These are the transnational networks of resistance associated with the counter-globalisation movements.[1]

These political movements have brought neo-liberal globalisation into contestation in diverse ways. Further, they have demonstrated that neo-liberal globalisation is produced through a set of practices that citizens can contest and shape rather than being 'piloted through'. These movements, however, have been defined through the dynamic and generative ways in which they have brought the geographies of power produced through neo-liberal globalisation into contestation. By geographies of power I mean the unequal connections, flows and networks which are integral to neo-liberal globalisation. The forms of political activity deployed through counter-global networks disrupt the theoretical and political positions of both Third Way politics and theorists like Mouffe, Swyngedouw and Žižek who define the contemporary epoch as 'post-political'. Movements such as the transnational opposition to the actions of companies such as Coca-Cola emphasise how contested forms of the political are still being generated.

The contestation of the Coca-Cola Corporation demonstrates that this is a productive process. It brings together different movements contesting the multinational on different terms and in different places.

Coca-Cola has been the subject of mobilisation around the rights of trade unionists because of its alleged links to the assassination of trade unionists in Colombia and the subject of contestation over its environmental record, particularly in India (Gill, 2006, 2007; Higginbottom, 2007). In Kerala the multinational has been accused of 'creating severe water shortage, of polluting its groundwater and soil, and also of distributing toxic waste as fertiliser to farmers in the area' (Raman, 2005: 2481). Such conflicts produce transnational alliances and articulations of grievances that exceed the arenas of nation-state politics that structure Mouffe's analysis. In this sense they have dragged into the terrain of contestation aspects of the neo-liberal constitution of globalisation that are placed outside the limits of the political consensus. Such a political consensus has been established strongly in countries like Britain and the USA, and is also significant elsewhere. In India, for example, the adoption of neo-liberal industrial policies by the Communist Party (CPI(M)) in West Bengal and Kerala, where it is the leading partner in the Left Front governments, has brought the CPI(M) within the political consensus shaped by India's economic liberalisation.

Following the political practices through which movements have brought powerful multinational companies and neo-liberal institutions such as the World Trade Organization and IMF into contestation, then, produces productive and generative geographies of contestation. Bringing these relations of power into contestation involves following and contesting relations of power that stretch beyond the nation state. These movements have often constructed political agency and identities through bringing into contestation such unequal geographies of power. Their significance in bringing the neo-liberal practices structuring contemporary forms of globalisation into visibility/contestation should not be underestimated, particularly in a context where contestation of these neo-liberal practices and conventions has all too frequently been placed outside of mainstream political debate. As David Graeber (2007: 4) has argued:

> The Washington consensus lies in ruins. So much so it's hard to remember what public discourse in this country was even like before Seattle. Rarely have the media and political classes been so completely unanimous about anything. That 'free trade', 'free markets', and no-holds-barred supercharged capitalism was the only possible direction for human history, the only possible solution for any problem was so completely assumed that anyone who cast doubt on the proposition was treated as literally insane. Global justice activists, when they first forced themselves into the attention of CNN or Newsweek, were

immediately written off as reactionary lunatics. A year or two later, CNN and Newsweek were saying we'd won the argument.

Recent events such as the financial crash and the resulting part-nationalisation of major banks on both sides of the Atlantic make this assessment more prescient. What, however, seems remarkable in the wake of the crash and the discrediting of neo-liberalism, even on its own terms as the only sound way to effectively run the global economy, is the lack of alternative voices and political agendas that have been articulated. This situation is beginning to change, however, with a marked politicisation of the crisis articulated through the resistances that are coalescing around the G20 summit in London.

There have been some significant attempts to shape the political agenda in progressive ways. The report of the Green New Deal group and the political alliances between trade unions, development NGOs and environmental groups that have supported this agenda is significant for example. Mainstream political discourse, however, has remained entrenched firmly within a Third Way agenda of articulating how best to manage the economy. It hasn't broached the implications of the failure of neo-liberalism to deliver as a means of economic governance let alone as a political/economic system that has entrenched and intensified inequalities and environmental destruction. Given that capitalism has shown itself to be adept at reinventing itself in periods of crisis, it is crucial that the Left uses the current moment to develop counter-hegemonic visions/projects. The next section takes up this challenge through engaging with key aspects of the political practices and alternatives shaped through the counter-globalisation movements.

Actually existing alternatives to neo-liberalism

The networked resistances to neo-liberal globalisation have been defined not only by bringing neo-liberalism into contestation. They have also been defined by their experiments with political alternatives to neo-liberalism and crucially with different ways of generating globalisation. These movements have not generated a singular alternative or programme. Rather, mobilising and engaging with a plurality of political strategies and alternatives has been central to their political identities and practices. Here I point to some key contributions that I think are of particular importance/relevance for the current conjuncture, while also engaging with some of the tensions generated through the activity of these movements.

Firstly, one of the most significant achievements of these movements is to have generated translocal connections through their organising against neo-liberal globalisation. Thus rather than producing oppositions to globalisation which are based on pitting bounded exclusionary notions of the local or national against an alien 'global', some of these movements have produced translocal articulations based around practices of solidarity between different struggles. Such solidarities have been generated through sites such as the World Social Forum and the alliances forged through campaigns such as those against Coca-Cola. This has demonstrated the possibility of producing forms of globalisation based around ethics of solidarity and connection, rather than around exploitation and profit. These geographies of connection are a central part of the actually existing alternatives to neo-liberal globalisation shaped by these movements.

Secondly, the counter-globalisation movements have articulated forms of political identity, struggle and solidarities where environmental concerns and issues of social justice are combined in innovative and significant ways. Thus the transnational organising against Coca-Cola has linked grievances in relation to Coca-Cola's environmental and human rights record in distinctive ways. Through such imaginative connections and alliances and through foregrounding questions of environmental and social injustice, these movements have contested the terms on which environmentalism is defined. These alliances have articulated environmentalisms of the poor, for example, which contest dominant assumptions that environmental politics is the domain of privileged middle-class groups.

These antagonistic articulations of environmental politics have particular resonance in relation to the dominant way in which debates on climate change have been constructed. Erik Swyngedouw (2007), drawing on the 'post-political thesis' of Mouffe and Žižek, has interpreted the politics of climate change as a manifestation of such depoliticisation. Swyngedouw, however, shares Mouffe and Žižek's nation-centred account of the political and ignores the antagonisms constructed by different activists and social/political movements in relation to climate change. These antagonisms have disrupted the consensual framing of the climate change debate and directly related climate change to the unequal geopolitics of neo-liberal globalisation. Thus groups like Platform have articulated climate change politics directly to the forms of social and environmental injustice associated with transnational oil companies. They illuminate the ways in which environmentalisms have engaged with struggles against the unequal social and environmental relations made through neo-liberal practices, which are absolutely central to climate change politics. These cuts into the contested geographies of power associated with climate change have forged distinctive alternatives to the unjust and wasteful social and environmental relations produced through neo-liberal globalisation. Such attempts to make issues of social and environmental injustice central to a politics of climate change are deeply antagonistic to mainstream/environmental modernisation approaches.

Thirdly, these struggles are generative of new ways of articulating social and environmental relations. Neo-liberalism generates particular relations between humans and non-humans through neo-liberal conventions and practices. The contestation of neo-liberal practices like privatisation has frequently been dismissed as merely being defensive reactions to such neo-liberal conventions and projects. Through such struggles, however, innovative forms of ordering such relations are being generated. A good example here are the struggles against water privatisation in Bolivia. The disputes over water privatisation in Cochamba where different social movements/unions successfully mobilised against Bechtel have been well publicised. This took place in a context where transnational water policy networks have shaped a pro-privatisation consensus.

These movements were successful in bringing into contestation attempts to privatise water. They were not, however, just movements about defending an existing status quo against privatisation. Movement intellectuals/leaders like Oscar Olivera, of the Cochamba Federation of Factory Workers, mobilised around not just a rejection of water privatisation, but also around a critique of existing state-led provision. Their contestation of privatisation opened up spaces for experimenting with new forms of common ownership/participatory control that were seen as alternatives to both privatisation and existing state-led provision. This was related to a particular kind of organisational politics that has also been a key contribution of such movements and is central to their political identities. Olivera argued that 'We managed to build a movement that doesn't have *caudillos* or untouchable leaders, doesn't have decisions made from above, but rather is transparent and honest. Most important it empowered a people' (Oscar Olivera, cited by Kohl and Farthing, 2006: 167).

Finally, these movements have intervened in important ways in how local resistances/practices of localisation are envisioned. This is a set of political interventions which are likely to be crucial given the twin challenges of a global economic downturn combined with the ecological crisis associated with climate change. One of the major tensions associated with opposition to neo-liberal globalisation has been that many political movements, often but not exclusively connected with the political Right, have mobilised bounded, exclusionary notions of the local or national against globalisation. These are frequently based around the mobilising of extremely regressive gender/race politics. Right-wing political parties such as the Hindu Nationalist BJP have also shown themselves to be adept at co-opting struggles such as popular resistance to Enron in India and using them to build their own political agendas. Given Eric Hobsbawm's (2008) argument that the chief beneficiaries of the current political and economic crisis may well be the far-Right, the significance of intervening in these debates in ways which articulate 'resistance' in a progressive direction is not to be underestimated.

Particularly significant in this regard are ways of envisioning local resistances and practices of localisation, not in isolation, however, but as part of alternative practices of globalisation from below. Thus experiments with localisation can be defined through mobilising connections rather than just retreating into atavistic or chauvinistic versions of the local. The localisation strategies developed by the Brazilian land rights movement Movimento Sem Terra, for example, have been directly linked to various internationalist struggles against neo-liberal globalisation. They have been forged through connections with other movements such as the French peasant movement Confédération Paysanne and through Via Campesina, the influential international network of peasant movements. Such alternatives suggest ways of developing low carbon alternatives, but whilst generating internationalist political identities and imaginaries. This emphasises the possibilities opened up by articulating local resistances and practices of localisation in solidaristic ways.

Conclusions

This chapter has sought to engage with the significance of movements that have brought the neo-liberal structuring of globalisation into contestation. I have argued that the diverse and generative geographies of contestation shaped by such movements are central to contemporary radical politics. I have drawn upon the critique of the radical centre offered by Mouffe and Žižek. However, I have also argued that their characterisation of contemporary politics as 'post-political' is problematic. There is a need to engage with the diverse ways in which the geographies of power of neo-liberal globalisation have been brought into contestation and the implications this has for generating radical political agendas. This unsettles the rather nation-centred account of the political that structures the work of Mouffe and Žižek.

These political movements have constituted elements of actually existing alternatives to neo-liberal globalisation. These alternatives are necessarily fragmentary, diverse and contested. Developing such alternatives will also necessarily be a fraught process. As I emphasised through the story that starts this chapter the construction of common-sense as neo-liberal is partial, unfinished and open to contestation. Recognising this allows the shaping of forms of common-sense beyond neo-liberalism. The actually existing alternatives discussed here suggest some elements of such a common-sense. Articulating forms of localisation and local resistance in internationalist ways will be particularly important for the coming times.

Note

1. Mouffe does point to the importance of these movements in struggling for another globalisation, but her analysis of the current conjuncture has little analytical space for the ways in which these movements have brought neo-liberalism into the terrain of contestation.

References

Featherstone, D. J. (2008) *Resistance, Space and Political Identities: the Making of Counter-Global Networks* (Oxford: Wiley-Blackwell).

Giddens, A. (1998) *The Third Way: the Renewal of Social Democracy* (Cambridge: Polity Press).

Gill, L. (2006) 'Fighting for Justice, Dying for Hope: On the Protest Line in Colombia', *North American Dialogue*, 9(2): 9–13.

Gill, L. (2007) ' "Right there with you": Coca-Cola, Labor Restructuring and Political Violence in Colombia', *Critique of Anthropology*, 27(3): 235–60.

Graeber, D. (2007) 'The Shock of Victory', *Rolling Thunder*, August: 4.

Gramsci, A. (1985) *Selections from Cultural Writings* (London: Lawrence & Wishart).

Higginbottom, A. (2007) 'Killer Coke', in W. Dinan and D. Miller (eds), *Thinker, Faker, Spinner, Spy: Corporate PR and the Assault on Democracy* (London: Pluto Press), pp. 278–94.

Hobsbawm, E. (2008) 'After Crisis, a Mixed Economy', BBC Interview with Eric Hobsbawm 14 December, http://news.bbc.co.uk/today/hi/today/newsid_7677000/7677683.stm

Kohl, B. and J. Farthing (2006) *Impasse in Bolivia: Neo-liberal Hegemony and Popular Resistance* (London: Zed Books).

Mouffe, C. (2005) *On the Political* (London: Routledge).

Raman, R. (2005) 'Corporate Violence, Legal Nuances and Political Ecology: Cola War in Plachimada', *Economic and Political Weekly*, 18 June: 2481–5.

Swyngedouw, E. (2007) 'Impossible "Sustainability" and the Post-political Condition', in D. Gibbs and R. Krueger (eds), *Sustainable Development* (New York: Guilford Press), pp. 13–40.

Žižek, S. (1999) 'Carl Schmitt in the Age of Post-Politics', in C. Mouffe (ed.), *The Challenge of Carl Schmitt* (London: Verso), pp. 18–37.

28

Democracy, the State and Capitalism Today

Alejandro Colás and Jason Edwards

Many forms of contemporary politics are radical in that they seek a root and branch transformation of mainstream politics, or aim to challenge power from the bottom up. They are seen as radical either because they engage in different ways of doing politics (e.g. direct action, publicity stunts, creating 'transversal' alliances) or because they offer fresh and subversive ways of thinking about politics – or both. But not all these expressions of politics are progressive. Across the world political movements and organisations adopt religious fundamentalism, racism, sectarianism, xenophobia or misogyny as their guiding programme in ways that can objectively be considered radical. Moreover, some contemporary political movements and organisations are radical in their actions, but not in their thinking (and vice-versa).

We are not interested in this chapter in exploring reactionary or regressive forms of radicalism – powerful as these often are – but are principally concerned with progressive ways of doing and thinking about radical politics. From this perspective, the most progressive forms of radical politics today are rooted in struggles for substantive or radical democracy (we use these terms interchangeably). What this means concretely will vary from one place to the next (this is in fact one marker of progressive radicalism). Yet the common denominator in the politics of radical democracy involves individuals obtaining greater collective control over our everyday lives: securing basic human needs to work, education, health and housing; extending the rights to, and realm of, collective decision-making in the workplace; generating greater personal autonomy, particularly with regard to control over our own bodies; and fostering mechanisms to collectively combat diverse forms of public and private oppression, discrimination and prejudice.

These are among the political objectives which, for most of the world's population, remain radical aspirations, both because they are often still very distant and also because achieving them requires radically upsetting existing power relations. Such political objectives certainly draw on and defend the apparatus of formal democracy – competitive elections for office, guarantee of civil liberties, separation of powers and so forth. But underlying such radical aspirations is the conviction that purely formal democratic procedures remain mere institutional shells if they are not given substance by the kinds of collective control over our everyday lives mentioned above.

Two modern political structures lie at the root of struggles for the kind of radical democracy just described. The first is global capitalism. Since its inception in Europe during the 'long' sixteenth century (1450–1650), the capitalist market has acted both as a radical force of socio-economic and cultural change and as a powerful social mechanism of domination, wanton despoliation and violence – a dialectic famously labelled as 'creative destruction' by Joseph Schumpeter (1975). Capitalism has uprooted vast populations from their immediate access to land and water as sources of livelihood, and thrown them into the maelstrom of market dependence mediated through the cash nexus. This has enabled many millions previously shackled to the arbitrary whims of landlords, patriarchs, arcane customs or even nature itself to at the very least fight for, and often obtain, some semblance of substantive democracy. Successive democratic struggles for working-class enfranchisement, gender equality, national liberation or just and sustainable development across the world have cashed in some of the prosperity, freedom and equality promised by global capitalism.

The extent of such prosperity, freedom and equality has generally been conditional upon the degree of resistance to capitalism displayed by the peoples subject to this new market logic. In those societies where workers and other subaltern classes have managed to sustain a popular mobilisation against market forces – in Europe after both world wars, in the USA during the New Deal and the Civil Rights era, in the erstwhile Third World during the protracted processes of decolonisation – radical democracy has made considerable strides. Plainly, such progress is rarely linear and never definitive. Securing radical democracy requires constant social mobilisation and political vigilance. Democratic gains are eminently reversible. Still, 'progress' understood as the consolidation of democratic gains over the capitalist market and its accompanying forms of oppression and discrimination, warrants talk of a tradition of radical politics which today continues to combat and undermine such expressions of power.

The second political structure which is central to the realisation of radical democracy is the state. This may at first sight appear paradoxical. Agents and institutions of the modern state have after all been responsible for some of the most heinous forms of oppression and violence in modern times. Progressive radicalism can quickly degenerate into authoritarianism and dictatorship if the state becomes the sole vehicle for defending and mobilising substantive democracy. Yet equally, without the powerful resources of the modern state – its capacity to collect and reinvest revenue; to regulate the economy and redistribute wealth; to provide for or coordinate the delivery of the necessary infrastructure in securing basic human needs – struggles for radical democracy can get stuck in the debilitating treadmill of constant protest, perpetual mobilisation and ubiquitous antagonism. This latter understanding of radical politics as 'pure movement' misses the critical point that the greatest contemporary obstacle to substantive democracy – capitalism – itself thrives on constant movement, on the uninterrupted process of exchange and the destabilisation of community. In contrast, the creation of an inclusive substantive democracy requires a large degree of institutional stability and continuity. The logic of capital is a fundamentally temporal one: capitalist profit derives from exchanging labour-time for a money wage; in generating future returns on current investments; in anticipating sharp movements in the money markets. The logic of radical democracy on the other hand is essentially spatial: it requires access to and redistribution of wealth generated within delimited spaces; it involves the territorial definition of a specific political community (the 'demos', the people); above all, it necessitates the territorial authority of the state when protecting democracy from the footloose logic of the market, or at the very least democratically harnessing the dynamics of the international capitalist market to the needs and interests of the majority of citizens in any given political community.

The crisis in international financial markets that started with the collapse of Lehman Brothers in September 2008 highlights this fundamental tension between democratic stability and capitalist mobility. It moreover demonstrates the centrality of the state to contemporary politics and society. Capitalism has, not for the first, and probably not for the last time, been saved by the economic resources and political power of the state. And it's already becoming evident (we write in October 2008) that the kind of capitalism emerging out of this crisis is likely to be a very different beast than that we have become used to over the last thirty years.

We may therefore well be witnessing the death of neo-liberalism. Its demise presents new opportunities but also great dangers. The extent of these dangers rests largely on the severity of the economic downturn that will now inevitably follow the financial crisis. The Great Depression brought in its wake the ascendancy of extreme nationalism and fascism. The democracy of citizens and civility gave way to the democracy of blood and land. Economic protectionism, now as then, can all too readily lend itself to the promotion of national, ethnic and racial enmities. Factor into a severe economic depression conflict between states over energy resources, land and water in an era of dangerous and unpredictable climate change, and we are presented with a potentially bleak picture of the future.

Of course, it may well be the case that the world escapes with a relatively minor recession. But even if so, it seems unlikely that neo-liberal voices claiming it all to be a blip will carry the day. The current crisis was a direct product of the liberalisation of international financial markets that has taken place over the last thirty years. The warning signs for the West were clearly there in the shape of the Asian crisis of 1997 and the collapse of the Argentinian economy in 2002. The Asian and Argentinian economies were bailed out by the IMF, subject to the stringencies of neo-liberal structural adjustment policies. But the IMF has nothing like the resources to rescue the financial institutions of the West, and there is now no appetite in Western governments for the further deregulation of money markets demanded by the IMF in its interventions. Any governing party proposing to extend the life of the neo-liberal project after September 2008 is likely to be routed at the polls.

Whether what lies ahead is minor recession, major depression, or something in between, the international political landscape is clearly changing. The progressive Left will need to figure out in the next few years where it fits into this transformed terrain. It cannot hope to learn much from itself in the last thirty years. Whether that period in its history proves to be farce or tragedy is yet to be determined. But what is now starting to stand out in relief is that the two main models of progressive politics that have come to dominate in recent years are destined to share the fate of neo-liberalism, in large measure because of their own uncritical privileging of global movement over the territorial polity in the formulation of their radicalism.

This seems most obviously the case for the Clinton–Blair Third Way. The political Third Way embraced the ideology of globalisation, blithely accepting the arguments of authors like Anthony Giddens (1998) about the inexorable compression of space by time under global capitalism. Giddens saw the liberalisation of financial markets as having eliminated the capacity of nation states to effectively intervene in economic management and, by so doing, to maintain and extend radical democracy within any given territory. A politics of state coordination of production and consumption had to be replaced by a politics of personal life and identity in cultures transcending and subverting territorial boundaries. In the runaway world, the only way ahead for the Left was full-steam towards the global cosmopolitan society, accepting the market as the solution to the problem of distribution, and transforming the state into one of numerous vehicles for personal realisation in a world saturated by information and new communications technology, and where identities are unstable and subject to rapid change.

A decade after the intellectual Third Way was at its most politically influential, the idea of a global cosmopolis seems as fanciful as ever. Economic globalisation has not solved the problem of distribution, either within or between states, but has rather served to embolden and entrench the interests of national political and economic elites. For most people in the world, questions of material security have a clear priority over questions of personal identity when it comes to their expectations of public power. Most people still look to the state – as the ongoing financial crisis amply demonstrates – as the last resort for providing economic security and political stability.

When it comes to the track record of Third Way governments – in the USA, Britain and Germany – they hardly followed an agenda to clearly distinguish them from the neo-liberal Right. Indeed, they continued to pursue deregulatory financial and labour policies, the privatisation of public bodies, and a movement away from universal welfare schemes – all of which have undermined the prospects for radical democracy. While there was some redistribution of wealth via the taxation system, the clear winners under Third Way governments were the wealthiest, particularly those holding executive positions in the financial services.

The fundamental error of Third Way progressives was to conceive of international markets as being decoupled from state institutions and political will. Increased capital flows, operating out of the reach of states, were regarded as the driver of global social and political change. What the advocates of the Third Way failed to understand – or at least failed to appreciate the full implications of – was that it was the most powerful states that primed 'globalisation' and then pressed the trigger.

It was states, firstly under Margaret Thatcher in the United Kingdom and then Ronald Reagan in the USA, who unleashed globalisation by deregulating financial and labour markets. Globalisation was promoted through the international financial institutions of the Bretton Woods system – the International Monetary Fund and the World Bank – whose executives came to be dominated by state appointees versed in the shibboleths of free-market economics. At bottom, globalisation was a *political* phenomenon driven by the most powerful states in the international system, and principally by the USA. Like all previous expansions of trade and commerce in the modern world, it was led by the projection of domestic state power onto the international system. Colonialism and imperialism may not be exactly the right words to express the spread of neo-liberalism, but they are not too far away.

The second model of Leftist politics in recent times (though 'model' might be too strong) involves the often nebulous movements and ideas that have been seen to fall under the umbrella of 'alter-globalisation'. In general, alter-globalisation thinkers have been right to reject the notion that neo-liberal globalisation represents the Holy Grail of the end of history, and tend to view it as a political project crafted and implemented by powerful political and economic elites. Yet like proponents of the Third Way, many supporters of alter-globalisation have tended to grossly exaggerate the extent to which transnational agencies and processes have weakened state power. In the work of authors like Naomi Klein (2008), states appear as the instruments of powerful multinational corporations. Politics is reduced to the interests of corporations, and political activism to focalised resistance to corporations and their political allies. The result is a moral fable, in which the global bad guys – the currency speculators, hedge-fund gamblers, corporate profiteers and venal politicians – hijack the state and use it in their own material interests. But while it is undoubtedly true that the interests of finance and business have exercised disproportionate leverage over governments, this is nothing particularly new. It does not follow from this leverage, as many anti-corporate, antiglobalisers seem to believe, that the most powerful states are simply in hock to the multinationals. If we want to explain what has made neoliberal globalisation possible over the past thirty years, we must look to the economic and ideological changes in states and the international system rather than assuming that what has taken place is just another corporate takeover. Real changes in the economic structure of Western states – the relative decline of Fordist heavy industry, the emergence of new, smaller but more complex manufacturing industries requiring flexible specialisation and high levels of technological investment, and an increasingly open and competitive international economy – made national economic management less viable and successful. At the same time policy-makers in advanced states, both on the Right and the Left, came to embrace the argument put forward by economists like Milton Friedman that the free market was both a more efficient *and* equitable means of wealth production and resource allocation.

Some alter-globalisation theorists have indeed attempted to construct an analysis of the economic and ideological underpinnings of neo-liberal globalisation and how it might be transformed. Probably the most famous of these efforts is Michael Hardt and Antonio Negri's (2001) book *Empire*. In the world today, 'Empire' represents a new form of decentred and deterritorialised sovereignty corresponding in turn to the widening and deepening of market influence in politics and society. Hardt and Negri famously argue that 'There is No More Outside' to Empire. By this they mean that social cleavages of race, gender and sexuality have become more fluid and indeterminate under Empire, undermining forms of exclusion to a specific space (the ghetto, the household or the 'scene'), and replacing them with a 'differential inclusion' across different places. But Hardt and Negri assume, rather than demonstrate, this 'flattening out' of global social relations, thereby paradoxically mirroring the neo-liberal utopia of a placeless, unmediated capitalist market. At the same time, their claim that Empire creates its own grave-diggers in the form of an amorphous and elusive 'Multitude' is pure fantasy. It speaks little to the practical political strategies that the progressive Left will need to implement at the level of states and the international system if it is to expand and deepen radical democracy in the future.

The Third Way and the discourse and ideology of alter-globalisation are inextricably linked to the fortunes of the neo-liberal project. They will likely share in its failure. What models of radical politics might we look to, then, to consider how progressives can shape the world in the wake of the current crisis of capitalism?

The biggest threat and obstacle to radical democracy today is not the state per se but the 'self-regulating' international markets that the most powerful states have supported over the last thirty years. These markets have privatised public space and have further empowered unaccountable economic and political elites. The most radical expressions of progressive politics today are those that seek to challenge these elites through the democratic (re)appropriation of public space and political and economic decision-making. On this reading, radical politics has two broad contemporary expressions. In urban, industrialised settings, it involves struggles over the democratic organisation and control of time and public space. Here radical politics revolves around clawing back time from the market through struggles for greater control over collective decision-making and labour-time allocation in the workplace; campaigns for more affordable, sustainable and efficient use of transport and communication within any given town or city; initiatives aimed at freeing up time for a more equal distribution of childcare and care of the elderly, ill and disabled; guaranteeing secure and free or inexpensive access for all to recreational spaces – be these open-air or indoor; and consequently, the extension of public or collective management of the built environment so as to provide the bulk of citizens with affordable and dignified housing in neighbourhoods that offer a diverse range of services and cultural amenities within reasonable proximity of their homes.

In more rural contexts, radical politics is generally about reappropriating concrete spaces by way of redressing historical injustices. In the post-colonial world, this has involved campaigns for the restitution of communal or customary rights over land and other resources, to peoples and communities (or their descendants) that were historically marginalised or were once expropriated by colonial authorities and settlers. Across the global South, such mobilisations have involved organisations of landless rural workers who, through direct action, squatting, occupation or tactical alliances with other progressive political forces, have sought to stem the ecological, social and economic devastation wrought by agribusiness and industrial logging, mining and fishing concerns.

Clearly, such tidy distinctions between industrial and agricultural, urban and rural, temporal and spatial contexts do not obtain in reality. Many contemporary forms of progressive radicalism – from the protests against the privatisation of water and other basic utilities in Andean Latin America, to the campaigns for free and direct access to anti-retroviral drugs in southern Africa – straddle the terrain between town and country, or the primary and other economic sectors. Indeed, one of the ambitions of progressive radicalism is surely to minimise the power differentials between centre and periphery, town and country or the formal and informal economy in any given territory. The point is, rather, that radical politics today requires thinking about and articulating the spatial and temporal dimensions of democratic power. Specifically, this means harnessing the public and democratic authority invested in various branches of the sovereign territorial state to facilitate the development of democratic forms of social and economic governance as the alternative to rule by the market and unaccountable public and private bureaucracies. This is arguably what has been getting underway – not without its own serious flaws and contradictions – in Venezuela's Bolivarian revolution over the past decade.

Two final provisos obtain in this formulation of radical politics today. First, such public and democratic authority must always have an explicitly internationalist component. Progressive radicalism cannot afford to uncritically celebrate political community or cultural identity – these are powerful mobilising structures but they are neither natural nor immutable, and can, as already noted, readily be instrumentalised by conservative and reactionary forces. Moreover, any viable radicalism must always carry with it an implicit universalism – a sense, as conveyed by the foreign policy of revolutionary states through the centuries, that democratic solidarity never stops at the borders of a given polity. Second, and following on from this, different political communities will identify different political priorities in their struggles for substantive democracy. A radical universalism can thus also ill afford the artificial homogenisation of political programmes in different parts of the world. Capitalist markets, no less than other social structures, have given specific character to inequality, injustice, oppression and violence in different parts of the world. It is therefore always up to those at the point of struggles for radical democracy to collectively decide which specific combination of political objectives and organisational form best responds to their political predicament at any given time.

References

Giddens, A. (1998) *The Third Way: the Renewal of Social Democracy* (Cambridge: Polity Press).

Hardt, M. and A. Negri (2001) *Empire* (New York: Harvard University Press).

Klein, N. (2008) *The Shock Doctrine: the Rise of Disaster Capitalism* (London: Penguin).

Schumpeter, J. A. (1975) *Capitalism, Socialism and Democracy* (New York: Harper).

29
Tackling the Supplicant State

David Boyle

History has not been kind to radicals. There is something about the powerful radical groups that do manage, against all the odds, to attract support for their different interpretation of the world that is politically unstable. The Populists in the USA at the turn of the century, the campaign that gave us the Wizard of Oz, became white supremacists. The Social Credit movement that rose to political prominence in Canada and New Zealand between the wars had become anti-Semitic by the 1940s (though they are now reborn and are not any more). Something about frustrated radicalism makes it bitterly intolerant.

Perhaps that is hardly surprising considering the indifference the mainstream tends to show to radicals. Despite their best efforts, the vast weight of evidence, their sheer common sense, most radical campaigns do not succeed in shifting the world. Perhaps the truth about radicalism is that it has to carry this weight of suspicion and rage simply because it is so hard to break out of the political margins, with any new slant on what is really wrong with the world. This chapter is an attempt to set the problem more clearly, and to suggest a way out – a genuinely radical populism that could break the paradox.

The problem for radicals is particularly hard in the UK, where we make pets of our scientific cranks, but we have a particular horror – especially in the establishment – of political cranks, still more of economic cranks, with their plastic bags full of badly printed leaflets. Radical movements worthy of the name have to not just interpret the political problem differently, they have to gather the evidence for it, name the problem, gather around themselves the sense of momentum, chip away successfully at the indifference, and of course this defeats most of them.

Worse, they have to pedal their new interpretation of our crisis based on obscure topics that many of their most obvious potential supporters have never considered before: that the problems of the world are based on debt, or the financial system, or business conspiracies, or obscure kinds of pollution.

There remains a yearning among people of radical bent for some kind of movement that speaks to ordinary people, and to their lives, which will ignite the anger that radicals believe they share deep down. G. K. Chesterton (1907) talked about 'the people of England, who never have spoken yet'. They are still yet to speak, and Chesterton's Distributist campaigns – though they were forerunners of aspects of the anti-globalisation movement – also petered out in strange byways of Roman Catholic conservatism.

Given those difficulties, it is extraordinary that radical movements do emerge, often diffuse and diverse. The Jubilee Debt campaign succeeded in getting 70,000 demonstrators onto the streets of Birmingham during the G8 summit in 1998, and created a political opening for change. The anti-globalisation movement stopped the WTO summit in Seattle the following year, and succeeded in galvanising opposition among the negotiators of the developing countries which did largely prevent further global deregulation. The green movement, the corporate responsibility movement, the feminist movement, have all in their different ways risen out of the mush of mass media to change the world, even if it hasn't been changed very much.

But these are successes where radicals and pragmatists find themselves in uneasy alliance, as they nearly always do in successful movements. The corporate responsibility movement has shifted the way business success is measured, launched a flurry of international standards and ethical institutions from FTSE4Good to ETI and GRI, and other bizarre acronyms. But radicals will complain, and rightly, that it never quite addressed the fundamental issues of corporate power. Equally, it could not have succeeded at all were it not for the background noise that radicals were making, that persuaded the corporates to listen to the pragmatists for fear of something worse.

The same paradox applies to radical innovations. Healthy Living Centres ushered in a whole new approach to public health outside the NHS, funded by the National Lottery, and were allowed to wither on the vine. The Expert Patient Programme ushered in a new approach to doctor–patient relationships, in the same radical tradition, but without the radical ambition and inside the NHS. That has thrived.

The added problem is that radicals and pragmatists often loathe each other, especially when they are tackling the same issue. They often fail to recognise the role of the other in their own success, and they drive a disabling wedge between each other that saps their effectiveness as campaigners and agents of change.

This is one of the causes of the current miserable state of politics in the UK, where mainstream politicians are forced to perform a televised ritual so shorn of any radicalism, except in the vaguest possible terms, that it alienates – not just radicals – but anybody who looks to politicians for a lead. Radicalism remains outside the topics and rituals that are considered safe to expose to Jeremy Paxman. Political parties are increasingly fearful of appealing to radical ideas. This is disastrous for both sides: the radicals are excluded from mainstream political debate, along with their interpretations of the world and their ideas, while the politicians find themselves shuffling towards irrelevance, using a language shorn of meaning in the real world, often ignorant of the world outside their own bubble.

This paradox, and this division between radicals and pragmatists, makes genuinely radical interventions increasingly difficult. There are exceptions: the green movement has succeeded in getting its world view widely accepted, but mainly outside mainstream politics. Most exceptions are radical campaigns based on direct action rather than new ideas, which do still galvanise support, or internet-based paranoia, conspiracy theories and bizarre theories that modernise discredited radicalism of the past.

I have been involved in radical campaigning, albeit from the safe distance of an economics think tank, for more than two decades, and I have struggled with this paradox myself. Radicalism as the word implies goes to the roots of a problem. Radical campaigns by their very nature imply that the mainstream has ignored the basic causes. Often radical ideas are based on scientific facts (green radicalism) or engineering insights (economic radicalism) or medical statistics (complementary health), which gives campaigners the veneer of rival technocrats rather than purveyors of major solutions.

Is it possible any more for a new radical interpretation of everyday frustrations and problems to grab mainstream attention, without becoming populist, and force its way onto the carefully spun mainstream political agenda? Is there an issue that can fuse the various fragmented elements of a successful radical campaign again to genuinely shift the way we live? Is there something, as Chesterton put it – so dangerously and ambiguously – that could make the people of England speak?

I would like to suggest one possible way out of the paradox. It certainly isn't the only one, but it could provide a way forward for a widely held critique of the way our lives are lived for us, and I recommend it. I would like to nominate a topic for a powerful radicalism of the future, which goes to the heart of why so little works in the modern world: the tentacles of technocratic power, corporate and bureaucratic, which have us so miserably and deadeningly in its grip.

The trigger for this sudden realisation of our predicament is the after-effects of the Gershon Review, which the government accepted in 2004, with recommendations on public service efficiency, which subjected our institutions to unprecedented savings, streamlining and modernisation. Nearly four years later, there are serious doubts about whether the £20 billion in savings that were planned are real at all – and increasing evidence that these costs have simply been passed on to clients and individuals, often the poorest people, who face the barrage of new bureaucracy, call centres and obfuscation that were defined by two Liberal Democrat MPs as 'Faceless Britain'.

That was the trigger, but thanks to increasing centralisation in the UK, business and administrative, and the technocratic ideas emanating from the Harvard Business Review, we find ourselves suddenly unexpectedly disempowered, supplicants to distant government agencies and monopolistic corporates.

All radical campaigns emerge from a new intellectual breakthrough: this one is based on two new understandings. One is that being supplicants to public and private IT systems is not that different. Their public or private status is not important here; what is important for the new radicalism is their dehumanised and dehumanising nature. The other big idea is that this sclerotic centralisation is a major reason our services are so ineffective. They are why, despite six decades of welfare spending, Beveridge's giants remain with us. The new radicalism is a challenge to both the private and the public sector, because it attacks an insidious combination of them both: the idea that people are defined narrowly by their needs, and should be administered by giant agencies part-public, part-private, by huge databases and remote call centres.

This is the new centralised supplicant state, and it is a more fundamental problem for our public services than the traditional debate about whether we should tax more to pay for them or not. The problem is not that they are too public or too private. It is because they are grinding to a halt. They are doing so because of the massive inefficiencies of centralisation, the disempowering targets and the externalities of giant organisations. They are doing so because centralisation causes sclerotic bureaucracy that tries to exclude the vital human element – the very element that actually makes things happen in schools and hospitals. And they are doing so because they refuse to share responsibility with their clients, preferring them passive and silent.

This is the real story of public services in the twenty-first century. They feel unnervingly inauthentic, and you can see the symptoms everywhere:

- The patients of factory hospitals who never see the same doctor twice, one in ten of whom will suffer real harm from hospital mistakes or viruses.
- The new claimants who have to hold on so long at the call centre on their pay-as-you-go mobile phones just to make a claim that it costs them £35.
- The A&E nurses who know what the patients in front of them need so urgently, but who have to go through more than 20 pages on their IT system before they can help each of them.
- The public service managers who struggle to manipulate their expensive recruitment IT systems just to make sure the people they know would be best get interviewed.
- The teachers who know what they need to say in their pupil's report, but have to choose from a series of approved phrases in their approved report-writing system.

Politicians see these problems of course, but they ignore them because these issues are not couched in the impoverished political language they have to use. They do not fit neatly into the conventional divisions between government departments, or differentiate politicians from rival parties, or any of the conventional entry points into mainstream debate. So it is up to radicals to stitch these concerns together, name them as one problem: which is about how inefficient centralised systems downgrade human skills and human needs.

This is a radicalism that goes to the heart of the problem, but it requires a new kind of political language to make it sing – when politicians tend to debate what differentiates themselves traditionally from other parties, but steer clear of areas where their opponents have no track record. Or they debate what they have the clear power to do something about – thanks to globalisation, a dwindling list. This makes for a strange categorisation of issues. Politicians debate the size of school classes endlessly, but for some reason not the size of schools. They debate hospital waiting lists, but not the obsession with pills and gizmos.

But while political language shuffles the designated issues, real lives face challenges which include balancing work, mortgage and family life. They include the question of buying fresh, healthy vegetables from nearer than 4,000 miles away. Or what levers can persuade their local hospital consultants not to ask people to come at 8 a.m. for an appointment at noon. But most of all, excluded issues include the interactions with the supplicant state and its corporate outriders.

Behind these issues lies a major trend which is already affecting radicalism today: the revolt by a sizeable minority of people against what is spun, marketed, one-dimensional and 'rationally' inhuman. In short, the new demand for authenticity. This is partly a revolt against modern, rationalised organisations which remove the small and apparently irrelevant details that make dealing with them bearable and human: conversation, flexibility, humanity.

Those who run the world do not believe it is important for hospital patients to see the same doctor they saw yesterday. Or that call centre staff should be able to help, even if your particular problem does not have a corresponding box on their software. I recently watched one old gentleman, forced into the supermarket by the closure of his local shop, enrage queue and staff alike by trying to chat to the check-out person, as he used to do. I don't think we are wealthier for the loss of that very little human service.

But then the corporate giants do not believe human beings have three dimensions. It is only human, for example, to need a lavatory occasionally on the train. But because train companies believe we need only to get from A to B, they don't bother to mend them. A friend of mine announced at a dinner party that he had bought a flat in Paris because the shops there were 'real', and everyone seemed to know immediately what he meant – locally owned, personal, baking on the premises, odd smells and so on. These are among the aspects of modern life that accountants and chief executives earn bonuses for abolishing, that make life authentic and three-dimensional, and therefore human.

Modern, rational systems are too shallow to be authentic. Yet you only have to look at adverts these days to see how much people want their products and services real. They may not want authenticity as much as they say they do, but the massive growth of real ale, natural yoghurt, complementary medicines, farmers' markets, slow food, organic vegetables, unmixed music and much else besides, shows that they still want it. But what enough people want, in a market economy, they will eventually start to get.

So this radicalism today, constrained, fragmented, excluded from the mainstream, but succeeding sometimes despite all that, and seeking for the breakthroughs and insights that can gather up the frustrations and dreams of ordinary people to take on the mainstream. The new radicalism is, I believe, going to go back to people's lives to find the source of our malaise – in the sclerotic disease known variously as centralisation, rational modernisation, streamlining, Faceless Britain – and to construct a radical human way forward. The task for radicals in the next generation is to articulate this process of dehumanisation, to research its effects, and to find a language with which to talk about it to the mainstream and the political establishment. And to do so using the stuff of everyday life, aware that the material is there.

Radicals are often inconvenient people to take around. They always see some deeper cause than the one you are engaged on. They are awkward in their failure to join in quite the way intended. They are so seriously off-message that they find few places in modern politics. But we need them in the same way that we need bards and poets – because they push forward the language that makes people see things they never saw before.

Reference

Chesterton, G. K. (1907) 'The Secret People', http://www.chiark.greenend.org.uk/
~martinh/poems/SECRET

30
The Potential for a Progressive State?

Saskia Sassen

Accepting that my argument may seem uncomfortable for many of those who call themselves 'radical', in this chapter I argue for the importance of the state as a potentially positive force for change.[1] I start with some preliminary remarks on the nature of 'power', as this is naturally important for debates in radical politics today.

Power is made, and hence can be unmade. The work of making power varies across time and space. And so does the success, effectiveness and durability of this work of making. This means also that powerlessness is constructed. Powerlessness is not simply the absence of power or mere victimhood, as is so often believed. Hence it is variable rather than fixed. From there, then, comes the possibility that powerlessness can range from elementary to complex. This variability does not simply depend on the characteristics of individuals: the settings also matter. For instance, the powerlessness of a specific undocumented immigrant will be quite elementary in the context of a California commercial farm but can become complex in a city like New York or Los Angeles. In that complexity of powerlessness lies the possibility of a politics.

Here I examine one particular aspect of a larger project that seeks to recode power and powerlessness (Sassen, 2008a, 2008b). It is the fact that corporate economic globalisation is far more dependent on national states and national spaces than the typical arguments in the globalisation scholarship allow for. This is one way of researching the limits of power, in this case, corporate global power. The work of national states has been far more important than is usually recognised. Much has been said about the USA and the UK as the key states producing the design for the new standards and legalities needed to ensure protections and guarantees for global firms and markets.[2] But here it is important to emphasise that the imposed 'consensus' in the community of states to further globalisation is not merely a political decision: it entails specific types of work by a large number of distinct state institutions in each of the 150 plus countries that have joined (willingly or not) the global economy. Legislative items, executive orders, adherence to new technical standards, and so on, will have to be produced through the particular institutional and political structures of each state. All these states worked at it, and in that process installed global logics deep inside their national institution. Precisely because of this, I see a possible radical politics in using state capacities for a politics not only of resistance, but of remaking without the violence of armed conflict, without war.

I argue that neo-liberal globalisation has, ironically, forced specific state institutions to learn how to do global work and has produced a particular type of state authority and power, one geared to global projects. States have historically been nationalist. One challenge for a radical politics today is to get states to redeploy that learning and that particular type of power towards the pursuit of alternative global projects – towards an alternative globalisation. We need to push states to use that learning and emergent global power for projects aiming at social justice and human security in its many different settings. It will take political action to get states to reorient their international work away from the corporate global economy and from war. These global agendas include eliminating economic violence, strengthening human rights, protecting the environment, fighting racisms and intolerance. None of these is likely to be achieved fully. But we can do better with our massive resources. The world need not be this grim.

Any working state is a complex organisation with major capacities to handle an enormous variety of challenges and disparate political alignments. Not even the richest corporation is as complex a capability as a working state. Pity that just about most states are in the hand of regressive forces when it comes to the larger agendas that would humanise the world. If we add to this organisational complexity the fact that states have shown a willingness to be more internationalist, albeit on the wrong terrain, it becomes clear that states are key actors to address our global challenges, from the environment to socially just economic development. We cannot give up on this type of capability. We need to reorient these vast organisations within each country towards addressing these urgent challenges, some of which can only be addressed through collaborations and concerted action among a majority of states.

Using national instruments to fight for an alternative globalisation

The most common interpretation in the literature on globalisation is that citizens and states have lost power confronted with global firms and global finance.[3] But in my work I have researched the multiple ways in which even the most powerful global firms and financial exchanges actually need particular agencies and capacities of states in order to develop, implement and guarantee a range of conditions and protections (Sassen, 2008a: chapter 5). You would not know that when reading most of the globalisation texts. Rarely do those texts mention, for instance, that there is no such legal persona as a global firm; there is not even a legal entity such as a European firm, even though the EU is well-positioned to develop such a persona. Yet we know there are firms that conduct themselves as if such a legal persona existed. What enables this? It is the hard and politically contentious work of state after state around the world to make a space for foreign firms inside each nation state where these firms can conduct themselves as if they were global. One way of describing this state work is as an active denationalising of particular institutional settings – by which I mean not a privatising but literally a denationalising of what has historically been constructed as national, a condition that cannot simply be subsumed under the global. Providing such a denationalised space for foreign firms is often at the cost of destroying their national firms and markets.

I am interested in capturing this dependence of powerful firms on state work so as to mark the limits of their power, the new kinds of power that accrue to the national state, and, importantly, that states have learnt to act together internationally, without much negotiating, towards a single aim. Thus I argue that particular parts of the state have actually gained power *because* of globalisation (Sassen, 2008a: chapter 4). This goes against the prevalent notion that states have lost power; certain components of national states have lost much ground, notably legislatures and state agencies linked to the social wage and broad welfare functions benefiting the working and middle classes. But for the possibility of the kind of radical politics I am positing here, it is important to emphasise the growing power of ministries of finance, central banks and the executive (and, in some cases, judiciary) branch of government: these have done the state work necessary to secure a global capital market, a global trading system, the needed competition policies, and so on.

Secondly, in detecting this type of 'internationalist' state work to set up a global corporate economy, and by inference the possibility of regearing state work towards higher order goals for the common good, I am also arguing against the prevalent notion in globalisation texts that the global and the national are mutually exclusive. Even if many components of each, the national and the global, are separate and mutually exclusive, I argue that this still leaves a specific set of conditions or components that deborders this dualism. One key implication of the fact that the concerted action of national states to enable the growth of a global corporate economy has taken place through particular parts of national states, is that developing novel, more enlightened forms of state internationalism can begin through the work of specific state parts, such as environment and development agencies and legislatures and courts; having an enlightened president or prime minister can help enormously, given the vast structural power increase of the executive branch of government over the last twenty years. But the main point I am trying to make is that this political project can start through the work of specific parts of the state; it is not dependent on first reorienting state work *in toto*, which would seem an almost impossible task without a French, American or Russian style classical revolution. We can start working on it now.

Thirdly, one key implication is that this new type of internationalist power of national states can become a structural bridge for citizens, who are today still largely confined to the national for maximising their rights and powers, to do global politics from inside the national. A critical point in the larger project (Sassen, 2008a: chapters 6–8) is that citizens can fight for an alternative globalisation using *national* instruments (besides existing international instruments, such as the International Criminal Court, global civil society organisations, and so on). To do global politics they need not wait for some putative global state – an unlikely development – nor are they confined to work through the supranational system where states are the dominant actors and much of the agenda is regressive (e.g. WTO and IMF policy goals). But this option to do global politics from inside the national requires active *making*, including reorienting the work of states and the making of new types of global jurisdictions.

Critical to the type of radical politics I think is possible using the capacities of states is whether this specific type of state power that has emerged can in fact extend to global domains beyond the global corporate economy – such as the environment, human rights, socially just economic development – and be used to contain rather than promote the powers of global economic corporate actors.

But first a brief illustration of this new type of structural power of particular components of the state, a power that opens up the possibility of effective use of the state for a new type of global politics – if the needed kind of governing classes control those parts of the state – and that takes us beyond the notion that the global corporate economy has rendered national states and citizens irrelevant or at least, powerless.

The structural growth of executive power: beyond the state of exception

The growing power of the executive branch of government is, in my reading, a structural development that is part of the historical evolution/adaptation of the so-called liberal state. This structural development needs to be distinguished from the state of emergency or the state of exception – an anomalous condition that can return to 'normal' once the emergency is over. Much of the commentary on the rise of executive power (whether presidential or prime ministerial) today focuses on the state of emergency (e.g. the Patriot Act in the USA, or the new emergency anti-terrorist policies in the EU member states). Because of this focus there is a failure to recognise this second, structural trend of greater executive power, one which is not anomalous, but rather the new norm of the liberal state. I see this trend beginning in the 1980s: that is the time of Reagan in the USA, Thatcher in the UK, Mitterand in France, and so on. But again, it is a mistake to see this as party politics – that is why the mix of party politics represented by the inclusion of a socialist premier in France helps us recognise that deeper trend. Party politics matters, but there is also a realignment of the modern liberal state that is in fact part of what is often referred to as the neo-liberal era or, more generally, globalisation.

One illustration of this structural trend is the case of the positioning of the executive branch of government in the USA in matters outside the emergency state. In my research I identified at least five trends in the global economy that feed executive power:

1. As already mentioned, certain parts of the administration (the Treasury, the Federal Reserve, the office of the Trade Representative, and so on, and the equivalent institutions in other countries) have played a critical role in building a global corporate economy. This pattern repeats itself across the world as states become incorporated, willingly or not, into the global economy. At the same time, the policies associated with this incorporation – deregulation and privatisation – remove various oversight functions from Congress, as has been widely noted. Less noted is that

deregulation and privatisation have added functions to the domain of the executive branch. Thus the deregulating of finance and telecommunications, for example, brought about the loss of oversight functions in the legislature and, at the same time, the formation of special commissions on finance and on telecommunications within the executive branch – commissions where most members are from these economic sectors!

2. Intergovernmental networks centred largely in the executive branch have grown well beyond matters of global security and criminality. The participation by the state in the implementation of a global economic system has engendered a whole range of new types of cross-border collaborations among specialised government agencies focused on the globalisation of capital markets, international standards of all sorts, and the new trade order.

3. The major global regulators, notably the International Monetary Fund and World Trade Organization, as well as many lesser known ones, negotiate only with the executive branch. As the global corporate economy and the supranational system expand, executive power grows.

4. A critical component of economic deregulation beginning in the 1980s is the privatisation of formerly public functions. In the USA, privatising prisons and outsourcing of particular welfare functions to private providers are probably the most familiar cases. Today we can add the outsourcing of soldiering to private contractors even in war theatres, as is the case in Iraq. This privatisation has reduced the oversight role of Congress but added to the role of the executive through specialised commissions. One recent case that brings some of these issues to light is the extent to which Congress has not been given information by the executive branch as to the amount of taxpayers' money going to private contractors who now handle a growing range of the USA's military activities. The executive branch can actually handle private contractors with little if any oversight by Congress.

5. A final bundle of issues makes visible the alignment of the executive with global corporate logics in a range of domains – which is not always negative, by the way. The case of the Dubai Ports World corporation, which was meant to acquire control over the security of several American port operations, was strongly supported by George W. Bush. This points to the executive branch becoming partly denationalised, with Bush in a position to want a corporation from an Islamic country to be in charge of port security in the USA, quite a positive turn for a president who had declared war on much of Islam. More recently,

and not as positive, was Bush's insistence that no environmental and labour standards be included in the new set of free trade agreements under discussion in the autumn of 2008. Yet another such example was Bush's willingness to allow long-haul Mexican trucks access to American highways with minimum public notice and safety guidelines, privileging global free trade over national road safety. Finally, we have the Treasury's positive reaction to the acquisition of shares in American financial firms by foreign governments – among them China, Dubai and Singapore – with several other such acquisitions in the making.

The particular kinds of executive power growth I describe here are not exceptions. They are structural developments within the liberal state that are part of the implementation of a global corporate economy. In the USA they began with Ronald Reagan and continued under Clinton. Nor are they simply a result of the Patriot Act and an administration willing to abuse its power – these are separate sources of executive power. A new president genuinely willing to respect the balance of power and willing to cancel the Patriot Act will still be in a structural position of growing power in today's liberal state. Obama, with a different politics from Bush, has more power than most preceding presidents, not because he is grabby or charismatic, but because of the structural evolution of the liberal state. A hollowed-out Congress confined to domestic matters weakens the political capacity of citizens to demand accountability from an increasingly powerful and globally oriented executive. Today, the liberal state produces its own democratic deficit.

Returning to the argument in this chapter about the need to reorient state work, there is an ironic possibility in all of this. Can a president intent on fighting for a better and juster democracy actually use that expanded executive power to do this? And could the emergent internationalism of the executive branch, now used to further the global corporate economy, be used for addressing some of our pressing global challenges?

Using state power for a new global politics

These post-1980s trends towards a greater interaction of national and global dynamics are not part of some unidirectional historical progression. There have been times in the past when they may have been as strong in certain aspects as they are today (Sassen, 2008a: chapter 3). But the current positioning of national states is distinctive precisely because the national state has become the most powerful complex organisational entity in the world, and because it is a resource that citizens, confined largely to the national, can aim at governing and using to develop novel political agendas. It is this mix of the national and the global that is so full of potential.

The national state is *one* particular form of state: at the other end of this variable the state can be conceived of as a technical administrative capability that could escape the historic bounds of narrow nationalisms that have marked the state historically, or colonialism as the only form of internationalism that states have enacted. Stripping the state of the particularity of this historical legacy gives me more analytic freedom in conceptualising these processes and opens up the possibility of the denationalised state.

As particular components of national states become the institutional home for the operation of some of the dynamics that are central to globalisation they undergo change that is difficult to register or name. In my own work I have found useful the notion of an incipient denationalising of specific components of national states, i.e. components that function as such institutional homes. The question for research then becomes what is actually 'national' in some of the institutional components of states linked to the implementation and regulation of economic globalisation. The hypothesis here would be that some components of national institutions, even though formally national, are not national in the sense in which we have constructed the meaning of that term over the last hundred years.

This partial, often highly specialised or at least particularised, denationalisation can also take place in domains other than that of economic globalisation, notably the more recent developments in the human rights regime which allow national courts to sue foreign firms and dictators, or which grant undocumented immigrants certain rights. Denationalisation is, thus, multivalent: it endogenises global agendas of many different types of actors, not only corporate firms and financial markets, but also human rights and environmental objectives. Those confined to the national can use national state institutions as a bridge into global politics. This is one kind of radical politics, and only one kind, that would use the capacities of hopefully increasingly denationalised states. The existence and the strengthening of global civil society organisations becomes strategic in this context. In all of this lie the possibilities of moving towards new types of joint global action by denationalised states – coalitions of the willing focused not on war but on environmental and social justice projects.

Notes

1. For full development of the various issues raised here and the pertinent sources and bibliographies, see Sassen (2008a) and http://www.columbia.edu/~sjs2/.
2. This dominance does not only affect poorer and weaker countries. France, for instance, ranks among the top global powers, but it has found itself at an increasing disadvantage in legal and accounting services because Anglo-American law and standards dominate in international transactions. Anglo-American firms with offices in Paris do much of the servicing of the legal needs of firms, whether French or foreign, operating out of France. Similarly, Anglo-American law is increasingly dominant in international commercial arbitration, an institution grounded in continental traditions of jurisprudence, particularly French and Swiss.
3. The scholarship on the state and globalisation contains three basic positions: one finds the state is victimised by globalisation and loses significance; a second one finds that nothing much has changed and states basically keep on doing what they have always done; and a third, a variant on the second, finds that the state adapts and may even be transformed, thereby ensuring that it does not decline and remains the critical actor. There is research to support critical aspects of each one of these three positions, partly because much of their difference hinges on interpretation. But notwithstanding their diversity these scholarships tend to share the assumption that the national and the global are mutually exclusive.

Reference

Sassen, S. (2008a) *Territory, Authority, Rights: From Medieval to Global Assemblages* (Princeton: Princeton University Press).
Sassen, S. (2008b) http://www.opendemocracy.net/article/globalisation/world_third_spaces

Index